25x ARTICLES | 25x GUIDED NO
25x HIGH-LEVEL REFLECTION QUESTION SETS
25x HYPOTHETICAL SETS | 25x VOCABULARY SETS
25x CROSSWORDS | 25x WORD SEARCHES

Aligned to National Standards in K-12 Personal Finance Education developed by the Jump$tart Coalition for Personal Financial Literacy

25x

25x: Personal Finance

version 2.0 - October 15, 2024

For more information: 3andB.com | email: info@3andB.com

Welcome & Instructions

Welcome to 3andB's *25x: Personal Finance* workbook. Our workbook is an ideal resource for parents and educators who are looking to introduce students to important concepts and terminology related to personal finance.

As a parent or teacher, we suggest reviewing and familiarizing yourself with the workbook content to facilitate a more engaging learning experience. We recommend assigning a designated time each week for the student to complete the assigned reading, guided notes, hypotheticals, reflection questions, and term definitions, followed by word search and crossword activities.

Our workbook is strategically structured with 25+ topics that offer a comprehensive overview of important personal finance concepts, terminology, and best practices. Each section includes a short and engaging article followed by guided notes, hypotheticals, and thought-provoking reflection questions, allowing students to internalize the material and apply it to their daily lives.

To enhance the learning experience, we suggest discussing the concepts with the students and encouraging them to brainstorm real-life scenarios where they can apply the concepts learned. This approach brings theoretical concepts to life, leading to a more meaningful and engaging experience for the students.

The workbook also includes 10 terms per section that the students are encouraged to define. We recommend that educators reinforce the importance of finding the best answer when defining these terms, as it will aid the students in understanding and internalizing the concepts.

As a career-oriented and professional organization, 3andB recognizes the importance of a high-quality education that prepares students for future success. Our workbook seeks to introduce personal finance concepts that empower students to navigate real-life situations with confidence and a greater understanding of their capabilities.

Finally, we encourage feedback from our users to better understand how we can improve our products and services. Thank you for choosing 3andB's *25x: Personal Finance* workbook. We believe our workbook offers a great foundation for a fulfilling, successful future for our youth.

Very truly yours,
The 3andB Team

TABLE OF CONTENTS
25x: Personal Finance

Aligned to National Standards in K-12 Personal Finance Education developed by the Jump$tart Coalition for Personal Financial Literacy

Unlocking Your Financial Future:
What is Personal Finance?

Imagine you're about to embark on a cross-country road trip. You wouldn't just jump in the car and start driving without a plan, would you? You'd need to know your destination, map out your route, and budget for gas, food, and lodging. Personal finance is a lot like planning that road trip, but instead of a vacation, you're planning your financial future.

What exactly is personal finance? It's the art and science of managing your money to achieve your goals and dreams. Whether you're saving up for your first car, planning for college, or dreaming about starting your own business, personal finance gives you the tools to turn those dreams into reality.

Personal finance is crucial as it empowers individuals to manage their money effectively, make informed financial decisions, and plan for a secure future.

Understanding Personal Finance

At its core, personal finance is about making smart decisions with your money. It encompasses a wide range of financial activities that affect your daily life and long-term future. These include:

1. Budgeting: This is like creating a spending roadmap. It helps you understand where your money comes from and where it goes.

2. Saving: Think of this as putting money aside for future you. It's like packing an emergency kit for your financial journey.

3. Investing: This is how you make your money work for you, like planting seeds that can grow into a money tree over time.

4. Managing debt: Sometimes you need to borrow money, but managing debt is about keeping those loans under control, so they don't derail your financial plans.

5. Insurance: This is your financial safety net, protecting you from unexpected financial setbacks.

Personal finance isn't just about numbers and spreadsheets. It's about understanding your values, setting goals, and making choices that align with what's important to you.

Why Personal Finance Matters to You

You might be thinking, "I'm just a high school student. Why should I care about personal finance now?" The truth is, the financial habits you develop today will shape your future in significant ways.

Consider this: according to a 2022 Bankrate survey, 56% of Americans couldn't cover a $1,000 emergency expense from their savings. By learning about personal finance now, you're giving yourself a head start on avoiding such financial stress in the future.

Moreover, understanding personal finance empowers you to make informed decisions about your education, career, and lifestyle. It gives you the tools to:

• Choose a college or career path with a clear understanding of the financial implications
• Start building credit responsibly, which can help you secure better rates on future loans
• Begin saving and investing early, taking advantage of compound interest
• Develop healthy money habits that will serve you well throughout your life

Personal Finance in Action

Let's look at a real-world example of how personal finance knowledge can make a difference. Meet Alex, a high school junior who wants to buy a car. Without understanding personal finance, Alex might be tempted to buy the flashiest car on the lot, maxing out a high-interest auto loan.

But Alex has been learning about personal finance. So instead, they:

1. Set a realistic budget based on their part-time job income
2. Researched the total cost of car ownership, including insurance, maintenance, and fuel
3. Shopped around for the best auto loan rates
4. Decided to buy a reliable used car that fits their budget
5. Set up an automatic savings plan for future car expenses

By applying personal finance principles, Alex not only got a car but also avoided financial stress and started building good financial habits for the future.

Taking Control of Your Financial Future

Personal finance isn't about restricting your life or saying "no" to everything. It's about making informed choices that allow you to say "yes" to the things that matter most to you. It's about creating a life where money works for you, not the other way around.

As you begin your personal finance journey, remember that it's okay to start small. Begin by tracking your spending for a month. Set a small savings goal. Learn about different types of bank accounts. Each step you take builds your financial knowledge and confidence.

Personal finance is your roadmap to financial freedom and security. By understanding and applying its principles, you're setting yourself up for a future where you're in control of your money, rather than letting it control you. As you continue through this course, you'll gain the knowledge and skills to navigate your financial journey with confidence. Every financial decision you make is a step towards your future. Make it count!

Did You Know?

• The concept of compound interest is so powerful that Albert Einstein allegedly called it the "eighth wonder of the world."
• April is designated as Financial Literacy Month in the United States, highlighting the importance of personal finance education.

X. What is Personal Finance?
GUIDED NOTES

I. Key Terms

1. Personal Finance: _____

2. Budgeting: _____

3. Investing: _____

II. Main Concept Overview

Personal finance is the art and science of _____ your money to

achieve your _____ and _____. It involves making smart

_____ with your money that align with your values and goals.

III. Components of Personal Finance

Match each term with its description:

_____ Budgeting   A. Protecting you from unexpected financial setbacks

_____ Saving   B. Making your money work for you

_____ Investing   C. Creating a spending roadmap

_____ Debt   D. Putting money aside for future you

_____ Insurance   E. Keeping loans under control

IV. Importance of Personal Finance

1. Empowers you to make informed decisions about:

    a) _____

    b) _____

    c) _____

2. Helps you avoid financial stress by: _____

3. Allows you to start: _____ early

V. True or False

_____ Personal finance is only about numbers and spreadsheets.

_____ Understanding personal finance can help you choose a college or career path.

_____ Personal finance is mainly about restricting your life and saying "no" to everything.

_____ The financial habits you develop today will shape your future in significant ways.

_____ It's best to wait until after high school before learning about personal finance.

VI. Real-World Application

Fill in the table below based on the example of Alex buying a car:

Personal Finance Action	Description
Set a realistic budget	
Researched costs	
Shopped around	
Made a wise choice	
Set up savings plan	

VII. Reflection/Summary

1. In your own words, explain why personal finance is important for high school students:

_____

_____

_____

_____

_____

_____

2. List two small steps mentioned in the article that you could take to start your personal finance journey:

a) _____

b) _____

X. What is Personal Finance?

1

How might your current spending habits affect your future financial goals?

Think about your recent purchases. Are you saving any money? How could your current habits help or hinder future plans like buying a car or paying for college?

2

How could learning about personal finance now help your future education or career plans?

Think about the costs associated with college or starting a career. How might personal finance knowledge help you make better decisions? What financial challenges might you face?

3

How do you expect your attitude towards money to change as you learn more about personal finance?

How do you feel about money now? Why do you think learning about personal finance might change these feelings? What aspects of money management interest or worry you most?

The Summer Job Opportunity

You're offered a part-time job at a local store for the summer. This would be your first job.

Questions:
a) How might having a job change your approach to money?
b) What personal finance skills would be important to have in this situation?
c) How could this job impact your financial goals?

_____

_____

_____

_____

_____

_____

_____

_____

_____

_____

The Budgeting Challenge

Your parents suggest you start managing your own money for things like clothes and entertainment.

Questions:
a) What steps would you take to start managing your own money?
b) What personal finance concepts would be most helpful in this situation?
c) How might this change affect your spending and saving habits?

_____

_____

_____

_____

_____

_____

_____

_____

_____

_____

TERM	DEFINITION
Personal Finance	
Budget	
Saving	
Investing	
Debt	

TERM	DEFINITION
Insurance	
Financial Goals	
Credit	
Financial Literacy	
Compound Interest	

What is Personal Finance?

```
S Z A H A E V C A N I C B S U G F T E B B F I Y
J O W R Z Q N J V Y C W M U K G G U P J R I V X
P S A V I N G Z W N M C A G T M K Z W V N N S N
B G N G E P H M Z L V T E J V A B G L I M A K A
J P Z Z U L C I B P E M Y C V M G N R P K N Q G
J N E C O Q N F N L E N K K V W H F L Y D C V F
E S D R H Y F C R S V U F F N I W M J H E I G F
Y O P V S H J C S M U Z M Y T X T J R U B A W H
L C K A M O H S K I X R R Q H Q S E Z X T L Y S
W O V L N U N D E Y Z W A P J G S D U X F L Q B
G M M L W E C A F Z H C W N B V S N D V L I P V
E P V L O S R H L G P Q E B C F Z D K C C T W R
M O L V E J E U T F F G Y A A E U U V V R E B U
S U S D G T D F Q H I H U O B V X B F W X R E S
B N C R O R I N L F W N H G I O D U O C R A I C
E D R X A U T E O J M I A C G O B D T P R C N F
O I M K L N I N V E S T I N G G Z G S O W Y Q U
J N U J S V H K K E P X U I C W F E G X B U L X
N T O I N Q B X P B Q C K S C E A T X H Q W X Y
B E N Y S F A K J T H T Q T J U S Z H U D X M A
P R F I R H L F Q N N G X M C U E Q B G G C J A
S E N S E D G S I C F H W H P G Q L E D Q X C
W S C W L G K Z V K W Z G W R Y J W R F H U G I
W T R X F I N A N C I A L G O A L S Y B Z N O W
```

Financial Goals	Financial Literacy	Compound Interest
Credit	Insurance	Debt
Investing	Saving	Budget
Personal Finance		

What is Personal Finance?

Across

5. A form of risk management primarily used to protect against the risk of potential financial loss.

6. Interest calculated on the initial principal and the accumulated interest from previous periods, _____ Interest

7. The ability to understand and effectively use various financial skills, including personal financial management and budgeting, Financial _____

8. A plan for managing income and expenses over a specific period.

9. The act of setting aside money for future use rather than spending it immediately.

10. Money owed or due to another party.

Down

1. The practice of managing one's money, including earning, spending, saving, investing, and protecting financial resources. (2 words)

2. Specific, measurable objectives related to money management and future financial well-being, Financial _____

3. Putting money into financial schemes, shares, property, or other ventures with the expectation of achieving profit.

4. The ability to borrow money or access goods or services with the understanding that payment will be made in the future.

The Money-Values Connection: How Your Beliefs Shape Your Wallet

Have you ever wondered why you splurge on concert tickets but hesitate to buy new school supplies? Or why your best friend seems to always be saving for the future while you prefer to live in the moment? The answer lies in your personal values – the core beliefs that guide your decisions and behaviors, including how you handle money. Let's explore the fascinating connection between personal values and financial decisions, and how understanding this link can help you make smarter choices with your cash.

What Are Personal Values?

Personal values are the fundamental beliefs and principles that shape your identity and guide your actions. They're like an internal compass, helping you navigate life's choices – big and small. Some common personal values include:

1. Family: Prioritizing relationships and family well-being
2. Freedom: Valuing independence and personal autonomy
3. Security: Emphasizing stability and safety
4. Adventure: Seeking new experiences and excitement
5. Achievement: Striving for success and personal growth

Your unique set of values influences every aspect of your life, including your approach to money. Let's dive deeper into how these values impact your financial decisions.

The Value-Money Connection

Your personal values play a crucial role in shaping your financial behaviors and decisions. Here's how:

1. Spending Priorities: Your values determine what you consider worth spending money on. For example, if you value experiences over material possessions, you might choose to spend more on travel than on buying the latest gadgets.
2. Saving Habits: Values like security and future-orientation might lead you to prioritize saving and investing, while values like spontaneity might make you more likely to spend in the moment.
3. Financial Goals: Your long-term financial objectives are often a direct reflection of your values. Someone who values family might prioritize saving for their children's education, while someone who values independence might focus on building a business.
4. Risk Tolerance: Your attitude towards financial risk is influenced by your values. If you value security, you might prefer low-risk investments, while someone who values growth might be more comfortable with higher-risk options.
5. Career Choices: The career path you choose is often aligned with your values, which in turn affects your earning potential and financial decisions.

Real-World Example: The Tale of Two Friends

Let's consider two high school friends, Alex and Jordan, who have different personal values:

Alex values adventure and new experiences. When she receives her paycheck from her part-time job, she often spends it on concert tickets, trying new restaurants, or saving for a summer road trip. She believes in living in the moment and creating memories.

Jordan, on the other hand, values security and future success. He saves most of his earnings from his weekend job, investing in a savings account for college. He's careful with his spending and often researches before making purchases to ensure he's getting the best value.

Neither approach is inherently right or wrong – they simply reflect different values. Alex's choices align with her value of adventure, while Jordan's align with his value of security. Understanding these differences can help both friends make more intentional decisions and find a balance that works for them.

Aligning Your Money with Your Values

Now that you understand the connection between values and financial decisions, how can you use this knowledge to your advantage? Here are some steps:

1. Identify Your Values: Reflect on what's truly important to you. What drives your decisions? What makes you feel fulfilled?

2. Examine Your Spending: Look at your recent purchases. Do they align with your identified values? Are there areas where your spending doesn't reflect what you claim to value?

3. Set Value-Based Goals: Create financial goals that support your values. If you value education, your goal might be to save for college or additional courses.

4. Make Mindful Decisions: Before making a purchase, ask yourself if it aligns with your values. This can help you avoid impulse buys and make more satisfying financial choices.

5. Seek Balance: Remember, it's possible (and often necessary) to balance multiple values. You can value both fun and security – the key is finding the right balance for you.

Understanding the link between your personal values and financial decisions is a powerful tool for managing your money more effectively. By aligning your spending, saving, and financial goals with what truly matters to you, you can create a more satisfying and purposeful financial life. There's no one-size-fits-all approach to personal finance – the key is to make choices that reflect your unique values and priorities.

Knowing your personal values is important because they shape how you spend, save, and invest your money based on what matters most to you.

I. Key Terms

1. Personal Values: _____

2. Spending Priorities: _____

3. Risk Tolerance: _____

II. Main Concept Overview

Personal values are like an internal _____ that guides our actions

and decisions, including how we handle _____. They influence our

_____ priorities, _____ habits, financial _____, and

attitude towards financial _____.

III. Matching Section

Match each value with its correct description:

_____ Family

_____ Freedom

_____ Security

_____ Adventure

_____ Achievement

A. Seeking new experiences and excitement

B. Emphasizing stability and safety

C. Prioritizing relationships and family well-being

D. Valuing independence and personal autonomy

E. Striving for success and personal growth

IV. The Value-Money Connection

Fill in the table with information from the article about how values influence financial behavior:

Aspect of Finance	How Values Influence It
Spending Priorities	
Saving Habits	
Financial Goals	
Risk Tolerance	
Career Choices	

V. True or False

_____ Personal values remain constant throughout a person's life.

_____ Values like security might lead to prioritizing saving and investing.

_____ People who align their spending with their values report higher levels of financial satisfaction.

_____ It's impossible to balance multiple values when making financial decisions.

_____ Your attitude towards financial risk is influenced by your personal values.

VI. Real-World Application

Read about Alex and Jordan from the article and answer the questions:

1. What value does Alex prioritize? How does this affect her spending?

_____

_____

2. What value does Jordan prioritize? How does this affect his financial behavior?

_____

_____

3. According to the article, is one approach better than the other? Explain.

_____

_____

VII. Reflection/Summary

In your own words, explain how understanding your personal values can help you make better financial decisions:

_____

_____

List the steps mentioned in the article for aligning your money with your values:

1. _____   2. _____

3. _____   4. _____

5. _____

1

How do your current spending habits reflect your personal values?

Think about your recent purchases. Do they align with what's truly important to you? Are there areas where your spending doesn't match your values?

2

How have your family, friends, or culture influenced your values about money?

What messages about money did you grow up with? How does your community view spending and saving? Are there any money beliefs you've adopted that you might want to change?

3

How can understanding the link between values and finances help you make better money choices?

Think of a financial decision you might face soon, like choosing a college or buying a car. How could knowing your values help? Which steps from the article could you use?

The Summer Job Dilemma

Scenario: You've been offered two summer jobs. Job A pays $15/hour at a local office, doing mostly data entry. Job B pays $12/hour at a community center, working with kids on art projects. You enjoy working with children and value creativity, but you also want to save money for college.

Questions:
a) What personal values are at play in this scenario?
b) How might each job choice reflect different financial priorities?
c) What long-term impacts could each choice have on your financial future?

_____

_____

_____

_____

_____

_____

_____

_____

_____

The Windfall Decision

Scenario: Your grandparents give you $5000 for your high school graduation. Your parents suggest you invest it all for your future. Your friends think you should use it for a fun trip to celebrate graduation. You're torn between these options and also considering donating some to a cause you care about.

Questions:
a) What personal values are reflected in each potential use of the money?
b) How might your decision impact your financial situation now and in the future?
c) Can you think of a way to balance multiple values in this situation? What might that look like?

_____

_____

_____

_____

_____

_____

_____

_____

TERM	DEFINITION
Personal Values	
Financial Decisions	
Spending Priorities	
Saving Habits	
Financial Goals	

TERM	DEFINITION
Risk Tolerance	
Impulse Buying	
Mindful Spending	
Financial Satisfaction	
Value-Based Budgeting	

Personal Values and Their Impact on Financial Decisions

```
F L X G Y T S P E N D I N G P R I O R I T I E S
I I S E U M J Y H T P E R S O N A L V A L U E S
R G N T V M O S M J A W S G E L E Q D P L J H U
Z L O A R A M K R I U D P F X C S M D E H I S W
J Z Y V N Q L H C Y N R L F T A E S V N P F Q F
N M P S C C X U U W A D H A O E U N A S I O L I
P L C G E M I R E V K M F H U P K E W I Q S U N
C J M P E B S A Y B P G D U U X O I U A U F T A
O T D Y S V D A L V A A A X L M I F V O M T E N
Q G B Y P V R K V S V S A X X S R Q F L Z M Z C
R G Y H F K I Y A I A P E Q R J P O W T V J H I
M F W R I E S M R O N T O D Y C I E S T D B O A
R N E V N I K I P G C G I D B Q D A N J L C V L
L C I Z A R T W P U D V H S S U L I N D R T P D
M W H A N U O S D R L Z V A F N D R M N I Y N E
Z A D Q C S L K V E Z S D J B A J G D M V N K C
D M J O I R E L F X V N E Y Z I C V E R W E G I
L B U V A F R J I K U G J B Z Y T T K T P V K S
L K U X L Y A M D H M M B I U Z E S I V I C U I
R S Z E G I N Q K I P W F G F Y C L I O Z N D O
P F G U O J C U I W E U N U P F I O B N N C G N
A T U P A V E J E M X B P V U S U N W R Q N L S
R D C X L X G B S O O V B Q N K H L G Z T S G Z
Y V F A S O T S M U S K J U W X F D Y B H G N A
```

Value-Based Budgeting	Financial Satisfaction	Mindful Spending
Impulse Buying	Risk Tolerance	Financial Goals
Saving Habits	Spending Priorities	Financial Decisions
Personal Values		

Personal Values and Their Impact on Financial Decisions

Across

4. Making unplanned purchases based on sudden desires rather than thoughtful consideration, _____ Buying

5. The items or experiences on which an individual chooses to spend their money, based on personal preferences and values, Spending _____

6. The practice of making conscious, deliberate decisions about purchases that align with personal values and financial goals, _____ Spending

7. A method of creating a spending plan that prioritizes allocating money to areas that align with personal values and goals, Value-Based _____

9. Regular patterns of setting aside money for future use or goals, Savings _____

10. Choices made regarding money management, including earning, spending, saving, and investing, Financial _____

Down

1. These core beliefs act as your internal compass for decision-making, Personal _____

2. The degree of variability in investment returns that an individual is willing to withstand, often influenced by personal values, Risk _____

3. A sense of contentment and fulfillment derived from one's financial situation and decisions, Financial _____

8. Specific objectives related to money management, often reflecting personal values and life aspirations, Financial _____

Setting SMART Financial Goals:
Your Path to Financial Success

Imagine you're standing at the edge of a vast financial landscape, filled with opportunities and challenges. How do you navigate this terrain and reach your desired destination? The answer lies in setting SMART financial goals. Whether you're saving for a new gaming console, planning for college, or dreaming of your first car, understanding how to set and achieve financial goals is a crucial life skill that will serve you well beyond high school.

Let's explore the concept of SMART financial goals, why they're important, and how you can use them to take control of your financial future. By the end, you'll have the tools to turn your financial dreams into reality, one SMART goal at a time.

What Are SMART Financial Goals?

SMART is an acronym that stands for Specific, Measurable, Achievable, Relevant, and Time-bound. This framework helps you create clear, attainable goals that can guide your financial decisions. Let's break down each component:

1. Specific: Your goal should be clear and well-defined. Instead of saying "I want to save money," specify "I want to save $500 for a new smartphone."

2. Measurable: You need to be able to track your progress. How will you know when you've reached your goal? In our example, you can easily measure your progress as your savings grow towards $500.

3. Achievable: While it's good to aim high, your goal should be realistic given your current situation. Saving $10,000 in a month might not be achievable for most high school students, but saving $500 over several months could be.

4. Relevant: Your goal should align with your values and long-term objectives. Ask yourself why this goal matters to you and how it fits into your bigger picture.

5. Time-bound: Set a deadline for your goal. This creates a sense of urgency and helps you stay focused. For example, "I want to save $500 for a new smartphone in 5 months."

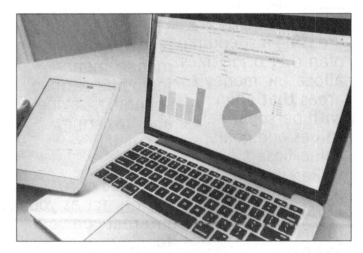

Setting SMART financial goals— Specific, Measurable, Achievable, Relevant, and Time-bound—ensures that your financial plans are clear and attainable, helping you stay focused on your objectives.

Why SMART Financial Goals Matter

Setting SMART financial goals is like having a GPS for your money. Here's why it's so important:

1. Direction: Goals give you a clear direction, helping you focus your efforts and resources where they matter most.

2. Motivation: When you have a specific target and can see your progress, it's easier to stay motivated and resist impulsive spending.

3. Decision-making: Clear goals make it easier to decide whether a purchase aligns with your priorities.

4. Financial literacy: The process of setting and working towards financial goals helps you better understand budgeting, saving, and managing money.

5. Sense of achievement: Reaching your goals, no matter how small, builds confidence and encourages you to set and achieve bigger goals in the future.

Real-World Example: Sarah's SMART Goal

Let's look at how high school student Sarah uses the SMART framework to save for college textbooks:

- *Specific:* Save $600 for first-semester college textbooks
- *Measurable:* Track savings in a dedicated bank account
- *Achievable:* Save $100 per month from part-time job earnings
- *Relevant:* Aligns with goal of being financially prepared for college
- *Time-bound:* Reach goal in 6 months, before the semester starts

Sarah creates a budget, cutting back on eating out and putting her babysitting money directly into her savings account. She tracks her progress weekly, celebrating small milestones along the way. By breaking her goal down into manageable steps and staying focused, Sarah successfully saves $600 for her textbooks, feeling confident and prepared for her first semester.

Applying SMART Goals in Your Life

Ready to set your own SMART financial goals? Here's a simple exercise to get you started:

1. Identify a financial goal you want to achieve.
2. Use the SMART criteria to refine your goal.
3. Write down your goal and put it somewhere visible.
4. Create a simple action plan with specific steps to reach your goal.
5. Track your progress regularly and adjust as needed.

Starting small is okay. As you achieve your initial goals, you can set more ambitious ones. The key is to start the process and build the habit of setting and working towards SMART financial goals.

Setting SMART financial goals is a powerful tool that can help you take control of your financial future. By making your goals Specific, Measurable, Achievable, Relevant, and Time-bound, you create a clear roadmap for financial success. Whether you're saving for something small or planning for major life expenses, the SMART framework can guide you towards making informed financial decisions and achieving your dreams.

2. Setting SMART Financial Goals
GUIDED NOTES

I. Key Terms

1. SMART Goals: _____

2. Financial landscape: _____

3. Financial literacy: _____

II. Main Concept Overview

SMART is an acronym that stands for:

S: _____

M: _____

A: _____

R: _____

T: _____

These components help create _____ and _____ financial goals.

III. Matching Section

Match each SMART component with its correct description:

_____ Specific   A. You can track your progress

_____ Measurable   B. Aligns with your values and long-term objectives

_____ Achievable   C. Clear and well-defined

_____ Relevant   D. Has a deadline

_____ Time-bound   E. Realistic given your current situation

IV. True or False

_____ SMART financial goals are like having a GPS for your money.

_____ Setting a deadline for your goal creates a sense of urgency.

_____ It's better to set vague goals to allow for flexibility.

_____ SMART goals can help with decision-making about purchases.

_____ You should only set ambitious, large-scale financial goals.

V. Fill in the Table

Complete the table with information from Sarah's example in the article:

Goal Description	Total Amount	Time Frame	Monthly Savings
College textbooks			

VI. Application Question

Using the SMART framework described in the article, create a goal for saving for a new smartphone:

Specific: _____

Measurable: _____

Achievable: _____

Relevant: _____

Time-bound: _____

VII. Reflection/Summary

List three reasons why SMART financial goals matter, according to the article:

1. _____

2. _____

3. _____

How can you apply the process of setting SMART financial goals in your life, based on the article's suggestions?

_____

_____

_____

_____

1

How might SMART goals change your spending habits?

Think about your current spending patterns and how you decide what to buy. Consider how having clear, measurable goals might influence these decisions. Reflect on the difference between things you need and things you want, and how SMART goals could help you prioritize.

2

How could achieving a SMART financial goal boost your money confidence?

Remember a time when you accomplished a goal and how it made you feel. Think about how confident you currently feel about handling money. Imagine how successfully reaching a financial target might change your outlook on managing money in the future.

3

How might setting SMART goals now help you in adulthood?

Think about your plans and dreams for the future. Consider the financial responsibilities you know adults have, like budgeting or saving for big purchases. Reflect on how developing good money habits now, through setting and achieving SMART goals, could impact your financial well-being as an adult.

Summer Job Savings

Alex just got a summer job at the local ice cream shop. He want to save money for a laptop for college next year but isn't sure how much he can save.

Questions:
a) How could Alex use the SMART framework to set a savings goal?
b) What factors should Alex consider when deciding how much to save each month?
c) How might setting this SMART goal affect Alex's spending decisions this summer?

_____

_____

_____

_____

_____

_____

_____

_____

_____

_____

Long-term Planning

Taylor wants to start saving for a car they plan to buy in three years when he turns 18.

Questions:
a) How can Taylor use the SMART framework to create a long-term savings plan?
b) What challenges might Taylor face in sticking to a long-term financial goal?
c) How could setting and working towards this long-term goal benefit Taylor beyond just getting a car?

_____

_____

_____

_____

_____

_____

_____

_____

_____

_____

TERM	DEFINITION
SMART Goals	
Financial Literacy	
Budget	
Savings	
Financial Decision-making	

TERM	DEFINITION
Short-term Goal	
Long-term Goal	
Financial Planning	
Impulse Spending	
Financial Priorities	

Setting SMART Financial Goals

```
H N L K O I N L V B Y C T I H C B M A R W Z N M
F G C I M P U L S E S P E N D I N G E P A S N R
I Z G H T Q N F I N A N C I A L P L A N N I N G
N Q G G Z E A R I P I H I X G U Q Y N B C A W X
A K E W M J W B Z N G W R P O Y V X P E L Z J W
N S I L F B U B K P A I J A N Y W H F I F Y J A
C Z M Q M J A H R X H N X G Y Q E U D P I P Q B
I P O A E X D D D P P W C I C T E I L I N C H U
A P F X R V X L H N A S E I U M Z E N Y A R A D
L Y Y F W T I I S Q K G A M A C U Y L V N C G G
D Z I X F X G E D R Z Y O W G L E I W U C M H E
E J G S Z Y Z O O S I Z R L V Z L S C T I E K T
C G C H B Y E A A Z K R P J I Q R I S F A O U Z
I B G O H V R A S L N Z Z N O 'M E I T G L U W H
S Z R R U K C U J I S Y H P X U O C E E P K Z V
I Y N T F E E P G J W Q U V N O K I U U R I Q S
O R S T H D J B J N B D G D W S C R L A I A O N
N C A E W E K O V V U W L O O C U F K P O K C C
M V V R D W E S O E H Z T P W L E J U T R B B Y
A F I M N Y W O T C X G K T Q R N E D A I M Q E
K V N G T Y K J V R C M D N T L A F D Y T C X E
I K G O O L O N G T E R M G O A L E X Z I K N I
N E S A V U B N I M I W A C K J P O J Z E M U M
G L B L S R V O Q H E H J B W E Z A M D S W J L
```

SMART Goals

Short-term Goal

Impulse Spending

Budget

Financial Literacy

Long-term Goal

Financial Priorities

Financial Decision-making

Financial Planning

Savings

Setting SMART Financial Goals

Across

4. Money set aside for future use rather than spent immediately.

5. The ability to understand and effectively use various financial skills, including personal financial management, budgeting, and investing, Financial _____

7. Unplanned or unnecessary purchases made without careful consideration of financial consequences, _____ Spending

8. The process of managing your money to achieve personal economic satisfaction and meet life goals, Financial _____

9. An acronym for Specific, Measurable, Achievable, Relevant, and Time-bound goals used to guide goal setting, _____ Goals

10. A financial objective that can be achieved in a relatively short period, typically less than a year, ____-____ Goal

Down

1. The order of importance assigned to various financial goals or expenses based on personal values and circumstances, Financial _____

2. A financial objective that requires more time to achieve, often several years or more. ____-____ Goal

3. The process of making choices about how to manage money and financial resources, _____ Decision-Making

6. A financial plan for a defined period, typically a month or a year, that outlines estimated income and expenses.

Mastering Your Money:
The Power of Personal Budgeting

Money management is a crucial life skill, and at its core lies the personal budget. Just as a GPS guides you to your destination, a personal budget directs you toward your financial goals. Whether you're saving for a new smartphone, planning for college, or simply trying to make your allowance last, understanding how to create and use a personal budget is key. Let's explore the ins and outs of budgeting, a skill that will set you up for financial success now and in the future.

What is a Personal Budget?

A personal budget is a plan for managing your money over a specific period, usually a month. It's a simple yet powerful tool that helps you track your income, plan your expenses, and make informed decisions about your spending and saving habits. Think of it as a financial snapshot that shows you where your money is coming from and where it's going.

Key Components of a Budget

1. Income: This is all the money you receive, including allowances, part-time job earnings, or gifts.
2. Expenses: These are your costs, divided into fixed (like a phone plan) and variable (like entertainment) categories.
3. Savings: The money you set aside for future goals or emergencies.
4. Debt Payments: If applicable, any money owed on loans or credit cards.

Creating Your Personal Budget

Step 1: Track Your Income and Expenses

Start by recording all your income sources and every penny you spend for a month. This might seem tedious, but it's eye-opening! Use a notebook, spreadsheet, or budgeting app to make this easier.

Step 2: Categorize Your Expenses

Group your expenses into categories like food, transportation, entertainment, and savings. This helps you see where your money is really going.

Step 3: Set Financial Goals

What do you want to achieve financially? Maybe you're saving for a new gaming console, a car, or college tuition. Having clear goals will motivate you to stick to your budget.

Step 4: Create Your Budget Plan

Based on your income, expenses, and goals, allocate specific amounts to each category. A popular method is the 50/30/20 rule:
• 50% for needs (essential expenses)
• 30% for wants (non-essential expenses)
• 20% for savings and debt repayment

Step 5: Implement and Adjust

Put your budget into action and track your progress. Remember, a budget is a living document. You'll need to adjust it as your income, expenses, and goals change over time.

Using Your Budget Effectively

Once you've created your budget, the real work begins. Here are some tips to make the most of it:

1. Review Regularly: Check your budget weekly to ensure you're on track.
2. Use Cash Envelopes: For tricky categories like entertainment, use cash envelopes to limit overspending.
3. Automate Savings: Set up automatic transfers to your savings account on payday.
4. Find Ways to Increase Income: Look for part-time jobs or ways to earn extra money to boost your budget.
5. Cut Unnecessary Expenses: Identify areas where you can reduce spending without sacrificing quality of life.

Creating a personal budget involves tracking income and expenses to manage finances effectively and achieve savings goals.

Real-World Application: The Coffee Shop Conundrum

Let's say you love buying a $4 latte every day. That's $120 a month! Your budget might reveal that this habit is eating into your savings goals. You have options:
1. Cut out the lattes entirely (saving $120)
2. Reduce to twice a week (saving $80)
3. Learn to make lattes at home (potentially saving $100)

By using your budget, you can make an informed decision that aligns with your financial goals without completely giving up something you enjoy.

The Impact of Budgeting

Mastering the art of budgeting has far-reaching effects:

• It reduces financial stress by giving you control over your money.
• It helps you achieve both short-term and long-term financial goals.
• It prepares you for unexpected expenses or emergencies.
• It develops crucial life skills like discipline, planning, and delayed gratification.

Creating and using a personal budget is a fundamental skill that will serve you well throughout your life. It's not about restricting your spending, but about making conscious choices that align with your values and goals. As you become more comfortable with budgeting, you'll find it easier to make smart financial decisions, reach your goals, and build a secure financial future. The road to financial success starts with a single step – creating your first budget.

I. Key Terms

1. Personal Budget: _____

2. Income: _____

3. Expenses: _____

4. Savings: _____

II. Main Concept Overview

A personal budget is a _____ for managing your _____

over a specific period, usually a _____. It helps you track your

_____, plan your _____, and make informed decisions about

your _____ and _____ habits.

III. Matching Section

Match the terms with their correct descriptions:

_____ Fixed Expenses   A. Money set aside for future goals or emergencies

_____ Variable Expenses   B. All money received, including allowances, part-time job earnings, or gifts

_____ Income   C. Costs that change, like entertainment

_____ Savings   D. Regular costs that stay the same, like a phone plan

IV. True/False Questions

_____ 1. A personal budget is about making conscious choices that align with your values and goals.

_____ 2. The 50/30/20 rule suggests allocating 50% of your income to needs.

_____ 3. Tracking your expenses for a month is an important step in creating a budget.

_____ 4. A budget is a living document that needs to be adjusted as your income, expenses, and goals change.

_____ 5. Using cash envelopes can help limit overspending in certain categories.

V. Fill in the Table

Complete the table below with the steps for creating a personal budget:

Step	Description
1	
2	
3	
4	
5	

VI. Application Question

The article mentions "The Coffee Shop Conundrum." Describe this scenario and explain how using a budget can help make an informed decision in this situation.

_____

_____

_____

_____

VII. Reflection/Summary

Summarize the main points of the article in your own words. How do you think creating and using a personal budget could benefit you in your current life situation?

_____

_____

_____

_____

1

How might having a personal budget change your spending habits?

Think about your recent purchases. Would a budget have changed these decisions? Consider both small daily expenses and larger occasional buys. How might a budget help you prioritize your spending?

2

Do you think the 50/30/20 rule would work for you right now?

How might this change in the future? Look at your current income and expenses. How close are you to this allocation? How might moving out or starting a career affect this balance? What adjustments might you need to make?

3

How could technology help or hurt your budgeting efforts?

What budgeting apps or tools have you heard of? How might they make budgeting easier or harder? Think about how these tools could impact your awareness of spending and saving habits.

Unexpected Expense

Jordan has been following a budget for a few months and has saved some money for new soccer gear. Suddenly, her bike needs an expensive repair. Jordan's parents agree to pay half if Jordan covers the rest.

Questions:
a) How might this unexpected expense impact Jordan's budget?
b) What options does Jordan have for covering this expense while minimizing the impact on their soccer gear savings?

First Debit Card

Casey just opened her first checking account with a debit card. She is excited about the convenience but nervous about managing it responsibly.

Questions:
a) How could Casey incorporate debit card use into their existing budget?
b) What strategies could Casey use to ensure they don't overspend with the debit card?
c) How might using a debit card impact Casey's ability to track expenses in their budget?

TERM	DEFINITION
Budget	
Income	
Expenses	
Savings	
Fixed Expenses	

TERM	DEFINITION
Variable Expenses	
Financial Goals	
Cash Flow	
Debt	
Discretionary Income	

Creating and Using a Personal Budget

```
S M Z B U B J L U R O R K V Z B I M K I U H R F
T S G J M U A P B Y Q H B O G G M X G B D E B T
H Z P D H Y U F I M K T E D S Z F R X V S G S Q
S D Q M I B V A M Y P N Z N W S K S L B Z Y V J
G X O C O S O Z J S B W K U D U J E E R K B A S
B Z L D A Q C D S B G C H Y A O Y R N Y E G R E
J V F A M S P R I J Z F C L R T H B J Q K S I W
R B K P P F H D E G G Y I I Z D Q V P Z F V A M
D J B S K I C F I T U U F X L Z C F M V N H B S
X N S U C N M U L S I Q B K E G H C G E R M L F
T P A R N A J E D O C O G Z V D R D T M Z R E R
Y S A V I N G S M M W R N K C C E X S E B O E Q
A A O O R C G C T E Q Y E A U X Z X O Z I H X M
M C Q R P I J B T O J A P T R D O A P P G C P O
M D H Y U A L I J C P I T C I Y P Z X E Z G E M
G D F D W L P P H G F A N T W O I P G S N D N T
E B L Q B G D T A I O J U C I J N N W Y J S S V
P A C J P O X Z I S V L U D O G R A C E F A E Y
C V G H F A T E D D J U K B B M T V R O I K S S
V P M X K L C T M U Q I U N E C E U Q Y M R F F
Q A R V H S G H B T E B S M Y H V F Y F V E B Z
A E X P E N S E S R N V L J B U D G E T Z C H D
H P Q J O N C W W I L R R Y X B B O L C W V O X
E S P R H M L W B R G P J S L H A Q Z B H L L C
```

Discretionary Income   Financial Goals   Variable Expenses

Fixed Expenses   Debt   Cash Flow

Savings   Expenses   Income

Budget

Creating and Using a Personal Budget

Across

5. Money set aside for future use or for unexpected costs.

6. Money received, especially on a regular basis, for work or through investments.

8. A plan for managing money during a given period of time.

9. Regular expenses that generally remain the same each month, such as rent or a phone plan, _____ Expenses

10. Expenses that change from month to month, such as entertainment or groceries, _____ Expenses

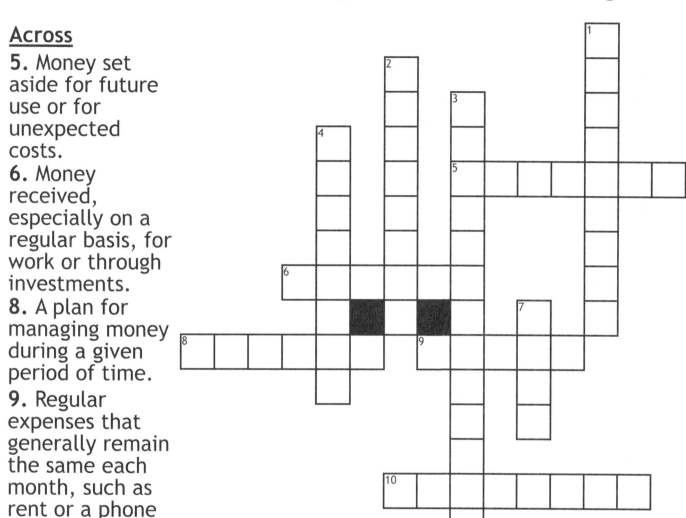

Down

1. Specific, measurable objectives related to money management, _____ Goals

2. The movement of money into and out of a budget. (2 words)

3. Money left over after paying for necessities, available for spending or saving as desired, _____ Income

4. The amount of money that is spent on goods and services.

7. Money owed to another person or institution.

The Power of Tracking:
Mastering Your Income and Expenses

In the world of personal finance, one skill stands out as absolutely crucial: the ability to track your income and expenses. This fundamental practice is the cornerstone of sound financial management and can set you on the path to achieving your monetary goals, whether they're short-term desires or long-term dreams.

Understanding Financial Tracking

At its core, tracking income and expenses is the process of recording all the money that comes into your possession (income) and all the ways you spend it (expenses). It's like creating a financial diary of your life, showing where your money comes from and where it goes.

For high school students, income might come from various sources such as part-time jobs, allowances, gifts, or entrepreneurial ventures like mowing lawns or tutoring. Expenses often include food and snacks, entertainment (movies, games, apps), transportation costs, clothing, and savings for future purchases.

The Importance of Tracking

Understanding the flow of your money is crucial for several reasons:

1. Awareness: It's easy to underestimate how much you're spending when you're not keeping track. A $5 coffee here, a $10 movie ticket there – it all adds up. Tracking makes these expenses visible.

2. Goal Setting: Whether you're saving for a new smartphone, a car, or college tuition, knowing your financial situation helps you set realistic goals and timelines.

3. Budgeting: Tracking is the first step in creating a budget. You can't plan for the future if you don't know where you stand today.

4. Financial Responsibility: Learning to track your finances now builds habits that will serve you well throughout your life, from managing student loans to buying a house.

5. Identifying Patterns: You might notice you're spending more than you thought on certain categories, allowing you to make informed decisions about where to cut back.

How to Track Your Finances

Now that we understand why tracking is important, let's explore how to do it effectively:

1. Choose Your Method: You have several options:
   - Pen and Paper: Simple and straightforward. Use a notebook to record all income and expenses.
   - Spreadsheets: Programs like Excel or Google Sheets allow for more detailed tracking and analysis.
   - Mobile Apps: Many free apps are designed specifically for financial tracking, offering features like category sorting and visual reports.

2. Record Everything: The key to effective tracking is to record every financial transaction, no matter how small. That $2 vending machine snack counts!

3. Categorize Your Expenses: Group your expenses into categories like food, entertainment, transportation, etc. This helps you see where most of your money is going.

4. Review Regularly: Set aside time each week to review your tracker. This habit helps you stay on top of your finances and spot any areas where you might be overspending.

5. Be Consistent: Tracking only works if you do it consistently. Make it a daily habit to update your records.

Real-World Application

Let's say you're tracking your expenses and notice you're spending $100 a month on fast food. That's $1,200 a year! By packing lunch more often, you could potentially save hundreds of dollars annually – money that could go towards your other goals.

The Bigger Picture

Tracking your income and expenses isn't just about managing your money today; it's about setting yourself up for future success. As you grow older, your financial responsibilities will increase. You might need to manage student loans, rent, or even mortgage payments. The habits you form now will be the foundation for your financial future.

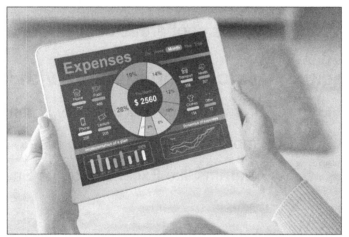

Tracking your income and expenses is important because it helps you understand where your money goes and teaches you to manage your finances wisely.

Understanding your financial patterns can help you make informed decisions about your career path. You might realize you need to look for higher-paying jobs or additional income streams to meet your financial goals.

Overcoming Challenges

Tracking finances isn't always easy. Here are some common challenges and how to overcome them:

1. Forgetting to Record: Keep your tracking tool (whether it's an app or a notebook) easily accessible. Set reminders on your phone if needed.

2. Losing Receipts: Take pictures of receipts with your phone or request digital receipts when possible.

3. Feeling Overwhelmed: Start simple. Begin by tracking just one category of expenses, then gradually add more as you get comfortable with the process.

4. Lack of Motivation: Set small, achievable financial goals. Watching your progress can be a great motivator to keep tracking.

Tracking your income and expenses is a powerful tool in your financial toolkit. It gives you clarity about your financial situation, helps you make informed decisions, and sets you on the path to achieving your monetary goals. While it may seem tedious at first, the insights and control you gain are invaluable. Every financial expert started somewhere – and this is your starting point.

By mastering the art of tracking your income and expenses, you're taking a crucial step towards financial literacy and success. Start today, and watch as your financial awareness and management skills grow over time.

I. Key Terms

1. Income: _____

2. Expenses: _____

3. Financial tracking: _____

II. Main Concept Overview

Financial tracking is the process of _____ all the money that

_____ into your possession and all the ways you _____ it.

III. Importance of Tracking (Fill in the blanks)

1. A_____: Makes all expenses visible

2. Goal S_____: Helps set realistic financial goals and timelines

3. B_____: First step in creating a financial plan

4. Financial R_____: Builds important lifelong habits

5. Identifying P_____: Helps spot areas of overspending

IV. Methods of Tracking (Match each method with its description)

_____ Pen and Paper   A. Offers features like category sorting and visual reports

_____ Spreadsheets   B. Simple and straightforward method using a notebook

_____ Mobile Apps   C. Programs like Excel or Google Sheets for detailed

analysis

V. Steps to Effective Tracking (True/False)

_____ You only need to record large expenses when tracking.

_____ Categorizing expenses helps you see where most of your money is going.

_____ It's enough to review your tracker once a month.

_____ Consistency is key to successful financial tracking.

_____ You should start by tracking all categories of expenses at once.

VI. Real-World Application (Fill in the table)

Monthly Fast Food Spending	Annual Cost	Potential Savings

VII. Overcoming Challenges (Match the challenge with its solution)

_____ Forgetting to Record   A. Take pictures of receipts or request digital ones

_____ Losing Receipts   B. Set small, achievable financial goals

_____ Feeling Overwhelmed   C. Keep tracking tool easily accessible, set reminders

_____ Lack of Motivation   D. Start with one category, then gradually add more

VIII. Reflection/Summary

1. How might tracking your income and expenses benefit you in the future?

_____

_____

_____

_____

_____

2. What method of tracking do you think would work best for you, and why?

_____

_____

_____

_____

_____

1

How might tracking your spending change your habits?

Think about your recent purchases. Would you make the same choices if you were recording every dollar spent? Consider areas where you might be overspending without realizing it.

2

How can tracking help you reach long-term financial goals?

Think of a big purchase you want to make in the future, like a car or a laptop. How could keeping track of your money help you save for it? Consider how it might influence your daily spending decisions.

3

How might tracking your finances affect your feelings about money?

Do you ever feel stressed about money? How could having a clear picture of your income and expenses change that? Think about both positive and negative ways it might impact your relationship with money.

The Forgotten Subscriptions

Sarah, a high school junior, starts tracking her expenses and realizes she's spending $50 a month on forgotten app subscriptions and streaming services she rarely uses. Some are free trials she forgot to cancel, while others are old subscriptions she no longer needs.

Questions:
a) How might tracking her expenses help Sarah in this situation?
b) What steps could Sarah take to address this issue?
c) How much could Sarah potentially save in a year by canceling unnecessary subscriptions?

_____
_____
_____
_____
_____
_____
_____
_____
_____
_____

The Savings Challenge

Jamie wants to buy a used car that costs $5,000 by the end of the school year, which is 10 months away. She decides to start tracking her income from babysitting and her monthly allowance, as well as all her expenses.

Questions:
a) How can tracking her finances help Jamie reach her goal?
b) What specific information should Jamie focus on in her tracking to help her save for the car?
c) If Jamie's average monthly income is $300, what strategies could she use to save enough for the car?

_____
_____
_____
_____
_____
_____
_____
_____
_____
_____

TERM	DEFINITION
Income	
Expenses	
Financial Tracking	
Budget	
Cash Flow	

TERM	DEFINITION
Financial Goals	
Overspending	
Financial Responsibility	
Categorization	
Financial Literacy	

Tracking Income and Expenses

```
V N Y L T T Z D A G U J E B D N C A S H F L O W
S B N R J Z A X U J Y B T C B B E F V M N Y G D
C Z O A F L Z Z A M K J V N G F I L P Q D F V U
P K A Z Y F J D Z R W H N I F R A N W G Z J M W
S L M C T X I T T L E Q Z K I G V S C Q H X E I
J L K Q G W U A P Z N E R S H N G S D O L H S B
P S G F U C B H F T X I X D P R A X J H M S B M
S R P T W C P P I R E R C P Z F Z X T Y V E C C
T E Y S A F S F N Y Z I M W E I H D H K A Y A D
Z F I N A N C I A L R E S P O N S I B I L I T Y
T P G X G Q L H N B E J W H E A S B T C S A E C
O T H Q T Z V M C K H Y R D P N O E V S S O G Q
O K K M I O U R I K F R D N Y C D H S Q P K O P
S V Y K Y F I N A N C I A L L I T E R A C Y R S
C Y E L O E V P L Q F K U U N A B G R W N Q I R
Z D Z R W X D Y G I H V X A Y L S P N Y K E Z W
Q C S X S U T E O O P V R W B T C B R I S J A S
O S Y V R P X B A S P F Y Y C R X M A Q B B T R
C F Z I J B E B L O K J U L B A A X B E I H I M
Y V G E B Q U N S I E R X G M C F E T P U J O A
Z T C L Q J B D D V I U K C X K R E I B Y N N H
M X N V C H M S G I T C H C R I B P O G X D U F
Q E P J M M D G G E N E F B K N D P Z K W C A C
K N G W E E V O F S T G M T S G N U I S T U Y D
```

Financial Tracking	Financial Goals	Financial Responsibility
Financial Literacy	Categorization	Overspending
Cash Flow	Budget	Expenses
Income		

Tracking Income and Expenses

Across

3. The ability to understand and effectively use various financial skills, Financial _____

5. This term refers to all the funds you receive, whether from a job, allowance, or gifts.

6. The movement of money into and out of your possession. (2 words)

7. The practice of managing money and financial decisions effectively, Financial _____

8. Specific objectives you aim to achieve with your money, Financial _____

9. The act of spending more money than planned or available.

10. This practice involves keeping a detailed record of your money's inflow and outflow, Financial _____

Down

1. The process of grouping expenses into specific types or classes.

2. These are the costs you incur in your daily life, from buying lunch to paying for a movie ticket.

4. This financial tool helps you allocate your money to different categories of spending and saving.

The Hidden Price Tag:
Understanding Opportunity Costs in Financial Decisions

Every financial decision we make comes with a hidden price tag – the opportunity cost. This concept is crucial for understanding the true impact of our choices and plays a vital role in shaping our financial future. Let's explore opportunity costs, their significance in financial decision-making, and how grasping this concept can empower you to make smarter choices with your money.

What Are Opportunity Costs?

An opportunity cost is the value of the best alternative you give up when making a choice. It's the "road not taken" in your financial journey. Every time you decide to spend money on something, you're also deciding not to use that money for something else. This "something else" is your opportunity cost.

Examples:

- When you buy a $5 latte, your opportunity cost might be $5 you could have saved towards a new bike.
- If you work a part-time job instead of joining a sports team, your opportunity cost is the potential athletic experience and skills you miss out on.
- When you save money for college instead of spending it on concert tickets, your opportunity cost is the immediate fun and memories from the concert.

Understanding opportunity costs helps you see the full picture of your financial decisions. It's not just about what you're getting, but also about what you're giving up in the process.

Why Opportunity Costs Matter

Recognizing opportunity costs is crucial for several reasons:

1. Better Decision Making: You're more likely to make choices that align with your long-term goals and values.

2. Budgeting Skills: It helps you prioritize your spending and saving, making budgeting more effective.

3. Long-Term Thinking: It encourages you to consider the future impact of your choices.

4. Resource Management: You learn to allocate your limited resources (money, time, energy) more efficiently.

5. Financial Awareness: It increases your overall financial literacy, helping you become more conscious of your money habits.

Calculating Opportunity Costs

Calculating opportunity costs can be straightforward. Here's a simple formula:

**Opportunity Cost =
Value of the Next Best Alternative -
Value of the Chosen Option**

For example:
You have $1,000 and are deciding between a savings account earning 2% interest annually or stocks expected to appreciate by 7% over the year.

If you choose the savings account:
Opportunity Cost = (7% of $1,000) - (2% of $1,000) = $70 - $20 = $50

Your opportunity cost is $50 – the additional return you could have potentially earned by investing in stocks.

Applying Opportunity Cost Thinking

Understanding opportunity costs can transform your approach to everyday financial decisions:

1. Spending Choices: Before buying something, ask yourself, "What else could I do with this money?"

2. Saving and Investing: Consider the long-term opportunity costs of not saving or investing early.

3. Education and Career: Weigh the costs and potential returns of different educational or career paths.

4. Time Management: Remember, time is a valuable resource too. Consider the opportunity costs of how you spend your time.

Opportunity Costs and Financial Goals

Thinking about opportunity costs naturally leads to setting and prioritizing financial goals. When you understand what you're giving up for each choice, you become more intentional about aligning your spending with your values and long-term objectives.

For instance, if your goal is to graduate college debt-free, recognizing the opportunity cost of small, regular expenses can motivate you to save more. That daily $5 latte might not seem like much, but when you consider that it could be $1,825 towards your college fund over a year, the choice becomes clearer.

Real-World Application

Consider this scenario: You're offered a summer job that pays $2,000, but it would mean missing a family vacation. The opportunity cost here isn't just monetary – it includes the experiences and memories you'd miss. On the flip side, the job could provide valuable work experience and networking opportunities. Weighing these factors against each other is the essence of considering opportunity costs.

Another example is choosing between two college majors. If you're deciding between engineering and business, you need to consider not just the cost of education, but also the potential future earnings, job satisfaction, and career growth opportunities in each field. The opportunity cost of choosing one major is the potential benefits you might have gained from the other.

Understanding opportunity costs is like having a financial superpower. It allows you to see beyond the surface of your choices and make decisions that truly serve your best interests. As you move forward in your financial journey, remember to ask yourself not just "What will I gain?" but also "What will I give up?" This mindset will guide you towards smarter financial choices and help you build a stronger, more secure financial future.

Every financial decision has a hidden price tag – the opportunity cost. By recognizing and evaluating these costs, you're taking a crucial step towards financial wisdom and success.

Analyzing opportunity costs in financial choices helps you understand what you give up when you make a decision, allowing you to make smarter choices about how to spend your money.

5. Analyzing Opportunity Costs in Financial Choices
GUIDED NOTES

I. Key Terms

1. Opportunity Cost: _____

2. Financial Awareness: _____

3. Long-Term Thinking: _____

II. Main Concept Overview

Opportunity cost is the value of the _____ _____ you give up when making a choice. It's the "_____ not _____" in your financial journey.

III. Matching Section

Match each term with its correct description:

_____ Budgeting Skills   A. Considering future impact of choices

_____ Resource Management   B. Prioritizing spending and saving effectively

_____ Long-Term Thinking   C. Allocating limited resources efficiently

_____ Time Management   D. Considering opportunity costs of how you spend time

_____ Financial Awareness   E. Being conscious of your money habits

IV. Fill in the Table

Complete the table with examples of opportunity costs from the article:

Decision	Chosen Option	Opportunity Cost
Buying a $5 latte		
Working a part-time job		
Saving for college		

V. True/False

_____ Opportunity costs only apply to monetary decisions.

_____ Understanding opportunity costs can lead to better decision making.

_____ The formula for calculating opportunity cost is: Value of Next Best Alternative - Value of Chosen Option.

_____ Opportunity costs encourage considering both immediate and future consequences of financial decisions.

_____ Time should be considered when evaluating opportunity costs.

VI. Application Question

The article mentions a scenario about a summer job offer. What are the opportunity costs involved in this decision? How does this example illustrate the concept of opportunity costs?

_____

_____

_____

_____

VII. Reflection/Summary

Based on the article, explain how understanding opportunity costs can help you make smarter financial choices and achieve your long-term goals:

_____

_____

_____

_____

1

How has learning about opportunity costs changed the way you think about spending money?

Think about your last purchase. What did you give up to buy it? Was it worth it? How might you decide differently next time?

2

Can you give an example of a non-financial opportunity cost in your life?

Look at how you spend your time. What activities do you choose, and what do you miss out on? How do you decide what's most important?

3

How might understanding opportunity costs change the way you approach your education or career choices?

What opportunities does your current path offer? What are you giving up? How could this concept help you make better choices about your future?

The Summer Job Opportunity

Sarah has been offered a summer job at a local restaurant. However, taking this job means she won't be able to attend a free coding camp that lasts for the same period. The coding camp could potentially lead to better job opportunities in the future.

Questions:
a) What are the immediate and long-term opportunity costs for Sarah in this scenario?
b) How might the concept of opportunity cost help Sarah make her decision?
c) What non-financial factors should Sarah consider in making her choice?

_____

_____

_____

_____

_____

_____

_____

_____

_____

_____

The College Choice

Alex has been accepted to two colleges. College A is a prestigious private university that will leave him with significant student loan debt after graduation. College B is a public university where he can graduate debt-free thanks to a scholarship, but it's less renowned in his field of study.

Questions:
a) What are the potential opportunity costs for Alex in choosing College A? In choosing College B?
b) How might considering opportunity costs help Alex make this decision?
c) What long-term implications should Alex consider for each choice?

_____

_____

_____

_____

_____

_____

_____

_____

_____

_____

TERM	DEFINITION
Opportunity Cost	
Financial Decision	
Long-Term Goal	
Budget	
Resource Management	

TERM	DEFINITION
Financial Awareness	
Spending Choice	
Saving	
Value	
Trade-off	

Opportunity Costs in Financial Decisions

```
N F V Y R I X L T E H V Y J D I R Y W N N K P A
N N I H C T R F Q A P Y W V W J I A O I F G G I
O V Z N T R R Y M Z T A U D U C B X P D Y L E J
P X V S A D Z N Z V P C I H Y U V Z T M Z R H D
P F J O J N C H N J T V X P S K E S N M B W U S
O B I Q F H C X O R W R H I K A S E K Z K U C B
R V M N M H L I X C U W A K A H V N L G S N I U
T T Y S A X X F A B T B G D K U P I O P P F B Q
U K N P Q N T G W L Y U P Q E T L C N Z E S W Y
N G I C T H C R D D D Q E Q B O U A G G N E C M
I P R V U N L I K Y F E Q P V R F B T F D S H W
T R E V T G R V A R Y V C X K K S F E D I F A J
Y Q J J L R U T O L X C H I L X N A R A N J W I
C K N B T C G C Z X A Q R X S W T P M M G S S M
O Y U U P J J F H Z L W J L Z I N Y G K C L S Y
S U S T N O O M I N E Z A E P E O Y O R H B V U
T W E N B F X N X Q F C W R I Y P N A W O F C X
L Y X X H N B Y J V X D P K E E P O L B I H Z I
V S U B B J Q N P B A F F P Z N G A Y A C O H O
B O Y R V R M C A Z U L U P O C E X E F E O C X
N J H R E O O D X G U U U E O O I S M B D Q J S
B G Z L G G W O D R C W Z E Y J K O S P B P Z P
O T M S R N H S B A B U D G E T Y I H I S X D P
E N D U R E S O U R C E M A N A G E M E N T Q R
```

Financial Decision	Long-Term Goal	Resource Management
Financial Awareness	Spending Choice	Trade-off
Value	Saving	Budget
Opportunity Cost		

Opportunity Costs in Financial Decisions

Across

2. Each of these involves an opportunity cost, _____ Choice

3. A choice made about money matters, Financial _____

5. The importance, worth, or usefulness of something.

7. An objective or desired result that requires time and planning to achieve, _____-_____ Goal

8. A plan for saving and spending money.

9. The efficient and effective deployment of an organization's resources when they are needed, _____ Management

10. Setting aside money for future use.

Down

1. The value of the best alternative given up when making a choice. (2 words)

4. Being conscious and knowledgeable about one's money habits and financial situation, Financial _____

6. A balance achieved between two desirable but incompatible features. (2-words)

Unlocking the Income Puzzle:
Exploring Various Ways to Earn

In today's dynamic economy, understanding the diverse landscape of income sources is crucial for financial success. Many individuals find themselves limited by relying on a single income stream, often unaware of the myriad opportunities available to diversify their earnings. This article will explore the various types of income that exist in our modern financial world. By gaining insight into these different income streams, you'll be better equipped to make informed financial decisions and plan for a secure financial future.

What is Income?

At its core, income is money received, typically on a regular basis, for work performed or through investments. It serves as the financial foundation that supports our daily lives, fuels our aspirations, and helps us achieve our dreams. However, it's essential to recognize that not all income is created equal. Understanding the nuances of different income types can provide you with a significant advantage in managing your finances and building long-term wealth.

Types of Income

1. Earned Income

Earned income is the most common type of income for the majority of people. It represents the money you receive for providing services or selling products directly.

• Wages and Salaries: This is the income you earn from working for an employer. It's typically paid on an hourly, weekly, or monthly basis.
• Self-Employment Income: If you run your own business or work as a freelancer, the money you earn is considered self-employment income.

• Tips and Commissions: Additional compensation based on performance or service quality falls under earned income.

2. Passive Income

Passive income is money earned with minimal ongoing effort. It often requires an upfront investment of time or money but can provide long-term financial benefits.

• Rental Income: Money earned from renting out property you own.
• Royalties: Income from allowing others to use your intellectual property, such as books, music, or patents.
• Dividend Income: Regular payments made to shareholders from a company's profits.

3. Portfolio Income

Portfolio income is derived from investments and the selling of investments.

• Interest Income: Money earned from savings accounts, certificates of deposit, or bonds.
• Capital Gains: Profit made from selling investments like stocks or real estate for more than the purchase price.

4. Residual Income

Residual income is ongoing income from work done once. It's similar to passive income but often requires more initial effort.

• Network Marketing: Income from building a team of distributors in a multi-level marketing company.
• Online Courses or E-books: Creating educational content that continues to sell over time.

The Impact of Income Types on Financial Planning

Understanding these different types of income is crucial for several reasons:

1. Tax Implications: Different types of income are taxed at different rates. For example, earned income is subject to payroll taxes, while some forms of passive income may have tax advantages.

2. Financial Stability: Diversifying your income sources can provide more financial security. If one income stream dries up, you have others to fall back on.

3. Retirement Planning: Building passive income streams can be an effective strategy for maintaining your lifestyle in retirement.

4. Wealth Building: Some types of income, like portfolio and passive income, have the potential to grow wealth more quickly than relying solely on earned income.

Applying Your Knowledge

Now that you're familiar with these income types, it's important to reflect on your own financial situation. Consider what types of income you currently have and whether there are opportunities to diversify your income streams.

Consider this scenario: Sarah, a high school teacher, earns a salary (earned income) but also creates and sells online lesson plans (residual income) and invests in dividend-paying stocks (portfolio income). By diversifying her income, Sarah has created multiple streams of revenue, increasing her financial stability and potential for wealth growth.

The Role of Financial Literacy in Income Diversification

Understanding different income types is just one aspect of financial literacy. To truly leverage this knowledge, it's important to continually educate yourself about personal finance, investment strategies, and economic trends. This ongoing learning process can help you identify new opportunities for income diversification and make more informed decisions about your financial future.

Understanding the different types of income is a crucial step in taking control of your financial future. Whether you're just starting your career or planning for retirement, knowing how to leverage various income streams can help you build a more secure and prosperous financial life. Remember, the key to financial success often lies not just in how much you earn, but in how diversified and strategic your income sources are. By exploring and potentially incorporating different types of income into your financial portfolio, you can create a more resilient and prosperous financial future for yourself and your family.

Understanding different types of income, such as earned, passive, and portfolio income, helps you recognize various ways to earn money and plan your finances better.

6. Understanding Different Types of Income
GUIDED NOTES

I. Introduction

A. Income is defined as: _____

B. Why is understanding different types of income important? (List two reasons)

   1. _____

   2. _____

II. Types of Income

A. Earned Income

   1. Definition: _____

   2. Examples:

      a. _____

      b. _____

      c. _____

B. Passive Income

   1. Definition: _____

   2. Examples:

      a. _____

      b. _____

      c. _____

C. Portfolio Income

   1. Definition: _____

   2. Examples:

      a. _____

      b. _____

D. Residual Income

   1. Definition: _____

   2. Examples:

      a. _____

      b. _____

III. Impact of Income Types on Financial Planning

List four ways understanding income types impacts financial planning:

A. _____

B. _____

C. _____

D. _____

IV. Applying Knowledge

Scenario: Sarah's Income Diversification

1. Earned Income: _____

2. Residual Income: _____

3. Portfolio Income: _____

V. True or False

_____ Different types of income are taxed at different rates.

_____ Passive income requires minimal ongoing effort.

_____ Diversifying income sources can provide more financial security.

_____ Portfolio and passive income have the potential to grow wealth more quickly than relying solely on earned income.

_____ Understanding different income types is crucial for effective financial planning.

VI. Matching

_____ Wages and Salaries   A. Portfolio Income

_____ Rental Income   B. Earned Income

_____ Interest   C. Residual Income

_____ Online Courses   D. Passive Income

_____ Capital Gains   E. Portfolio Income

VII. Reflection

1. What is the key to financial success according to the article?

_____

_____

2. How does financial literacy relate to income diversification?

_____

1

How might knowing about different income types affect your future job choices?

Think about what careers could offer multiple income streams. Consider how this knowledge might change your plans for college or training after high school. How could having various income types impact your long-term financial goals?

2

Why is having multiple income sources important for financial stability?

Reflect on how different income streams could help during tough economic times. Think about the pros and cons of relying on just one type of income versus having several. How might this affect your financial safety net?

3

How does passive income change the way we think about making money?

Consider the benefits and drawbacks of earning money with little ongoing effort. How might pursuing passive income change someone's daily life or work habits? Think about examples of passive income you might be able to create.

The Recent Graduate

Emma just graduated from high school and is considering her options. She's been offered a job at a local restaurant making $15 per hour. Her friend suggests she instead focus on building a YouTube channel about budget travel, which could potentially earn money through ads and sponsorships.

Questions:
a) What types of income are represented in each option?
b) How might Emma's short-term and long-term financial stability differ between these choices?
c) What factors should Emma consider when deciding between these options?

_____
_____
_____
_____
_____
_____
_____
_____
_____
_____

The Side Hustle

Mark works full-time as a teacher but wants to increase his income. He's considering either tutoring students after school or creating and selling educational materials online.

Questions:
a) Identify the types of income represented in Mark's current job and each of his potential side hustles.
b) How might each option impact Mark's overall financial picture differently?
c) What are the potential risks and benefits of each choice?

_____
_____
_____
_____
_____
_____
_____
_____
_____

TERM	DEFINITION
Income	
Earned Income	
Passive Income	
Portfolio Income	
Residual Income	

TERM	DEFINITION
Diversification	
Financial Stability	
Retirement Planning	
Wealth Building	
Financial Literacy	

Understanding Different Types of Income

```
F X X J U U A U P F J W O B E C K J Z V Z M Y Z
I B D M T L F I N A N C I A L L I T E R A C Y G
G J Q W X G C I Q F K S A U T W P R L N C J H E
N Q U N L W S W D B D J F D S U O Z H Y S E M G
G R E S I D U A L I N C O M E T R A E B K R N J
W W V G G D N A E N V F M K L O T I A T V N Q P
Z T R I N P K O I A Z E P F E R F M P O D F T V
S V E B K A E J T J R N R G J Z O O Q H S O T F
I E T C H X H W A M J N C S M F L B S H Y D U R
G A I J Y K H E W E J K E I I H I Y I T I M R S
B G R I T L Y A N H I M X D T F O L Z T Q X U N
M P E A A Q B L N Z N P P B I B I B F H Y U K U
I J M P B U O T J N C B D L O N N C H P Z B I D
I G E N N D R H M V O M S V Y Y C U A T Y Z N C
Q D N A E X X B O J M E S M U V O O S T S M H R
M A T O Q Z Q U H H E Z Y V W M K M L I C K G
O D P P A S S I V E I N C O M E E N Q E P O X R
A X L H E E D L R C Z T U Y F B F Y O K F K N I
G G A H E S D D V G H T D R F R W F T W U D P Z
Q K N V Y X Z I N K X N S E R R G Y O B Z P I M
F N N M C C E N M F M E X D M I R F Q S T D P O
K V I T H T P G G A D Q V T H I L T G Z U K K Y
A Y N G G F I N A N C I A L S T A B I L I T Y B
K N G S V E T F R Q X X E S J P N T R Q J V N Q
```

Earned Income	Passive Income	Portfolio Income
Residual Income	Financial Stability	Retirement Planning
Wealth Building	Financial Literacy	Diversification
Income		

Understanding Different Types of Income

Across

2. The ability to understand and effectively use various financial skills, including personal financial management, budgeting, and investing, Financial _____

5. The process of generating long-term income through multiple sources, often with a focus on creating assets that appreciate in value over time, _____ Building

8. Money received for providing services or selling products directly, such as wages, salaries, or self-employment income, _____ Income

9. The practice of varying income sources or investments to reduce risk and increase financial stability.

10. Money received, especially on a regular basis, for work or through investments.

Down

1. The state of having consistent income and manageable debts, allowing for financial security and the ability to meet financial obligations, Financial _____

3. The process of determining retirement income goals and the actions and decisions necessary to achieve those goals, _____ Planning

4. Ongoing income from work done once, such as royalties from books or revenues from online courses, _____ Income

6. Money earned with minimal ongoing effort, often from investments or business ventures that don't require active involvement, _____ Income

7. Income derived from investments and the selling of investments, including interest, dividends, and capital gains, _____ Income

Charting Your Future:
Navigating Career Choices and Financial Pathways

In today's dynamic job market, choosing a career is more than just picking a job—it's about crafting a financial future. As high school students, you stand at the threshold of countless possibilities, each with its own set of financial implications. Let's explore how your career choices can shape your economic landscape and equip you with the tools to make informed decisions.

Understanding the Career-Finance Connection

When we think about careers, we often focus on job descriptions and required skills. However, the financial aspect of a career choice is equally crucial. Your career doesn't just determine what you'll do from 9 to 5; it significantly influences your earning potential, lifestyle, and long-term financial health.

The Salary Spectrum

Different careers come with varying salary ranges. For instance, a software developer in the United States might earn an average of $107,510 annually, while a teacher could earn around $61,730. This difference of over $45,000 per year can dramatically impact your financial life, from the house you can afford to the vacations you can take.

Beyond the Paycheck

But salary isn't the only financial factor to consider. Some careers offer extensive benefits packages that can significantly boost your overall compensation.

These might include:

- Health insurance
- Retirement plans (like 401(k)s with employer matching)
- Paid time off
- Stock options
- Educational reimbursement

For example, a job offering a lower salary but comprehensive benefits could potentially provide more financial value than a higher-paying job with minimal benefits.

Education and Training: Investing in Your Future

The path to your chosen career often involves an investment in education or training. This investment can have substantial financial implications:

1. College Degrees: While a bachelor's degree can increase your earning potential, it also often comes with student loan debt. The average student loan debt in the U.S. is about $37,574.

2. Vocational Training: Some high-paying careers require specialized vocational training rather than a traditional four-year degree. Electricians, for instance, can earn a median salary of $56,900 after completing an apprenticeship program.

3. Certifications: In fields like IT, certifications can boost your earning potential. A Certified Information Systems Security Professional (CISSP) can earn an average of $116,900 annually.

Career Progression and Financial Growth

Your first job out of school is just the beginning. Many careers offer opportunities for advancement that come with financial rewards:

- *Promotions:* Moving up the corporate ladder often means salary increases and better benefits.
- *Specialization:* Developing expertise in a niche area can lead to higher pay.
- *Entrepreneurship:* Some careers provide knowledge and skills that can be leveraged to start your own business.

Consider a nurse who starts at $75,330 annually. With experience and additional certifications, they could become a nurse practitioner, potentially earning $117,670 or more.

The Impact of Location on Career Finances

Where you work can be as financially significant as what you do. The cost of living and job market vary greatly by location:

- A teacher in Mississippi might earn an average of $45,574, while the same position in New York could pay $87,543.
- However, the cost of living in New York is significantly higher, which could offset the salary difference.

Balancing Passion and Practicality

While financial considerations are important, they shouldn't be the sole factor in your career choice. Job satisfaction, work-life balance, and personal fulfillment play crucial roles in overall life satisfaction. The key is to find a balance between your passions and financial realities.

Planning for Your Financial Future

As you explore career options, consider these steps to ensure a sound financial future:

1. Research potential salaries and benefits for careers you're interested in.
2. Understand the education or training required and its associated costs.
3. Look into career progression opportunities within your chosen field.
4. Consider the impact of location on your career and finances.
5. Develop a budget based on potential earnings to understand what lifestyle you can afford.

Your career choice is one of the most significant financial decisions you'll make. By understanding the financial implications of different career paths, you can make an informed decision that aligns with both your passions and your financial goals.

As you stand on the brink of your professional journey, remember that knowledge is power. The more you understand about the financial aspects of your career choices, the better equipped you'll be to navigate your path to a successful and fulfilling future. Your career is not just a job—it's a key that can unlock the door to your financial dreams.

Exploring career options involves understanding the potential financial implications, such as salary expectations, job stability, and growth opportunities, to make informed decisions that align with personal goals and economic realities.

I. Main Concept Overview

The choice of career significantly impacts your _____ future.

It affects not just your job responsibilities, but also your _____

potential, _____, and long-term financial _____.

II. Matching Section

Match the term with its correct description:

_____ Salary   A. Additional job perks beyond base pay

_____ Benefits   B. Money owed for educational expenses

_____ Student Loan Debt   C. Base monetary compensation for work

_____ Entrepreneurship   D. Starting and running your own business

III. The Salary Spectrum

Fill in the table with information from the article:

Career	Average Annual Salary
Software Developer	
Teacher	
Nurse Practitioner	

IV. True or False

_____ The highest paying job is always the best financial choice.

_____ Location has no impact on career finances.

_____ All high-paying careers require a four-year college degree.

_____ Certifications can increase earning potential in some fields.

V. Beyond the Paycheck

List three examples of benefits that can boost overall compensation:

1. _____ 2. _____

3. _____

VI. Education and Training

Fill in the blanks:

1. The average student loan debt in the U.S. is about $_____.

2. An electrician can earn a median salary of $_____ after

completing an apprenticeship program.

3. A Certified Information Systems Security Professional (CISSP) can earn an

average of $_____ annually.

VII. Career Progression and Financial Growth
List two ways career progression can lead to financial growth:

1. _____

2. _____

VIII. The Impact of Location
How does location affect career finances? Provide an example from the article:

_____

_____

_____

IX. Application Question
The article mentions the importance of balancing passion and practicality in career choices. Explain why this balance is important and how it relates to both job satisfaction and financial considerations.

_____

_____

_____

X. Planning for Your Financial Future
List three steps the article suggests for planning your financial future as you explore career options:

1. _____

2. _____

3. _____

1

How might your dream career affect your future finances?

Think about your financial goals, like buying a car or a house. How could your career choice help or hinder these goals? Consider both salary and benefits in your reflection.

2

Is pursuing additional education worth it financially for your chosen career?

Compare the costs of extra education with potential salary increases. How long might it take to pay off student loans? Think about non-financial benefits too, like job satisfaction.

3

How might changing technology affect your career choice and finances?

Think about how your chosen field might change with new tech. Could some jobs disappear or new ones emerge? How could learning new skills impact your earning potential?

College vs. Coding Bootcamp

Jamie loves coding and has two options:

A) Go to college for 4 years, costing $100,000 in loans. Could lead to a $80,000/year job.
B) Do a 6-month coding bootcamp for $15,000. Might start at $50,000/year but could reach $80,000 in 3 years.

Questions:
a) What are the pros and cons of each choice?
b) How might each option affect Jamie's finances in 5 years?
c) Besides money, what else should Jamie think about?

_____
_____
_____
_____
_____
_____
_____
_____
_____
_____

Different Paths in Healthcare

Michael wants to work in healthcare. He's considering:

A) Become a nurse (4-year degree, start at $60,000/year)
B) Become a paramedic (2-year degree, start at $40,000/year)

Questions:
a) How do the costs and potential earnings of each path compare?
b) How might each job affect Michael's work-life balance?
c) Which path do you think is better financially? Why?

_____
_____
_____
_____
_____
_____
_____
_____
_____
_____

TERM	DEFINITION
Career	
Salary	
Benefits	
Investment	
Student Loan	

TERM	DEFINITION
Compensation	
Cost of Living	
Financial Implication	
Earning Potential	
Entrepreneurship	

Exploring Career Options and Their Financial Implications

```
N M K P W U F O X P W P H P R M J K G K I Z M Y
N H R C S H O X P C E Z F P U Z Y F I B Q E N M
A W P B R H Y N V T F E Q J H Z W L I X K F J F
L R F I N A N C I A L I M P L I C A T I O N T G
B T Q V S X N H G C O M P E N S A T I O N G E E
Z E G W U X G J T B A C Z G J I Q U A M R Z B A
O N N E O H V D W E H O L E P N N L I M Z M V V
E I I E I G I G G N E S L A D I Q W L Y I K M B
N N I V F I O N H T F T B R K A G D Q N O P R N
O S O N K I F F B R P O G N S J O I F V A W D A
D T M I V H T T J E E F J I O O K G P C R A R L
T U D E F E P S H P P L Q N E M C U X Z V X M H
S D S S R H S E A R K I C G I A V J A D K T H V
H E S C A H C T U E G V F P T C B B R Z Y V X B
Z N K R E L C W M N N I X O N U X G E H X C A F
Y T E K J N A N J E M N U T S U X W U D B Y G Y
T L C C N M V R Q U N G N E Q R X R K B X E G R
B O S W W T E R Y R P T I N J P T F S Y O B C X
R A G A O M T O Y S G P T N W L Z U K T X A O
V N W Z C F L S V H M D P I K Y U L O Y D Q R J
J O X O X A D P X I G F O A J N S D W Q X K E H
B B S L P M X X D P J X V L T X E Z H P R B E C
L K G L J N I M C T Q K R X G W Z T A R D Z R J
D R X B Q Y Z S J J T B Q L E U O C O J E U S P
```

Student Loan

Earning Potential

Investment

Career

Cost of Living

Entrepreneurship

Benefits

Financial Implication

Compensation

Salary

Exploring Career Options and Their Financial Implications

Across

4. The total amount of the monetary and non-monetary pay provided to an employee by an employer in return for work performed.

8. The action of investing money for future financial return.

9. The activity of setting up a business, taking financial risks in the hope of profit.

10. A fixed regular payment, typically paid on a monthly basis, made by an employer to an employee.

Down

1. A profession or occupation chosen as one's life's work.

2. The potential financial effect or consequence of a decision or action, Financial _____

3. Money borrowed to pay for educational expenses, Student _____

5. The amount of money a person has the ability to earn in their career over time, Earning _____

6. The amount of money needed to sustain a certain standard of living, including basic expenses such as housing, food, and healthcare, Cost of _____

7. Additional compensation provided to employees beyond salaries.

Decoding Your Paycheck:
A High School Student's Guide to Financial Literacy

Imagine this: It's your first payday at your new part-time job, and you're excited to see the fruits of your labor. But when you look at your paycheck, it's a maze of numbers and terms you don't understand. Don't worry; you're not alone! Many high school students (and even adults) find paychecks confusing at first. Let's demystify the components of a paycheck, helping you understand where your money goes and why. By the end, you'll be equipped with essential knowledge for your financial future.

Gross Pay: The Starting Point

Your journey begins with gross pay - the total amount you've earned before any deductions. If you're paid hourly, this is your hourly rate multiplied by the number of hours worked. For salaried positions, it's a portion of your annual salary. Remember, this isn't what ends up in your bank account!

Deductions:
Where Does the Money Go?

1. Taxes: Uncle Sam's Share

• Federal Income Tax: A percentage of your earnings goes to the federal government, based on your income level and filing status.
• State Income Tax: Most states also take a cut, though rates vary depending on where you live and work.
• FICA (Federal Insurance Contributions Act): This funds Social Security (6.2% of your gross pay) and Medicare (1.45% of your gross pay). These programs provide benefits for retirees, the disabled, and children of deceased workers.

2. Other Possible Deductions

• Health Insurance: If you're eligible for employer-provided health coverage, your contribution might be deducted from your paycheck.
• Retirement Contributions: Some jobs offer 401(k) plans, allowing you to save for the future. If you choose to participate, a percentage of your pay will be deducted and invested.

Net Pay: What You Actually Receive

After all deductions, you're left with your net pay or "take-home pay." This is the amount that will be deposited into your bank account or given to you as a physical check. It's crucial to understand that this is the actual amount you have available to spend or save.

Understanding Your Pay Stub

Your pay stub is like a receipt for your work. It typically includes:

• Pay Period: The specific dates you're being paid for.
• Year-to-Date (YTD) Totals: Cumulative earnings and deductions for the year so far.
• Personal Information: Your name, address, and sometimes the last four digits of your Social Security number.
• Employer Information: The company's name and address.
• Itemized Deductions: A breakdown of each deduction taken from your gross pay.

Why This Matters to You

Understanding your paycheck is crucial for several reasons:

1. Budgeting: Knowing your net pay helps you plan your spending and saving accurately. You can't budget effectively if you don't know how much money you're actually bringing home.

2. Tax Awareness: You'll understand why your take-home pay differs from your gross pay. This knowledge is essential when filing your taxes and planning for your financial future.

3. Career Planning: This knowledge helps you evaluate job offers and understand the true value of your compensation. A higher salary doesn't always mean more take-home pay if the deductions are significantly different.

4. Financial Responsibility: It's a key step in managing your personal finances. Understanding your paycheck is the foundation of financial literacy.

Real-World Application

Let's say you earn $12 per hour and work 20 hours a week. Your gross pay would be $240. However, after deductions for taxes (let's estimate 20% for simplicity), your net pay might be around $192. Understanding this difference is crucial for budgeting and financial planning.

Consider this: If you were planning to save $100 from each paycheck for a car, you'd need to base that goal on your net pay, not your gross pay. If you budgeted based on your gross pay, you might find yourself short on funds for other expenses.

Thinking Critically About Your Paycheck

As you start your working life, consider these questions:

• How do different deductions affect your take-home pay?
• What steps can you take to maximize your earnings and minimize unnecessary deductions?
• How might understanding your paycheck now benefit you in future career decisions?
• If you're offered a job with benefits like health insurance or a 401(k), how will that impact your take-home pay? Is the trade-off worth it?

Reading and understanding your paycheck is an essential life skill. It's not just about knowing how much money you're making; it's about understanding the broader picture of employment, taxes, and personal finance. As you move forward in your work life, this knowledge will be invaluable in making informed financial decisions.

Each paycheck tells a story – your story of work, earnings, and contributions to society. By understanding this story, you're taking a significant step towards financial literacy and independence. Whether you're saving for college, planning for a major purchase, or just managing your day-to-day expenses, the ability to read and understand your paycheck is a crucial tool in your financial toolkit.

Reading and understanding your paycheck is crucial for managing finances effectively, as it reveals essential details about your earnings, deductions, and contributions, ensuring you are accurately compensated for your work.

8. Reading and Understanding a Paycheck
GUIDED NOTES

I. Key Terms

1. Gross Pay: _____

2. Net Pay: _____

3. FICA: _____

II. Main Concept Overview

Paychecks consist of several components, including _____ pay, various

_____, and _____ pay. Understanding these elements is

crucial for effective _____ and financial planning.

III. Matching Section

Match the term with its correct description:

_____ Federal Income Tax   A. Funds Social Security and Medicare

_____ State Income Tax   B. The amount you actually receive

_____ FICA   C. Percentage taken by the federal government

_____ Gross Pay   D. Varies depending on where you live and work

_____ Net Pay   E. Total amount earned before deductions

IV. True/False

_____ Gross pay is what ends up in your bank account.

_____ Understanding your paycheck is only important for budgeting purposes.

_____ FICA stands for Federal Insurance Contributions Act.

_____ Your pay stub includes Year-to-Date (YTD) totals.

_____ All states have income tax.

V. Application Question

Using the example from the article:

If you earn $12 per hour and work 20 hours a week:

a) What is your gross pay? _____

b) Assuming 20% in deductions, what is your approximate net pay?

_____

How could you use this information for budgeting?

_____

_____

_____

VI. Reflection/Summary

1. List three reasons why understanding your paycheck is important, according to the article:

a) _____

b) _____

c) _____

2. How might understanding your paycheck benefit you in future career decisions?

_____

_____

_____

3. What are two questions you should consider when thinking critically about your paycheck?

a) _____

b) _____

1

Why is understanding your paycheck important for evaluating job offers?

Imagine comparing two job offers with different salaries and benefits. How would knowing about taxes and deductions help you decide? Think about which job might actually give you more take-home pay.

2

How do you feel about FICA deductions funding programs that you might not use until you're older?

These programs are designed to help people in the future, including your future self. How important do you think it is to contribute to these programs now? Consider both the personal and societal impacts of these programs.

3

What voluntary deductions might you choose to have on your paycheck in the future?

Think about things like health insurance or retirement savings. How might these deductions benefit you in the long run? Consider the trade-off between having less take-home pay now versus potential future benefits.

First Summer Job

You've just started your first summer job at a local ice cream shop. On your first payday, you're excited to see your earnings, but you notice the amount on your paycheck is less than you expected based on your hours worked and hourly rate.

Questions:
a) What factors might explain why your actual paycheck is less than you anticipated?
b) How might this realization about the difference between gross and net pay affect your summer spending plans?
c) What steps could you take to better understand your paycheck and plan your budget accordingly?

Comparing Job Offers

You're about to graduate high school and have received two job offers. Job A offers a higher salary with no benefits. Job B offers a lower salary but includes health insurance and a 401(k) plan with company match.

Questions:
a) Besides the salary, what other factors should you consider when comparing these two job offers?
b) How might the benefits offered by Job B affect your overall compensation compared to Job A?
c) Why is it important to consider more than just the salary when evaluating job offers?

TERM	DEFINITION
Gross Pay	
Net Pay	
FICA (Federal Insurance Contributions Act)	
Deductions	
Pay Stub	

TERM	DEFINITION
Federal Income Tax	
State Income Tax	
Year-to-Date (YTD)	
Withholding	
Pay Period	

Understanding Your Paycheck

```
I U S G T J D Z G T H X J Q J V G Q M O R V J X
I N A X M U G D Y S F L W O Z I Z R P C P Y R C
I F H T O C R X S P X F I C A S A F O H E K Z V
B O F V W F L E W D N V Q V R J J D Q S T L T G
W G Y F N M A I A I W X G T R L Z Z I D S H R X
H U P E T K E Q C J T Y Z I G N U F R U F P P C
K F Y U A W P L M F X H O T P L K N H P O R A W
U N V G R Q A P N X B H S U F V E Z U C J U Y
J G X D J I T S Y G Q W U O I K B T W A I S P N
F Z O O L K W O S P P T F V L K S P S U R R B Q
A Z N O E E G V D D E D W D D M A X M H G Y T
K J R A B P Z R W A T R P I D Y I Y K Z Y Z L B
Z S L H M S B Q Z O T J I W P F S N T Y L U O B
Y P Y V M I N K R E P E Z O F B Q F G A D U A P
Q U U R Z N O Q B A A O M Y D U R R J M C V U A
O D H N C Y J P S T A T E I N C O M E T A X X Y
U R M H N T U F F W M C C M K J D N D N N G L S S
I F R P D E D U C T I O N S Y R Y N K Y E X L T
M W W F E D E R A L I N C O M E T A X D S C W U
F Q J C O O U R A D S B O L U E S X T V T J R B
L Q A V Q E F T Q B A J K D K B B Y N F G C E B
N U U V J I B T L U I T E P U G W T H K H E D M
E H P M U G A Y W T T P S X U S I D W H K X E B
U K V L Z Q S K A M J A M P O A Z B X E P P Y D
```

Pay Period	Year-to-Date	State Income Tax
Federal Income Tax	Net Pay	Gross Pay
Withholding	YTD	Pay Stub
Deductions	FICA	

Understanding Your Paycheck

Across

2. A tax levied by the federal government on your earnings, withheld from each paycheck, _____ Income Tax

6. Amounts subtracted from your gross pay, including taxes, insurance premiums, and retirement contributions.

8. The recurring schedule on which you receive your paycheck and for which your wages are calculated (e.g., weekly, bi-weekly, monthly), Pay _____

9. The cumulative total of your earnings and deductions from the beginning of the calendar year to the current pay period. (Abbrv.)

10. Stands for Federal Insurance Contributions Act, which funds Social Security and Medicare through payroll deductions. (Abbrv.)

Down

1. A document that itemizes your pay, including gross wages, deductions, and net pay for a specific pay period. (2 words)

3. The amount of money taken out of your paycheck for taxes and other deductions before you receive it.

4. The total amount you've earned before any deductions are taken out, _____ Pay

5. Also known as "take-home pay," this is the amount you actually receive after all deductions have been subtracted from your gross pay, _____ Pay

7. A tax levied by most states on your earnings, also typically withheld from each paycheck, _____ Income Tax

Navigating the World of Personal Income Taxes: Your Financial Responsibility

As you step into the workforce and receive your first paycheck, you'll quickly discover that a portion of your hard-earned money is deducted before it reaches your bank account. This is your introduction to personal income taxes. While it might seem challenging at first, understanding how income taxes work is crucial for every young adult entering the job market. This article will demystify personal income taxes, explaining their purpose, how they're calculated, and why they're an essential part of your financial life.

What Are Personal Income Taxes?

Personal income taxes are a form of direct taxation imposed by the government on an individual's earnings. These taxes serve as a primary source of revenue for federal, state, and sometimes local governments. The funds collected through income taxes

Income taxes are mandatory financial charges imposed by the government on individuals' earnings to fund public services and infrastructure.

support various public services and programs, including education, healthcare, infrastructure, and national defense.

Key Components of Personal Income Taxes:

1. Taxable Income: This is the portion of your income subject to taxation. It includes wages, salaries, bonuses, and other forms of compensation.

2. Tax Brackets: The U.S. uses a progressive tax system, meaning tax rates increase as your income rises. Your income is divided into "brackets," each taxed at a different rate.

3. Deductions and Credits: These are tools that can reduce your taxable income or tax liability, potentially lowering the amount you owe.

4. Withholding: This is the amount your employer deducts from each paycheck to cover your estimated tax liability.

How Personal Income Taxes Work

When you start a new job, you'll typically fill out a W-4 form, which helps your employer determine how much tax to withhold from your paycheck. Throughout the year, this withholding serves as a pre-payment of your taxes.

Come tax season (usually January to April), you'll need to file a tax return. This process involves:

1. Calculating your total taxable income for the year
2. Determining your tax liability based on your income and tax bracket
3. Subtracting the amount you've already paid through withholding
4. Either paying any remaining balance or receiving a refund if you've overpaid

Why Understanding Personal Income Taxes Matters

Grasping the basics of personal income taxes is crucial for several reasons:

1. Financial Planning: Knowing how much of your income will go to taxes helps you budget more effectively.

2. Maximizing Your Money: Understanding deductions and credits can help you legally reduce your tax burden.

3. Avoiding Penalties: Filing your taxes correctly and on time helps you avoid costly fines and legal issues.

4. Civic Responsibility: Paying taxes is part of your duty as a citizen, contributing to the functioning of society.

Real-World Application

Consider Sarah, a recent high school graduate who just landed her first part-time job at a local café. She earns $12 per hour and works 20 hours per week. Her annual income would be approximately $12,480 (assuming 52 weeks of work). At this income level, Sarah falls into the 10% federal tax bracket for 2021.

However, Sarah's actual tax liability would likely be lower due to the standard deduction ($12,550 for single filers in 2021), which would reduce her taxable income to zero. While she may not owe federal income tax, she would still see deductions for Social Security and Medicare taxes on her paycheck.

Personal income taxes may seem complex, but they're an unavoidable part of adult life. By understanding the basics now, you're setting yourself up for financial success in the future. Remember, as your income grows and your financial situation becomes more complex, don't hesitate to seek advice from tax professionals or use reputable tax preparation software.

As you embark on your career journey, keep in mind that taxes are more than just a financial obligation—they're an investment in the society you live in. Your contribution, no matter how small, plays a part in shaping the world around you.

9. Introduction to Personal Income Taxes
GUIDED NOTES

I. Key Terms

1. Personal Income Tax: _____

2. Taxable Income: _____

3. Tax Bracket: _____

4. Deduction: _____

II. Main Concept Overview

Personal income taxes are a form of _____ taxation imposed by the

government on an individual's _____. They serve as a primary source of

_____ for federal, state, and sometimes local governments.

III. Matching Section

Match each term with its correct description:

_____ Withholding   A. The portion of your income subject to taxation

_____ W-4 Form   B. Amount deducted from each paycheck for estimated tax liability

_____ Taxable Income   C. Form that helps employers determine tax withholding

_____ Tax Brackets   D. Income divisions taxed at different rates

_____ Deductions   E. Tools that can reduce your taxable income

IV. Components of Personal Income Taxes

Component	Description
Taxable Income	
Tax Brackets	
Deductions and Credits	
Withholding	

V. True/False

_____ The U.S. uses a progressive tax system where tax rates increase as income rises.

_____ Filing your taxes correctly and on time helps you avoid costly fines and legal issues.

_____ Tax withholding serves as a pre-payment of your taxes.

_____ Understanding personal income taxes can help with financial planning.

_____ Personal income taxes only fund federal programs.

VI. Key Aspects of Personal Income Taxes

List four reasons why understanding personal income taxes is important:

1. _____

2. _____

3. _____

4. _____

VII. Application Question

Sarah, a high school graduate, earns $12 per hour working 20 hours per week at a café. Using the information provided in the article, explain why Sarah might not owe federal income tax despite earning an income. Show your calculations.

_____

_____

_____

VIII. Reflection/Summary

Summarize the main points of the article in your own words. How does understanding personal income taxes relate to your future financial decisions?

_____

_____

_____

1

How do you think paying income taxes will change your spending and saving habits?

Look at your current budget or spending habits. How might they change when you start paying taxes? Think about both your everyday expenses and long-term savings goals. How could you adjust your financial plans to account for taxes?

2

What's your view on the idea that paying taxes is a civic responsibility?

Reflect on the public services funded by taxes, like schools or roads. How do you benefit from these services? Think about your role as a future taxpayer. How does this relate to your ideas about being a good citizen?

3

What can you do now to prepare for managing your taxes in the future?

What habits could you start developing to make tax time easier? Think about keeping records of income and expenses. How could understanding your paycheck now help you later? What resources might be useful for learning more about taxes?

The Summer Job Surprise

Jake gets a summer job at the local ice cream shop. He works 20 hours a week for $10 an hour. When he gets his first paycheck, he's surprised to see it's less than he expected.

Questions:
a) Why is Jake's paycheck less than he calculated?
b) What might Jake learn about income taxes from this experience?
c) How could Jake better prepare for his next paycheck?

_____
_____
_____
_____
_____
_____
_____
_____
_____

The Part-Time Puzzle

Alex starts a part-time job at a local bookstore. He works 15 hours a week and earns $12 per hour. After a month, he compares his total hours worked with the amount on his paycheck and feels confused.

Questions:
a) Why might Alex's paycheck be different from his simple hourly wage calculation?
b) What deductions might Alex see on his paycheck stub?
c) How could understanding these deductions help Alex in his future financial planning?

_____
_____
_____
_____
_____
_____
_____
_____
_____

TERM	DEFINITION
Personal Income Tax	
Taxable Income	
Tax Bracket	
Withholding	
W-4 Form	

TERM	DEFINITION
Tax Return	
Deduction	
Tax Credit	
Progressive Tax System	
Standard Deduction	

Personal Income Taxes

```
P K F G 4 C T T A X A B L E I N C O M E P P W M
M R O R U Y X W A Y F S F W R L W W 4 L K W O A
X W O F T P E R S O N A L I N C O M E T A X I I
U R R G C A T A X B R A C K E T I C E G S D W M
I H E S R O X G G X P E B H F U D L M 4 A X 4 C
O H V X M E P R A G B T H G A F G H E H O A V W
X K S A H G S D E K D P V M T U L A M N N N C M
F 4 V G M L B S T T R U T P 4 W M F I H R C K G
W P M H C D S X I I U D E W I T H H O L D I N G
V U I C U R D U M V K R I T T S D A X P F O M B
M Y 4 N W I N C Y T E C N G W M R C D S I Y I D
Y H L K L G W E C L T T B 4 D E S U V P L A M U
V A X B N P D B L Y A R A I K E C U T T Y W G K
M R W U V S D L M H X K F X A R D S V L G X X K
H S R H 4 G 4 A A P C X I U S X C U I S M 4 A V
T E F R I 4 G T B G R A B H G Y G A C G F E E G
Y H K H W C A O W G E U W K U A S M K T G I G I
B K C B F U N I N D D C S 4 Y L I T B G I H K C
P I P K M I 4 M K S I S W N F S P F E A E O R O
F K K L 4 L M M 4 C T P 4 K E O G K E M S H N S
C H M N E I P D K D M P D I M G R E K X T G X N
K C N D H 4 W T G H W M B G A A H M Y A 4 X F U
V N F S T A N D A R D D E D U C T I O N S A K E
A A Y G K M X X N F S X S D A M I R F R D V B G
```

Deduction

Tax Credit

Taxable Income

Withholding

Standard Deduction

Tax Return

Personal Income Tax

Progressive Tax System

Tax Bracket

W-4 Form

Personal Income Taxes

Across

7. A form of direct taxation imposed by the government on an individual's earnings, _____ Income Tax

8. A reduction in the amount of tax owed, differing from a deduction which reduces taxable income, Tax _____

9. A specific dollar amount that reduces your taxable income, an alternative to itemizing deductions, Standard _____

10. The amount your employer deducts from each paycheck to cover your estimated tax liability.

Down

1. The portion of your income subject to taxation, including wages, salaries, and bonuses, _____ Income

2. A reduction in taxable income, potentially lowering the amount of taxes owed.

3. A form filled out when starting a new job that helps your employer determine how much tax to withhold from your paycheck. (__-__ _____)

4. A range of incomes taxed at a specific rate in a progressive tax system, Tax _____

5. A form filed with the tax authority that reports income, expenses, and other relevant tax information, Tax _____

6. A system where tax rates increase as the taxable amount increases, _____ Tax System

Employee Benefits and Their Value: More Than Just a Paycheck

When evaluating job offers, many people focus solely on the salary. However, employee benefits play a crucial role in determining the true value of a compensation package. These benefits, forms of non-wage compensation provided to employees in addition to their regular salary, can significantly impact your overall financial well-being and quality of life. This article explores various types of employee benefits, their value, and why they matter in your career decisions.

Understanding Employee Benefits

Employee benefits are additional compensations offered by employers to attract and retain talented employees. These benefits can be mandatory (required by law) or voluntary (offered at the employer's discretion). They often represent a substantial portion of an employee's total compensation package, sometimes accounting for up to 30% of the total value.

Types of Employee Benefits

1. Health Insurance
Health insurance is one of the most valuable and common employee benefits. It helps cover medical expenses, including doctor visits, hospital stays, and prescription medications. Some employers offer additional coverage for dental and vision care.

2. Retirement Plans
Employers may offer retirement savings plans such as 401(k)s or pension plans. These benefits help employees save for their future and often include employer contributions, effectively boosting your long-term savings.

3. Paid Time Off (PTO)
PTO includes vacation days, sick leave, and personal days. This benefit allows employees to take time off work while still receiving their regular pay, promoting work-life balance and employee well-being.

4. Life and Disability Insurance
These insurance policies provide financial protection for employees and their families in case of death or disability, offering peace of mind and financial security.

5. Educational Assistance
Some employers offer tuition reimbursement or professional development programs, supporting employees' continued learning and career growth.

The Hidden Value of Employee Benefits

While your salary might seem like the most important factor in job compensation, employee benefits can significantly increase the overall value of your employment package. Here's why:

1. Tax Advantages
Many benefits, such as health insurance premiums and retirement plan contributions, are often tax-deductible or tax-deferred. This means you can save money on taxes while receiving valuable benefits.

2. Cost Savings
Employer-sponsored health insurance plans are typically less expensive than individual plans, as employers can negotiate better rates with insurance providers due to group coverage.

3. Financial Security

Benefits like retirement plans and life insurance provide long-term financial security, helping you prepare for the future and protect your loved ones.

4. Work-Life Balance

Benefits such as paid time off and flexible work arrangements can greatly improve your quality of life, reducing stress and increasing job satisfaction.

Evaluating a Benefits Package

When considering a job offer or comparing different opportunities, it's crucial to look beyond the salary and evaluate the entire compensation package. Here's a simple exercise to help you assess the value of employee benefits:

1. List all the benefits offered by the employer.
2. Estimate the monetary value of each benefit (e.g., the cost of health insurance if you were to purchase it individually).
3. Add up the values of all benefits.
4. Add this total to the annual salary to get a more accurate picture of your total compensation.

Remember, some benefits may be more valuable to you depending on your personal circumstances. For example, if you have a chronic health condition, comprehensive health insurance might be particularly important to you.

Emerging Trends in Employee Benefits

As the workplace evolves, so do employee benefits. Some emerging trends include:

1. **Mental Health Support:** More companies are offering counseling services and mental health days.
2. **Flexible Work Arrangements:** Remote work options and flexible schedules are becoming increasingly common.

3. **Financial Wellness Programs:** Some employers provide financial education and planning services to help employees manage their money better.
4. **Student Loan Assistance:** With rising student debt, some companies offer help with loan repayments as a benefit.
5. **Wellness Programs:** These might include gym memberships, health screenings, or incentives for healthy behaviors.

Employee benefits play a crucial role in your overall compensation and can significantly impact your financial well-being and job satisfaction. By understanding and properly valuing these benefits, you can make more informed decisions about your career and maximize the value of your employment package. Remember, when it comes to job compensation, there's much more to consider than just the number on your paycheck.

As you enter the job market or consider career changes, take the time to thoroughly evaluate benefits packages. They can make a substantial difference in your overall job satisfaction and financial health. By considering the full picture of compensation, including both salary and benefits, you'll be better equipped to make choices that align with your personal and professional goals.

Employee benefits, such as health insurance, retirement plans, and paid time off, add significant value to compensation packages by enhancing financial security, well-being, and work-life balance.

10. Employee Benefits and Their Value

I. Introduction

A. Employee benefits are forms of _____ provided in addition to regular salary or wages.

B. Benefits can significantly impact your overall _____ _____ and quality of life.

II. Understanding Employee Benefits

A. Employee benefits can be:

   1. _____: required by law

   2. _____: offered at employer's discretion

B. Benefits can account for up to _____% of an employee's total compensation package.

III. Types of Employee Benefits

A. _____ Insurance: Covers medical expenses, sometimes including dental and vision care.

B. _____ Plans: Help employees save for the future (e.g., 401(k)s, pension plans).

C. Paid Time Off (PTO): Includes _____, _____, and personal days.

D. Life and _____ Insurance: Provides financial protection for employees and their families.

E. _____ Assistance: May include tuition reimbursement or professional development programs.

IV. The Hidden Value of Employee Benefits

A. _____ Advantages: Many benefits are tax-deductible or tax-deferred.

B. _____ Savings: Employer-sponsored plans are often less expensive than individual plans.

C. Financial _____: Benefits like retirement plans provide long-term security.

D. Work-Life _____: Benefits like PTO can improve quality of life and job satisfaction.

V. Evaluating a Benefits Package

Steps to assess the value of employee benefits:

1. _____

2. _____

3. _____

4. _____

VI. Emerging Trends in Employee Benefits

Match each trend with its description:

_____ Mental Health Support   A. Remote work options and flexible schedules

_____ Flexible Work Arrangements   B. Financial education and planning services

_____ Financial Wellness Programs   C. Help with loan repayments

_____ Student Loan Assistance   D. Counseling services and mental health days

_____ Wellness Programs   E. Gym memberships, health screenings, or

                                                                          incentives for healthy behaviors

VII. True or False

_____ Employee benefits account for about 31% of the total compensation for civilian workers on average.

_____ All employee benefits are mandated by law.

_____ Some companies offer pet insurance as an employee benefit.

_____ The salary is always the most important factor when evaluating a job offer.

_____ Employer-sponsored health insurance is usually more expensive than individual plans.

VIII. Matching

Match each term with its correct description:

_____ Health Insurance   A. Helps employees save for future

_____ Retirement Plans   B. Covers medical expenses

_____ PTO   C. Protects against loss of income due to illness or

                                                                          injury

_____ Educational Assistance D. Paid vacation, sick days, and personal time

_____ Disability Insurance   E. Supports continued learning and career growth

1

How could a good benefits package affect your job satisfaction and work-life balance?

How might benefits like paid time off or flexible work hours impact your daily life? Think about how these benefits could affect your stress levels and overall happiness at work. Consider the long-term effects on your career and personal life.

2

How does understanding total compensation (salary plus benefits) change how you look at job offers?

Compare a job with a higher salary but fewer benefits to one with a lower salary but better benefits. What factors would you need to think about? How might this affect your job choices in the future?

3

Why do you think some companies offer unique benefits like student loan help or pet insurance?

How do these benefits reflect changes in what employees want or need? What does this suggest about how work and society are changing? What new benefits do you think might become common in the future?

The Job Offer Dilemma

Alex, a recent high school graduate, has received two job offers:
Company A offers a salary of $35,000 per year with basic health insurance and 10 days of paid time off.
Company B offers a salary of $32,000 per year but provides comprehensive health insurance (including dental and vision), 15 days of paid time off, and a 401(k) plan with a 3% company match.

Questions:
a) How should Alex evaluate these two job offers?
b) What factors beyond the immediate salary should Alex consider?
c) How might Alex's decision impact their financial situation in the short term and long term?

_____

_____

_____

_____

_____

_____

_____

_____

_____

_____

The Start-up vs. Established Company

Jamie is deciding between two summer internship opportunities:
A well-established tech company offers a paid internship with a structured schedule, health insurance coverage, and the possibility of future employment.
A promising start-up offers a higher hourly wage but no additional benefits. However, they provide a more flexible schedule and the potential for rapid career growth.

Questions:
a) What are the pros and cons of each internship opportunity in terms of benefits?
b) How might the difference in benefits affect Jamie's overall experience and future career prospects?
c) In what ways could the flexible schedule be considered a benefit, and how does it compare to traditional benefits?

_____

_____

_____

_____

_____

_____

_____

_____

_____

TERM	DEFINITION
Compensation	
Benefits	
Health Insurance	
Retirement Plan	
Paid Time Off (PTO)	

TERM	DEFINITION
Financial Security	
Work-Life Balance	
Mandatory Benefits	
Voluntary Benefits	
Total Compensation	

Employee Benefits and Their Value

```
O P Q G C P F C F Y P J Z R K E J D D A D C G Y
T L M V H T A M G X Q H A E A F Q D R X U G R Y
M M S N W C E I J C O M P E N S A T I O N U V F
Q D C U D C M V D I P Q X N F E J R X A Z S O F
S O G E H J B Z J T D K O Q C Q H N X G Y I L G
R I F H L H P C G J I R C L T K E F T H F H U M
N V V H R X C W X P Q M Y K A K A A O T T B N A
H F C V C I N V G V G C E Q F Z L U T W V B T R
W I I M X R O Z K E O Z P O Z Y T P A G B M A O
O B Z N J Y E C C J S L W N F H H M L O O P R E
R Y R X A N N T B S W S U Q O F I A C J D E Y R
K Y Z G R N U A I W Z B J N S D N H O O Y M B O
L P V K C I C P F R W E Z C T P S Q M W T H E E
I J U M P D G I W I E X V B V A U E P C M A N O
F X U U X T P P A N N M D F S C R M E Q P Q E S
E T I Q C A O F G L J Q E L X A A Y N C G O F R
B K M Q X J N K T J S G Y N Y B N S S T M M I B
A A D Z P V M E K F B E S X T L C X A L N V T G
L B K V R A N Q M F K J C B S P E U T D F N S M
A Y I W Q D G Q X O X I G U B B L G I M K P F S
N M W V N H K X T N K Y C U R Y M A O Y T M F V
C M A N D A T O R Y B E N E F I T S N J A I R U
E Y I X P F L J R O U B S H P C T D I R N W Z O
F U V Q T P Z T G D X G Y H B X H Y A H Y Y H C
```

Compensation

Paid Time Off

Mandatory Benefits

Voluntary

Health Insurance

Financial Security

Voluntary Benefits

PTO

Retirement Plan

Work-Life Balance

Total Compensation

Employee Benefits and Their Value

Across

7. An arrangement to provide people with income during retirement, _____ Plan

8. Additional benefits offered at the employer's discretion, _____ Benefits

9. Payment or reward for services or employment.

10. Employee benefits required by law, _____ Benefits

Down

1. The equilibrium between one's job and personal life, _____-_____ Balance

2. The state of having stable income or resources to support one's standard of living, Financial _____

3. The complete pay package, including all benefits and salary, Total _____

4. Additional compensation provided to employees beyond regular salary.

5. Coverage that pays for medical and surgical expenses, _____ Insurance

6. Compensated leave from work for vacation, illness, or personal reasons. (Abbrv.)

Emergency Funds:
Your Financial Safety Net

Life is full of unexpected twists and turns. A sudden car repair, a medical emergency, or an unforeseen job loss can quickly derail your financial stability. This is where an emergency fund comes into play. Let's explore the concept of emergency funds, their importance, and how you can build your own financial safety net.

What Is an Emergency Fund?

An emergency fund is a dedicated savings account set aside specifically for unexpected expenses or financial emergencies. It serves as a financial buffer, protecting you from life's unpredictable events without derailing your regular budget or forcing you into debt.

Key Components of an Emergency Fund:

1. Liquidity: Your emergency fund should be easily accessible, typically in a savings account.
2. Separation: Keep it distinct from your regular savings to avoid temptation.
3. Adequacy: Experts typically recommend having 3-6 months of living expenses saved.

The Importance of Emergency Funds

Emergency funds are crucial for several reasons:

1. Financial Security: They provide a safety net during unexpected situations.
2. Stress Reduction: Knowing you have a backup plan reduces financial anxiety.
3. Debt Avoidance: Instead of relying on credit cards or loans, you can use your fund.
4. Flexibility: It allows you to make better financial decisions without the pressure of immediate need.

Consider Sarah, a recent high school graduate working her first job. She saves $50 from each paycheck for her emergency fund. Six months later, her laptop – essential for her online classes – crashes. Thanks to her emergency fund, Sarah can replace it without derailing her budget or resorting to high-interest credit card debt.

Building Your Emergency Fund

Creating an emergency fund might seem challenging, but it's achievable with the right approach:

1. Start Small: Begin with a goal of saving $500 or $1,000.
2. Automate Savings: Set up automatic transfers from your checking to savings account.
3. Use Windfalls Wisely: Allocate tax refunds or gift money to your fund.
4. Cut Unnecessary Expenses: Redirect money from non-essential spending to your fund.
5. Increase Gradually: As your income grows, boost your contributions.

The Impact of Emergency Funds

An emergency fund doesn't just provide financial security; it can significantly impact your overall well-being. It reduces stress, improves decision-making, and gives you the confidence to pursue opportunities without fear of financial setbacks.

An emergency fund is a stepping stone to broader financial health. Once you've established this safety net, you're better positioned to tackle other financial goals like investing, saving for major purchases, or planning for retirement.

Real-World Applications

Emergency funds can be lifesavers in various situations:

1. Job Loss: If you're laid off, your emergency fund can cover living expenses while you job hunt.
2. Medical Emergencies: Unexpected health issues can lead to high out-of-pocket costs.
3. Home Repairs: Sudden repairs like a leaky roof or broken furnace can be costly.
4. Car Troubles: Vehicle repairs or the need for a replacement can arise unexpectedly.
5. Family Emergencies: You might need to travel suddenly for a family crisis.

Common Misconceptions About Emergency Funds

1. *"I don't need one because I have insurance."* Insurance is crucial, but it doesn't cover everything and often involves deductibles or waiting periods.
2. *"I can always use my credit card."* Credit cards often come with high interest rates, potentially leading to long-term debt.
3. *"I don't make enough to save."* Even small, consistent contributions can build a significant fund over time.

Tips for Maintaining Your Emergency Fund

1. Regularly Review: Assess your fund periodically to ensure it still covers 3-6 months of expenses.
2. Replenish After Use: If you dip into your fund, make it a priority to rebuild it.
3. Adjust for Life Changes: Major life events like marriage, having children, or buying a home may require increasing your fund.

In the unpredictable journey of life, an emergency fund acts as your financial shock absorber. It's not just about being prepared for the worst; it's about empowering yourself to face life's challenges with confidence. By starting to build your emergency fund today, you're taking a crucial step towards financial stability and peace of mind.

Financial security isn't just for adults with established careers. As a high school student, developing the habit of maintaining an emergency fund now will set you up for a lifetime of financial wellness. Start small, stay consistent, and watch your financial safety net grow.

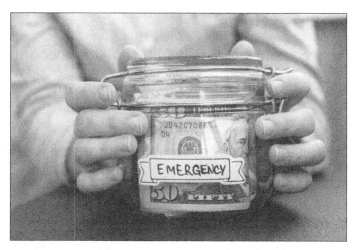

Personal finance is crucial as it empowers individuals to manage their money effectively, make informed financial decisions, and plan for a secure future.

Did You Know?

- According to a 2021 survey by Bankrate, only 39% of Americans could cover a $1,000 emergency expense from savings.
- The concept of an emergency fund gained popularity during the Great Depression when job security became uncertain for many Americans.

11. The Importance of Emergency Funds
GUIDED NOTES

I. Key Terms

1. Emergency Fund: _____

2. Liquidity: _____

3. Financial Security: _____

II. Main Concept Overview

An emergency fund is a _____ set aside specifically

for _____ or financial emergencies. It serves as a

_____ buffer, protecting you from life's unpredictable events.

III. Matching Section

Match the term with its correct description:

_____ 1. Liquidity   A. Keeping emergency funds separate from regular
                                        savings

_____ 2. Separation   B. Typically 3-6 months of living expenses

_____ 3. Adequacy   C. Easy accessibility of funds

_____ 4. Financial Security   D. Safety net during unexpected situations

_____ 5. Stress Reduction   E. Knowing you have a backup plan reduces this

IV. True/False Questions

_____ 1. An emergency fund should be easily accessible, typically in a savings account.

_____ 2. Experts typically recommend having 3-6 months of living expenses in an
            emergency fund.

_____ 3. Emergency funds are only necessary for adults with established careers.

_____ 4. Credit cards are always a better option than using money from an emergency
            fund.

_____ 5. Regular review and replenishment are important for maintaining an emergency
            fund.

V. Application Question

Sarah, a recent high school graduate, saves $50 from each paycheck for her emergency fund. After six months, her laptop crashes. How does her emergency fund help in this situation?

_____

_____

_____

_____

VI. Reflection/Summary

List three real-world situations where an emergency fund could be useful:

1. _____

2. _____

3. _____

How can starting an emergency fund as a high school student benefit you in the future?

_____

_____

_____

_____

1

How might having an emergency fund affect your daily spending choices?

Think about your current spending habits. Would you make different choices if you had an emergency fund? How might it change your approach to unexpected expenses?

2

As a high school student, how could starting an emergency fund now benefit you in the future?

What financial challenges might you face after high school? How could the habit of saving for emergencies help you later in life? Think about both money and peace of mind.

3

How might someone's emergency fund needs change as they get older?

How are a high school student's financial needs different from an adult's? What new expenses or risks might come with age? Think about how the size of an ideal emergency fund might change over time.

Unexpected Car Trouble

You're a high school senior with a part-time job and a used car for commuting. One day, your car breaks down and needs a $800 repair. You have $500 in your emergency fund and $200 in your checking account.

Questions:
a) How might having an emergency fund help in this situation?
b) What are your options for handling this expense?
c) How would this situation be different if you had no emergency fund at all?

Unexpected Opportunity

You're invited to attend a prestigious summer program related to your dream career. The program costs $1,500, and the deadline to register is in two weeks. You have $1,000 in your emergency fund and $300 in your regular savings.

Questions:
a) Should you consider using your emergency fund for this opportunity? Why or why not?
b) What are the potential risks and benefits of using emergency savings for this purpose?
c) If you decide to participate in the program, how would you adjust your financial plan going forward?

TERM	DEFINITION
Emergency Fund	
Liquidity	
Financial Security	
Budget	
Savings	

TERM	DEFINITION
Expenses	
Financial Stability	
Automatic Transfer	
Financial Goal	
Risk Management	

Emergency Funds

```
L H P O J M R I Y P R T F O J N W O K N X M D G
D I B F F I N A N C I A L S E C U R I T Y G X R
U V N U R R E H N I L G L L Y Y Y W D J Z E G F
M L G H D X F I N A N C I A L S T A B I L I T Y
K L W R Z G A P E E G A X D Z M B C V M I X H
Y I K Z X Q E O Z I Z Z G A W D M V S J Z T T E
Z K E T A W H T Y R E O C N L M Z E P B J A H X
V Q M D B A W Z O D I L R V K E Y I I G A I U P
R Y E A J N U D D M V S S S L O K O G H A E P E
U N R Z Z E Z T Y Q M V K P U L T G O I I D V N
L X G Y W Q B M O W J A N M K S U B F H A D B S
I R E S O D U X V M T D D P A L N S C Y R H J E
Q U N E X L O P U P A W D F W N P L K Q K U M S
U N C K E P G O X X A T D Z N L A L M R F V C X
I V Y J D Z S V H A D N I O B H L G L S M T H K
D U F C O W B X K T V Y C C C L H I E Q U A Q Z
I V U M Q B K F P R Q T I G T K C Z M M M E W N
T P N L U A D A M D F S H G Q R Y M I N E P D A
Y T D A H Q B T I F F N J V T A B L V C N Y O
O L K M J K I J A K H D T X R Q W N W P J M T D
K P H X F I N A N C I A L G O A L F S E C B A F
S C I C A L F D R E B H B I I Y Z V R F N Q U Q
N K I X O L F S A V I N G S A S E Q W E E A A I
R L N Q K O X Q M O H S D K C Z N J Q V Z R P N
```

Risk Management

Financial Stability

Expenses

Liquidity

Financial Goal

Financial Security

Savings

Automatic Transfer

Emergency Fund

Budget

Emergency Funds

Across

3. A specific, measurable objective related to money management, such as building an emergency fund, Financial _____

6. A financial plan that allocates income towards expenses, savings, and debt repayment.

7. Money set aside for future use, typically in a bank account or other low-risk, accessible location.

9. The practice of identifying, assessing, and controlling threats to one's financial well-being, _____ Management

10. The ease with which an asset can be converted into cash without significant loss in value.

Down

1. A pre-arranged movement of funds from one account to another, often used for regular savings contributions, _____ Transfer

2. The costs incurred for goods or services in daily living or to run a business.

4. A dedicated savings account set aside specifically for unexpected expenses or financial emergencies, Emergency _____

5. The state of having stability in one's financial situation, often achieved through proper planning and risk management, Financial _____

8. The ability to consistently meet financial obligations and weather unexpected financial challenges, Financial _____

Unlocking Your Financial Future:
The Power of Saving and Investing

Picture this: You're standing at the edge of a vast financial landscape, filled with opportunities and potential. This landscape represents your financial future, and the choices you make today will shape the path you'll walk tomorrow. Welcome to the world of saving and investing, where small decisions can lead to big rewards.

Saving and investing are two fundamental pillars of personal finance that can significantly impact your financial well-being. While they might seem intimidating at first, understanding these concepts is crucial for anyone looking to secure their financial future. In this article, we'll explore the basics of saving and investing, their importance, and how you can start your journey towards financial prosperity.

Saving: The First Step to Financial Security

Saving is the practice of setting aside a portion of your income for future use. It's like planting seeds in a garden – the more seeds you plant, the more bountiful your harvest will be. Here's why saving is essential:

1. Emergency Fund: Life is unpredictable. An emergency fund acts as a financial safety net, protecting you from unexpected expenses or income loss.

2. Short-term Goals: Saving allows you to achieve short-term goals, like buying a new smartphone or taking a vacation, without relying on credit.

3. Peace of Mind: Knowing you have savings provides a sense of security and reduces financial stress.

To start saving effectively, consider the following strategies:

• **Set Clear Goals:** Define what you're saving for, whether it's an emergency fund or a specific purchase.
• **Pay Yourself First:** Treat savings as a priority by setting aside money as soon as you receive your income.
• **Automate Your Savings:** Set up automatic transfers to your savings account to make the process effortless.

Investing: Growing Your Wealth Over Time

While saving is crucial, investing takes your financial game to the next level. Investing involves putting your money into assets that have the potential to grow in value over time.

Savings provide financial security for short-term needs, while investments aim to grow wealth over the long term through potential returns.

It's like planting a tree – with proper care and patience, it can grow into something much larger than the original seed.

Here's why investing is important:

1. Wealth Building: Investments can potentially earn higher returns than traditional savings accounts, helping your money grow faster.

2. Beating Inflation: Investing can help your money maintain its purchasing power by outpacing inflation.

3. Achieving Long-term Goals: Investments are particularly suited for long-term financial objectives, such as retirement or funding your children's education.

Common types of investments include:

- **Stocks:** Ownership shares in companies
- **Bonds:** Loans to governments or corporations
- **Mutual Funds:** Professionally managed collections of stocks, bonds, or other assets
- **Real Estate:** Property investments, including physical real estate or REITs (Real Estate Investment Trusts)

The Power of Compound Interest

One of the most powerful concepts in both saving and investing is compound interest. It's often called the "eighth wonder of the world" because of its ability to accelerate wealth growth. Compound interest is essentially "interest on interest" – you earn returns not just on your initial investment, but also on the accumulated interest over time.

Let's look at an example:

Imagine you invest $1,000 at an annual return of 7%. After one year, you'd have $1,070. But in the second year, you'd earn interest on $1,070, not just your original $1,000. This compounding effect can lead to significant growth over long periods.

Balancing Risk and Reward

While investing offers the potential for higher returns, it also comes with risks. Generally, investments with higher potential returns also carry higher risks. It's crucial to understand your risk tolerance – how much risk you're comfortable taking – and to diversify your investments to spread out risk.

Getting Started: Your Path to Financial Success

Ready to begin your saving and investing journey? Here are some steps to get started:

1. Assess Your Financial Situation: Understand your income, expenses, and financial goals.
2. Start with Saving: Build an emergency fund and save for short-term goals.
3. Educate Yourself: Learn about different investment options and strategies.
4. Start Small: Begin investing with amounts you're comfortable with, and gradually increase over time.
5. Seek Professional Advice: Consider consulting with a financial advisor for personalized guidance.

Saving and investing are lifelong practices. The key is to start early, be consistent, and stay informed. By understanding and applying these principles, you're taking a crucial step towards securing your financial future.

12. Introduction to Saving and Investing
GUIDED NOTES

I. Key Terms

1. Saving: _____

2. Investing: _____

3. Compound Interest: _____

II. Main Concept Overview

Saving and investing are two fundamental pillars of personal finance that can significantly impact your _____ _____. While saving is crucial for _____ and short-term goals, investing helps in _____ over time.

III. Matching Section

Match each term with its correct description:

_____ Emergency Fund   A. Ownership shares in companies

_____ Stocks   B. Financial safety net for unexpected expenses

_____ Bonds   C. Professionally managed collections of stocks, bonds, or other assets

_____ Mutual Funds   D. Loans to governments or corporations

_____ Real Estate   E. Property investments, including physical real estate or REITs

IV. Saving

A. Importance of Saving:

1. _____   2. _____

3. _____

B. Strategies for Effective Saving:

1. _____   2. _____

3. _____

V. Investing

A. Importance of Investing:

1. _____   2. _____

3. _____

B. Common Types of Investments:

1. _____ 2. _____

3. _____ 4. _____

VI. True or False

_____ Compound interest is essentially "interest on interest".

_____ Investments with higher potential returns usually carry higher risks.

_____ Diversifying your investments helps spread out risk.

_____ Saving is only important for long-term financial goals.

_____ It's recommended to start investing with large amounts of money.

VII. Fill in the Table

Complete the table comparing saving and investing based on information from the article:

Aspect	Saving	Investing
Primary Purpose		
Time Frame		
Examples		

VIII. Application Question

Explain the concept of compound interest using the example provided in the article. How does this demonstrate the power of investing over time?

_____

_____

_____

_____

1

How do your current spending habits align with the saving principles discussed in the article?

Think about your recent purchases. Were they needs or wants? How much of your income do you save? Consider how you might adjust your habits to save more effectively.

2

How might understanding compound interest change the way you think about saving and investing?

Reflect on the example given in the article. How does starting to save or invest early impact long-term growth? Think about how you could benefit from compound interest in your own life.

3

What steps can you take now to start building your financial future?

Consider your current financial situation. Which of the "Getting Started" steps from the article could you implement now? Think about any obstacles you might face and how you could overcome them.

The Summer Job Savings Challenge

Your friend Jamie just got their first summer job at the local ice cream shop. They're excited about earning their own money but aren't sure if they should save any of it. Jamie says, "I'm too young to worry about saving, right?"

Questions:
a) What advice would you give Jamie about saving some of their summer job money?
b) How could you explain the benefits of starting to save early?
c) If Jamie saved just $20 a week from their job, how might this add up over the summer?

_____

_____

_____

_____

_____

_____

_____

_____

_____

_____

The Phone Upgrade or Invest Debate

You've been saving up for a new smartphone that costs $600. You currently have $700 in your savings account. Your older sibling suggests you keep your current phone for another year and invest the money instead.

Questions:
a) What are some pros and cons of buying the new phone versus investing the money?
b) If you decided to invest, what are some options you could consider based on the article?
c) How might delaying the phone purchase impact your finances in the long run?

_____

_____

_____

_____

_____

_____

_____

_____

_____

TERM	DEFINITION
Saving	
Investing	
Compound Interest	
Diversification	
Risk Tolerance	

TERM	DEFINITION
Emergency Fund	
Stocks	
Bonds	
Mutual Funds	
Liquidity	

Saving and Investing

```
V  Z  C  U  C  L  C  S  U  R  I  C  H  P  Z  T  V  N  U  M  X  R  E  K
J  H  J  R  A  S  X  R  O  R  S  U  R  Z  J  S  R  T  Y  H  S  I  F  Q
F  T  B  P  Y  W  H  B  Y  H  G  O  B  H  Z  R  U  P  K  E  U  I  L  V
S  F  O  U  Y  Y  J  J  O  L  M  U  T  U  A  L  F  U  N  D  S  B  L  H
B  I  N  V  E  S  T  I  N  G  J  K  F  U  E  M  T  K  R  R  J  T  B  R
D  P  D  Z  Q  P  F  Z  M  S  S  M  G  G  V  A  L  X  C  I  Q  Y  F  Z
G  X  S  G  J  P  C  E  V  D  O  O  H  T  T  U  H  R  Z  S  V  D  D  N
Y  M  X  O  I  I  H  H  G  T  B  R  L  Z  P  B  D  O  R  K  E  P  Q  T
L  I  N  H  W  J  Q  M  P  P  Q  L  H  Z  R  B  X  R  D  T  Z  J  C  X
D  I  C  O  M  P  O  U  N  D  I  N  T  E  R  E  S  T  Z  O  F  Y  L  A
Z  I  Q  C  M  J  P  T  A  B  G  M  E  Y  X  A  O  A  F  L  Z  H  S  D
E  G  V  U  L  G  X  I  X  S  Y  W  B  S  H  G  E  V  I  E  V  R  O  B
M  D  P  E  I  Z  R  Q  E  A  P  S  V  B  E  G  W  R  R  Y  H  E  Y
E  M  L  W  R  D  Z  L  B  V  L  F  V  I  T  V  X  G  H  A  V  P  Z  A
R  M  E  X  Y  S  I  I  T  I  W  N  T  H  T  D  X  A  W  N  Z  T  D  D
G  W  R  X  B  H  I  T  K  N  O  V  I  S  C  R  Q  M  S  C  R  S  J  C
E  X  B  N  I  I  C  F  Y  G  Z  V  E  E  Y  J  H  T  E  T  I  F  G
N  Q  O  G  E  G  B  D  I  W  Y  I  T  U  V  I  O  K  O  P  A  R  T  F
C  R  K  I  X  Y  G  W  H  C  E  Y  B  G  S  D  C  Y  C  S  O  Q  T  Z
Y  R  B  U  G  I  Z  E  N  X  A  H  B  F  C  Y  H  V  K  S  M  A  D  H
F  E  N  Z  V  D  P  E  C  U  D  T  G  U  M  A  E  W  S  M  N  V  Q  D
U  O  R  W  Y  M  C  C  R  Y  I  I  I  A  Y  V  H  I  V  W  V  Y  P  T
N  K  X  K  Z  Y  S  U  S  Q  R  V  B  O  Z  S  J  K  M  E  G  A  M  I
D  A  K  O  M  Q  I  Y  J  D  K  W  T  F  N  D  A  R  X  X  C  K  F  E
```

Compound Interest

Liquidity

Stocks

Saving

Risk Tolerance

Mutual Funds

Diversification

Emergency Fund

Bonds

Investing

Saving and Investing

Across

2. The ease with which an asset can be converted into cash without significant loss in value.

3. The degree of variability in investment returns that an investor is willing to withstand, Risk _____

4. Ownership shares in a company.

7. Money set aside for unexpected expenses or financial emergencies, _____ Fund

8. Professionally managed collections of stocks, bonds, or other assets. (2 words)

10. Putting money into assets with the potential to grow in value over time.

Down

1. Spreading investments across various assets to manage risk.

5. Interest earned not just on the initial investment, but also on accumulated interest over time, _____ Interest

6. Loans made to governments or corporations.

9. The practice of setting aside a portion of income for future use.

Balancing Act: Navigating Risk and Return in Your Investment Journey

Have you ever wondered why some people seem to grow their money faster than others? Or why your parents might be hesitant about certain investment opportunities? The answer lies in understanding the delicate balance between risk and return in investments. This concept is crucial for anyone looking to make informed financial decisions, whether you're saving for college, planning for your first car, or dreaming about your future home.

What Are Risk and Return?

Risk: The Uncertainty Factor

In the world of investing, risk refers to the chance that an investment's actual return will be different from what you expected. This difference can be positive or negative, but generally, when we talk about investment risk, we're concerned with the possibility of losing some or all of the money we invest.

Return: The Reward for Investing

Return, on the other hand, is the gain or loss on an investment over a specific period. It's usually expressed as a percentage of the amount invested. For example, if you invest $100 and it grows to $110 in a year, your return is 10%.

The Risk-Return Relationship

Here's a key principle to remember: Generally, the higher the potential return of an investment, the higher the risk. This relationship is fundamental to understanding how investments work.

Low Risk, Low Return

Investments like savings accounts or government bonds are considered low-risk. Your money is safe, but the return is typically low. It's like choosing to walk instead of drive – you'll get there safely, but it might take longer.

High Risk, High Return

On the flip side, investments like stocks or cryptocurrency can offer higher returns but come with higher risks. It's like choosing to drive a sports car – you might get there faster, but there's a higher chance of accidents.

Types of Investment Risks

1. Market Risk: This is the risk that the entire market will decline, affecting most stocks and investments.

In investing, higher potential returns are typically associated with higher levels of risk, requiring careful evaluation of one's risk tolerance and investment goals.

2. Interest Rate Risk: Changes in interest rates can affect investment values, especially for bonds.

3. Inflation Risk: The risk that your investment returns won't keep pace with inflation, reducing your purchasing power.

4. Liquidity Risk: The risk of not being able to sell your investment quickly without a loss.

5. Company Risk: Specific to stocks, this is the risk that a company will perform poorly or go bankrupt.

Strategies for Managing Risk

Diversification:
Don't Put All Your Eggs in One Basket

By spreading your investments across different types of assets (like stocks, bonds, and real estate), you can reduce the impact of poor performance in any single investment.

Asset Allocation:
Balancing Your Portfolio

This involves dividing your investments among different asset categories based on your goals, risk tolerance, and investment timeline.

Time Horizon:
The Power of Long-Term Investing

Generally, the longer you can keep your money invested, the more risk you can afford to take, as you have more time to recover from market downturns.

Real-World Example:
The Tech Stock Rollercoaster

Imagine you invested $1,000 in a popular tech company's stock. In the first year, the stock price soared, and your investment grew to $1,500 – a 50% return! However, the next year, due to a market downturn, your investment dropped to $800. This scenario illustrates both the potential for high returns and the risk of losses in stock investments.

Applying Risk-Return Concepts

Think about your own financial goals. If you're saving for a short-term goal, like buying a laptop next year, you might choose a low-risk investment to ensure your money is there when you need it. For long-term goals, like saving for retirement (which might seem far off now, but it's never too early to start!), you might be able to take on more risk for the potential of higher returns.

Understanding risk and return is essential for making smart investment decisions. By grasping these concepts, you're taking an important step towards financial literacy and independence. Remember, there's no one-size-fits-all approach to investing – it's about finding the right balance for your individual goals and comfort level.

Did You Know?

• The stock market has historically provided an average annual return of about 10% over the long term, but with significant short-term ups and downs.
• Warren Buffett, one of the world's most successful investors, follows a strategy of investing in companies he understands, demonstrating that knowledge can help manage risk.

---

13. Understanding Risk and Return in Investments
GUIDED NOTES

I. Key Terms

1. Risk: _____

2. Return: _____

3. Diversification: _____

4. Asset Allocation: _____

5. Time Horizon: _____

II. Main Concept Overview

The relationship between risk and return in investments is that _____ risk generally leads to _____ potential return. This means that investments with higher potential returns usually come with _____ risk of loss.

III. Matching Section

Match the term with its correct description:

_____ Market Risk   A. Risk of not being able to sell quickly without loss

_____ Interest Rate Risk   B. Risk that returns won't keep up with inflation

_____ Inflation Risk   C. Risk that the entire market will decline

_____ Liquidity Risk   D. Risk specific to a particular company's performance

_____ Company Risk   E. Risk related to changes in interest rates

IV. Fill in the Table

Complete the table comparing low-risk and high-risk investments:

Aspect	Low-Risk Investments	High-Risk Investments
Example		
Potential Return		
Safety of Capital		
Best for		

V. True/False

_____ Diversification means investing all your money in one promising company.

_____ The longer your investment time horizon, the more risk you can generally afford to take.

_____ Low-risk investments always provide better returns than high-risk investments.

_____ Asset allocation involves dividing investments among different asset categories.

_____ The stock market has historically provided an average annual return of about 10% over the long term.

VI. Application Question

You have $1,000 to invest and you need the money in 6 months for a new laptop. Based on what you've learned about risk and return, what type of investment would you choose and why?

_____

_____

_____

_____

_____

VII. Reflection/Summary

Summarize the main points about risk and return in investments in your own words. How might understanding these concepts affect your future financial decisions?

_____

_____

_____

_____

1

How might your personality affect the investment choices you make?

Think about whether you're a cautious person or someone who likes to take risks. Consider how this might influence the types of investments you'd choose. Would you prefer safer options or riskier ones with potentially higher rewards?

2

Can you think of a way to explain investment risk to a friend using a comparison to a everyday activity?

Think of an activity you and your friends enjoy that involves some risk and reward. How is deciding to invest similar to deciding whether to participate in this activity? Consider how you weigh the potential benefits against the possible downsides.

3

How do you think new technology might change the way people invest in the future?

Consider how smartphones and apps have already changed how people manage money. How might future tech developments affect investing? Think about whether these changes could make investing easier or potentially more risky.

Savings Account vs. Stock Market

Your grandfather gives you $1,000 for your 16th birthday. You're trying to decide between putting it in a savings account with a 1% annual interest rate or investing it in a diverse stock market fund that has historically averaged 7% annual returns but can be volatile.

Questions:
a) How do the risk levels of these two options compare?
b) If you need this money in 6 months for a school trip, which option might be more suitable and why?
c) How might your decision change if you're saving this money for college in two years?

Allowance Investing

You save $20 from your allowance each month. You're thinking about investing it in either one company's stock or in a fund that includes stocks from many different companies.

Questions:
a) Which option do you think has more risk: investing in one company or many?
b) How could investing in many companies help protect your money?
c) If the stock market goes down, which option might lose less money? Why?

TERM	DEFINITION
Risk	
Return	
Diversification	
Asset Allocation	
Time Horizon	

TERM	DEFINITION
Market Risk	
Liquidity	
Volatility	
Inflation Risk	
Portfolio	

Understanding Risk and Return in Investments

```
Y D N S U E D U W D I V E R S I F I C A T I O N
W E H X O L B Y A T K F E Z U Q G L F A J I O J
U S U H C N B B O F W B V Y Q S R J J B M L Q S
M V O L A T I L I T Y Y P K C V T Y N M X H H H
D D P O R T F O L I O N S I P Z Z F I E G Y A G
I W T B M U M Z T Z A W F T J H T V A C H J A W
N G O D R A A G D V R J I H Z O C Z G J N U A R
F Q Y I K A R R B V R Y X V B O O O D O Q I J L
L C F U U N N K N H O D A H W J H X V J C K D I
A Y O J H I T E E O F H N V W A D S S E H B Q Q
T K G A H T Y E T T Q A Y N S Y F W L R U U U
I Y J M X Z V T Y V R Q H Z J S K X Q U I P E I
O T E P Z A J W W R V I A V N E C C S N Z I X D
N Y W N I V Q S M U E J S Y M T C J H R M E M I
Y I N F L A T I O N R I S K P A X J H X U B G T
O T H K K U B Y G I Y A F D D L R L R Z D F E Y
Y B Z H X Q C X O G G L A I O L E A O S S U K K
H B U V V R P H Q O X C C K L O T D B M I U Y H
Y E Q K Y Z G B F N S W J V J C U K T O Z H U P
F P P L R Q C V X C P I T G E A R T R R J H I F
E Z T I M E H O R I Z O N H S T N C Q N T O A U
R H Z H Q J W V F N O E N V Z I R Y P V H X M B
R R C D W G H F K Y J A F C I O Q H P U R M H S
T Q L P A O D N U T K N D I P N G S A O P L J H
```

Asset Allocation

Inflation Risk

Volatility

Return

Time Horizon

Portfolio

Liquidity

Market Risk

Inflation

Diversification

Understanding Risk and Return in Investments

Across

6. The gain or loss on an investment over a specific period, usually expressed as a percentage.

7. The risk that the entire market will decline, affecting most stocks and investments, _____ Risk

8. The length of time you plan to keep your money invested, Time _____

9. How quickly and easily an investment can be sold or converted to cash.

10. The risk that your investment returns won't keep pace with inflation, _____ Risk

Down

1. Spreading investments across different types of assets to reduce risk.

2. A collection of investments owned by an individual or organization.

3. Dividing investments among different asset categories based on goals and risk tolerance, _____ Allocation

4. The degree of variation in the price of an investment over time.

5. The chance that an investment's actual return will be different from what you expected.

Navigating the Investment Highway:
Understanding Stocks, Bonds, and Mutual Funds

In the world of personal finance, investing plays a crucial role in building wealth and achieving financial goals. Three primary investment vehicles - stocks, bonds, and mutual funds - form the foundation of many investment portfolios. Each of these vehicles offers unique characteristics, risks, and potential rewards, making them essential tools for investors of all levels.

Stocks: Ownership in Companies

Stocks represent ownership shares in a company. When you purchase a stock, you become a partial owner of that business, entitled to a portion of its assets and earnings. Companies issue stocks to raise capital for various purposes, such as expanding operations, developing new products, or paying off debt.

The value of stocks can fluctuate based on various factors, including:
- Company performance
- Economic conditions
- Industry trends
- Investor sentiment

Stocks offer two primary ways to make money:
1. Capital appreciation: The increase in the stock's price over time
2. Dividends: Regular payments made by some companies to shareholders

While stocks have historically provided higher returns compared to other investment vehicles, they also come with higher risk. Stock prices can be volatile, and there's always the possibility of losing some or all of your investment if a company performs poorly or goes bankrupt.

Bonds: Lending to Organizations

Bonds are debt instruments issued by corporations, governments, or other entities to raise funds. When you buy a bond, you're essentially lending money to the issuer. In return, the issuer promises to pay you interest at regular intervals and return the principal amount (face value) when the bond matures.

Key components of bonds include:
- *Face value:* The amount the bond is worth at maturity
- *Coupon rate:* The interest rate paid by the bond
- *Maturity date:* When the bond's principal is to be repaid

Bonds are generally considered less risky than stocks, as they provide a steady stream of income and return of principal at maturity. However, they typically offer lower potential returns. Risks associated with bonds include:
- *Interest rate risk:* Bond prices typically fall when interest rates rise
- *Credit risk:* The possibility that the issuer may default on payments
- *Inflation risk:* The risk that inflation will erode the purchasing power of the bond's payments

Types of investments include stocks, bonds, real estate, and mutual funds.

Mutual Funds: Pooled Investments

Mutual funds pool money from many investors to invest in a diversified portfolio of stocks, bonds, or other securities. Professional fund managers make investment decisions on behalf of the fund's shareholders.

Types of mutual funds include:
- *Stock funds:* Invest primarily in stocks
- *Bond funds:* Focus on fixed-income securities
- *Balanced funds:* Invest in both stocks and bonds
- *Index funds:* Aim to track the performance of a specific market index

Advantages of mutual funds include:

1. Diversification: Spreading risk across multiple investments

2. Professional management: Benefiting from experienced fund managers' expertise

3. Accessibility: Allowing investors to access a broad range of securities with a relatively small investment

However, mutual funds also have potential drawbacks:
- *Fees:* Management fees and other expenses can eat into returns
- *Lack of control:* Investors have no say in specific investment decisions
- *Potential tax inefficiency:* Fund trading can generate taxable distributions

The Importance of Understanding Investment Vehicles

Grasping the fundamentals of stocks, bonds, and mutual funds is crucial for several reasons:

1. Informed decision-making: Knowledge of different investment options allows you to make choices aligned with your financial goals and risk tolerance.

2. Risk management: Understanding the risks associated with each investment vehicle helps you create a balanced portfolio that matches your risk profile.

3. Goal achievement: Different investments can be used to meet various financial objectives, from short-term savings to long-term retirement planning.

4. Financial literacy: Familiarity with investment basics enhances overall financial literacy, empowering you to take control of your financial future.

Real-World Application: Building a Diversified Portfolio

Consider how these investment vehicles might work together in a practical scenario. Sarah, a young professional, decides to start investing for her future. She creates a diversified portfolio using the following approach:

1. Stocks: She allocates 50% of her investment to a mix of individual stocks and stock-focused mutual funds, aiming for long-term growth.

2. Bonds: 30% of her portfolio goes into bond mutual funds, providing stability and regular income.

3. Mutual Funds: The remaining 20% is invested in balanced mutual funds, offering a mix of stocks and bonds managed by professionals.

This diversified approach allows Sarah to balance potential growth with risk management, adapting her strategy as her financial situation and goals evolve over time.

Stocks, bonds, and mutual funds serve as fundamental building blocks for creating a robust investment strategy. By understanding the unique characteristics, potential benefits, and risks associated with each of these investment vehicles, you can make more informed decisions about your financial future. As you embark on your investment journey, remember that knowledge, careful planning, and regular review of your investment choices are key to navigating the complex landscape of personal finance and working towards your financial goals.

14. Types of Investment Vehicles
GUIDED NOTES

I. Key Terms

1. Stocks: _____

2. Bonds: _____

3. Mutual Funds: _____

II. Main Concept Overview

Investing plays a crucial role in _____ and achieving

_____. The three primary investment vehicles discussed are

_____, _____, and _____.

III. Stocks

A. Definition: _____

B. When you purchase a stock, you become a _____ of that business.

C. Two primary ways to make money from stocks:

1. _____   2. _____

D. Factors affecting stock value (list four):

1. _____   2. _____

3. _____   4. _____

IV. Bonds

A. Definition: _____

B. Key components of bonds:

1. Face value: _____

2. Coupon rate: _____

3. Maturity date: _____

C. Risks associated with bonds (list three):

1. _____

2. _____

3. _____

V. Mutual Funds

A. Definition: _____

B. Types of mutual funds (list four):

   1. _____   2. _____

   3. _____   4. _____

C. Advantages of mutual funds (list three):

   1. _____   2. _____

   3. _____

D. Potential drawbacks of mutual funds (list three):

   1. _____   2. _____

   3. _____

VI. Matching

Match each term with its correct description:

_____ Stocks   A. Lending money to organizations

_____ Bonds   B. Ownership shares in a company

_____ Mutual Funds   C. Pooled investments in various securities

VII. True or False

_____ Stocks have historically provided higher returns compared to other investment vehicles.

_____ Bonds are generally considered less risky than stocks.

_____ Mutual funds allow investors to benefit from professional management.

_____ Index funds aim to track the performance of a specific market index.

_____ Diversification is one of the disadvantages of mutual funds.

VIII. Reflection/Summary

List four reasons why understanding stocks, bonds, and mutual funds is crucial for personal finance.

1. _____   2. _____

3. _____   4. _____

1

How might understanding stocks, bonds, and mutual funds affect your future financial decisions?

Think about your current knowledge of saving and spending money. How could learning about these investments change the way you plan for college, a car, or your first job? Consider how different investment options might help you reach your goals faster or more safely.

2

Why do you think it's important for companies to issue stocks and bonds?

Imagine you're starting a business. How could selling stocks or bonds help your company grow? Think about the pros and cons for the company and for the investors. How might this impact the economy as a whole?

3

If you had $1000 to invest right now, how would you divide it among stocks, bonds, and mutual funds?

Think about your personal goals and how comfortable you are with risk. How might your age affect your decision? Consider how each type of investment could help or hinder your plans for the near future and long term.

New Tech Stock

A new tech company, InnovateTech, has just gone public. Their stock price has doubled in the first week of trading due to excitement about their innovative products.

Questions:
a) What factors might be driving the rapid increase in InnovateTech's stock price?
b) What are the potential risks of investing in a newly public company like InnovateTech?
c) How might including this stock in a diversified portfolio affect overall risk and potential returns?

_____

_____

_____

_____

_____

_____

_____

_____

_____

_____

Economic Downturn

News reports suggest that the economy might be heading into a recession. You have a diversified portfolio of stocks, bonds, and mutual funds.

Questions:
a) How might a recession potentially affect each type of investment in your portfolio?
b) What advantages might a diversified portfolio offer during an economic downturn?
c) If you were planning to invest more money during this time, how might you adjust your investment strategy?

_____

_____

_____

_____

_____

_____

_____

_____

_____

_____

TERM	DEFINITION
Stock	
Bond	
Mutual Fund	
Diversification	
Portfolio	

TERM	DEFINITION
Dividend	
Capital Appreciation	
Risk Tolerance	
Liquidity	
Asset Allocation	

Navigating the Investment Highway

```
U I O F Q Q F I R D H B E L J T K K L J J Y J Y
Q N W Z S F P H K N R B H Q Z P W I U P W W Z O
V E W K Y T D O A D K B S G B L G H R Q D D Q T
D U E M D I O Y M D I M M L Z K C E P B U U P Z
G X D Z B U D C B J Z V J O F K Z G M S N I D T
R L K B F Z R C K O B X E Q R A T Z U U Y O G S
O V G O D F T J K W N Z S R I N M B O M O X P R
L M D I V I D E N D U D N S S N E B I D D Q P X
Y L Y M K O W U B U R E Z B K I R I S B E W O D
A M F P E C E I W U X R W N T C F F P G S I R F
D Z U F S P O P Z B Q X W L O L L I R U R E T D
V U C T C L S A F P D E B B L I I U C Q Q N F H
N D U A U M R G P P S S V E M Y Q I A S G O S
O F T X U A N N U M N I B E R D H T U E T Q L E
U E T W M O L B D F P N C E A O A U A I I I M
V A F U N K B F M O R Y O F N Y M I L G D M O L
R H G E T S U X U N Y K F B C R W D L R Y I I N
S Q W P C W C X W N O N T Z E J Q M P J J A T U
Q H C O S S M F Z H D U E B Z B A X O V W O J Y
Q E M Q P J M U V R E J Q V V T K Y F A O I C X
L A J O C E C V A M A G H R I Y G V D H U C Y N
F W C V M V O A S S E T A L L O C A T I O N U B
D K R S Q C A P I T A L A P P R E C I A T I O N
O Q B O Z I O E P Z P S U N Q L B V I L J B R A
```

Capital Appreciation

Risk Tolerance

Asset Allocation

Liquidity

Dividend

Portfolio

Diversification

Mutual Fund

Bond

Stock

Navigating the Investment Highway

Across

6. The increase in the price or value of assets, Capital _____

8. The degree of variability in investment returns that an investor is willing to withstand, Risk _____

9. Ownership shares in a company.

10. A distribution of a portion of a company's earnings to shareholders.

Down

1. The practice of spreading investments among various financial instruments to reduce risk.

2. The ease with which an asset can be converted into cash without affecting its market price.

3. The process of dividing investments among different asset categories such as stocks, bonds, and cash, _____ Allocation

4. An investment vehicle that pools money from many investors to invest in a diversified portfolio of stocks, bonds, or other securities. (2 words)

5. A debt instrument issued by corporations, governments, or other entities to raise funds.

7. A collection of financial investments like stocks, bonds, commodities, cash, and cash equivalents.

The Basics of Insurance: Safeguarding Your Future

Insurance is a crucial aspect of financial planning that often goes overlooked, especially by young adults. However, understanding the fundamentals of insurance is essential for protecting your assets, health, and loved ones. This article will explore the basics of three primary types of insurance: auto, health, and life insurance.

The Concept of Insurance

At its core, insurance is a contract between you and an insurance company. You pay regular premiums, and in return, the insurer agrees to cover specific financial losses you might face. This arrangement is all about managing risk and providing peace of mind in the face of life's uncertainties.

Auto Insurance: Protection on the Road

Auto insurance is mandatory for drivers in most states, and for good reason. It provides financial protection in case of accidents, theft, or damage to your vehicle. Here are the key components of auto insurance:

1. Liability Coverage: This is the foundation of any auto insurance policy. It covers damages you cause to others in an accident, including both property damage and bodily injury. Most states require a minimum level of liability coverage.

2. Collision Coverage: This pays for damage to your own vehicle in the event of a collision with another vehicle or object, regardless of who's at fault.

3. Comprehensive Coverage: This protects your car from non-collision related incidents such as theft, vandalism, natural disasters, or damage from falling objects.

4. Personal Injury Protection (PIP): Available in some states, PIP covers medical expenses for you and your passengers, regardless of who caused the accident.

5. Uninsured/Underinsured Motorist Coverage: This protects you if you're in an accident with a driver who doesn't have insurance or doesn't have enough coverage.

When choosing auto insurance, consider factors like your car's value, your personal assets, and your risk tolerance. The minimum required coverage may not be sufficient to fully protect you financially.

Health Insurance: Investing in Your Well-being

Health insurance is a vital component of personal finance, helping to manage the high costs of medical care. Here's what you need to know:

Insurance is a financial product that provides protection against potential future losses or damages in exchange for regular premium payments.

1. *Premiums:* These are the regular payments you make to maintain your insurance coverage. They can be paid monthly, quarterly, or annually.

2. *Deductibles:* This is the amount you must pay out-of-pocket for covered services before your insurance starts to pay. Generally, plans with higher deductibles have lower premiums, and vice versa.

3. *Copayments and Coinsurance:* Copayments are fixed amounts you pay for specific services, while coinsurance is a percentage of the cost that you're responsible for after meeting your deductible.

4. *Network:* Most health insurance plans have a network of healthcare providers who have agreed to provide services at negotiated rates. Using in-network providers typically results in lower out-of-pocket costs.

5. *Coverage Types:* Common plan types include Health Maintenance Organizations (HMOs), Preferred Provider Organizations (PPOs), and High Deductible Health Plans (HDHPs).

For young adults, it's worth noting that you can often stay on your parents' health insurance plan until age 26. However, it's important to understand your options as you transition to independent coverage.

Life Insurance: Protecting Your Loved Ones

Life insurance provides financial protection for your dependents in the event of your death. While it may seem unnecessary for young people, securing a policy early can be advantageous. Here's what life insurance can cover:

• Funeral and burial expenses
• Outstanding debts and mortgages
• Living expenses for your family
• Future costs like college tuition for your children

There are two main types of life insurance:

1. *Term Life Insurance:* This provides coverage for a specific period, typically 10, 20, or 30 years. It's generally more affordable and straightforward.

2. *Whole Life Insurance:* This covers you for your entire life and includes an investment component known as cash value. It's more expensive but offers lifelong coverage and potential for cash accumulation.

Choosing the Right Insurance

When selecting insurance policies:

1. Assess your needs and potential risks
2. Compare policies from different providers
3. Understand the coverage details, including any exclusions or limitations
4. Consider your budget for premiums
5. Review and update your coverage regularly as your life circumstances change

Insurance might seem like a complex and unexciting topic, but it's a crucial part of your financial health. By understanding the basics of auto, health, and life insurance, you're taking an important step towards protecting your future. The right insurance provides not just financial security, but also peace of mind as you navigate life's uncertainties.

Insurance needs vary from person to person. What works for your friend or family member may not be the best fit for you. Take the time to educate yourself, ask questions, and make informed decisions about your insurance coverage. Your future self will thank you for the protection and peace of mind that comes with being properly insured.

15. Basics of Insurance (Auto, Health, Life)
GUIDED NOTES

I. Key Terms

1. Insurance: _____

2. Premium: _____

3. Deductible: _____

4. Copayment: _____

5. Coinsurance: _____

II. Main Concept Overview

Insurance is a _____ between you and an _____

company. You pay regular _____, and in return, the insurer agrees to

cover specific _____ losses you might face.

III. Types of Insurance

A. Auto Insurance

1. Liability Coverage: _____

2. Collision Coverage: _____

3. Comprehensive Coverage: _____

B. Health Insurance

1. Premiums: _____

2. Deductibles: _____

3. Copayments: _____

4. Network: _____

C. Life Insurance

1. Term Life Insurance: _____

2. Whole Life Insurance: _____

IV. Matching Section

Match the term with its correct description:

_____ Liability Coverage   A. Covers damage to your own car in an accident

_____ Collision Coverage   B. Pays for damage you cause to others in an accident

_____ Comprehensive Coverage   C. Protects against theft and non-collision incidents

_____ Term Life Insurance   D. Provides coverage for a specific period

_____ Whole Life Insurance   E. Covers you for your entire life and includes an investment component

V. True/False

_____ Auto insurance is mandatory for drivers in most states.

_____ Young adults can stay on their parents' health insurance until age 26.

_____ Term life insurance provides coverage for a specific period.

_____ Premiums are the regular payments you make to maintain your insurance coverage.

_____ It's important to review and update your insurance coverage regularly.

VI. Application Question

You're about to choose a health insurance plan. List three components of health insurance mentioned in the article and explain why each is important to consider.

_____

_____

_____

VII. Reflection/Summary

Based on the article, explain why understanding insurance is crucial for your financial health. How can insurance provide both financial security and peace of mind?

_____

_____

_____

1

What are some risks in your daily life that insurance could help protect against?

Look at your daily activities and possessions. What could potentially go wrong? How might insurance help if something unexpected happened?

2

How would you explain the importance of insurance to a friend who thinks it's a waste of money?

Remember the main purposes of insurance mentioned in the article. How does insurance provide both financial protection and peace of mind? Can you think of a real-life example where insurance would be helpful?

3

Why might choosing the cheapest insurance plan not always be the best decision?

Think about the different components of insurance coverage discussed in the article. How do factors like deductibles and coverage limits affect the overall value of an insurance plan? What might you be giving up with a cheaper plan?

New Driver Dilemma

You just got your driver's license and your parents are adding you to their auto insurance policy. The insurance company offers three coverage options: basic liability, mid-level coverage with some additional protections, and comprehensive coverage with the highest limits.

Questions:
a) What factors should you and your parents consider when choosing the level of coverage?
b) How might choosing only the basic liability coverage affect you in the event of an accident?
c) Why might comprehensive coverage be beneficial, even if it's more expensive?

Health Plan Choices

You're starting your first job after college, and your employer offers two health insurance options: a plan with a low monthly premium but high deductible, and a plan with a higher monthly premium but lower deductible and copayments.

Questions:
a) How would your current health and financial situation influence your choice between these plans?
b) In what circumstances might the high-deductible plan be a better option?
c) How could your choice affect your out-of-pocket costs for a minor health issue versus a major medical event?

TERM	DEFINITION
Insurance	
Premium	
Deductible	
Liability Coverage	
Comprehensive Coverage	

TERM	DEFINITION
Copayment	
Network	
Term Life Insurance	
Whole Life Insurance	
Risk Management	

The Basics of Insurance

```
A L S G M J T A U H X U J Q D S V Q T U W A T Q
C Q J O B N F G D I G V Z F E P F S A D M K J U
X C S C W H O L E L I F E I N S U R A N C E L K
T Y O X G Q O Y D P K P V L E W O C W E S U T P
P J Y M C E F I I P B D E D U C T I B L E T W X
C L J I P J L P D I N S U R A N C E O U T T C E
E B Z M I R V L Q L A O H Y U D V L G R E E G Z
M Z Y I F Q E F V P E V R G V I L I U N X R D I
N S X O X F C H H U E W D Z M Y Y A S V V M K N
Q X G W K R W O E Z K P D S U Y V B T T U L L P
T Y I C L M I A P N N K F Y C Y C I V K Y I D T
R K P K J E L J W A S C Z O G Z L L D H S F M P
F G S T B Y I J R L Y I M E J D C I L R M E B H
Y B X Q D D N N F C O M V U F R V T V G Z I R P
F F U C X X J K S Z U V E E E Z Y Y P O E N B B
S P B Z N K M F O M C V Z N C G S C X B C S X B
G W R W Y T D T P M C I N W T O J O G A Q U J N
T F W E H X T J Q L U P R Y O I V V P W H R D S
P D P H M N H C Q N Q X Y K I R B E T X K A S U
R E I X Z I H T X T O C F D O C O R R Y E N X O
J U L R O V U S B Q E T F T M E X A B A X C H X
C O J R Q A P M Q U N E T W O R K G G V G E K W
X W V V Z H R Y A V Z W I K Z N N E K L H E T B
R I S K M A N A G E M E N T V Q P R T B P D H A
```

Liability Coverage

Comprehensive Coverage

Term Life Insurance

Whole Life Insurance

Risk Management

Network

Copayment

Deductible

Premium

Insurance

The Basics of Insurance

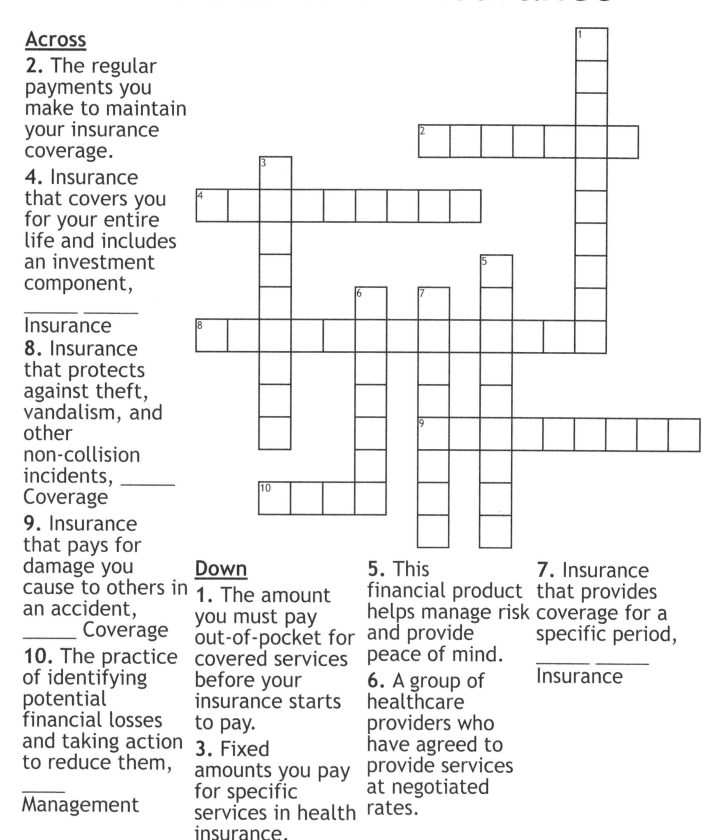

Across

2. The regular payments you make to maintain your insurance coverage.

4. Insurance that covers you for your entire life and includes an investment component, _____ _____ Insurance

8. Insurance that protects against theft, vandalism, and other non-collision incidents, _____ Coverage

9. Insurance that pays for damage you cause to others in an accident, _____ Coverage

10. The practice of identifying potential financial losses and taking action to reduce them, _____ Management

Down

1. The amount you must pay out-of-pocket for covered services before your insurance starts to pay.

3. Fixed amounts you pay for specific services in health insurance.

5. This financial product helps manage risk and provide peace of mind.

6. A group of healthcare providers who have agreed to provide services at negotiated rates.

7. Insurance that provides coverage for a specific period, _____ _____ Insurance

Unlocking Financial Success:
The Impact of Credit Scores and Reports

Credit scores and credit reports play a crucial role in shaping your financial future. These powerful tools serve as a financial report card, influencing everything from loan approvals to job opportunities. Understanding how credit scores and reports work is essential for building a strong financial foundation.

The Basics of Credit Scores

A credit score is a three-digit number, typically ranging from 300 to 850, that represents your creditworthiness. This score acts as a financial trust indicator – the higher the number, the more trustworthy you appear to potential lenders. Credit scores are determined by complex algorithms that analyze your credit report, considering various factors:

1. Payment history (35% of your score)
2. Credit utilization (30%)
3. Length of credit history (15%)
4. Types of credit accounts (10%)
5. Recent credit inquiries (10%)

Your payment history carries the most weight in determining your credit score. Consistently paying bills on time can significantly boost your score, while late payments can have a severe negative impact.

Demystifying Credit Reports

While your credit score is a quick snapshot of your creditworthiness, your credit report provides the full picture.

A credit report is a detailed record of your credit history, including:

- Open and closed credit accounts
- Payment history on each account
- Credit limits and balances
- Personal information like addresses and employment history
- Public records such as bankruptcies or tax liens

Credit reports are compiled by three major credit bureaus: Equifax, Experian, and TransUnion. These reports form the basis for calculating your credit score. It's important to regularly review your credit reports for accuracy, as errors can negatively impact your credit score.

A credit score is a numerical indicator of an individual's creditworthiness, influencing their ability to obtain loans and secure favorable financial terms in the future.

The Real-World Impact of Your Credit Score

Your credit score isn't just a random number – it has tangible effects on various aspects of your life:

1. Loan Approval and Interest Rates: A higher credit score often leads to easier loan approvals and lower interest rates on mortgages, car loans, and credit cards.

2. Renting an Apartment: Many landlords check credit scores to assess potential tenants' reliability in paying rent.

3. Employment Opportunities: Some employers may review credit reports as part of the hiring process, especially for financial positions.

4. Insurance Premiums: In some states, insurance companies may use credit scores to determine premiums for auto and homeowners insurance.

5. Utility Deposits: A good credit score might help you avoid deposits on utilities when moving to a new place.

To illustrate the impact of credit scores, consider two individuals applying for a $20,000 car loan. Alex, with a credit score of 750, might be approved for a 5-year loan at 3.5% interest rate, resulting in a monthly payment of $364 and total interest of $1,834 over the loan term. In contrast, Jordan, with a credit score of 600, might only qualify for a 10% interest rate, leading to a monthly payment of $425 and total interest of $5,496 – a difference of $3,662 in interest alone.

Did You Know?

- Checking your own credit report does not affect your credit score – it's considered a "soft inquiry."
- The concept of credit scoring was introduced by the Fair Isaac Corporation (FICO) in 1989, revolutionizing the lending industry.

Building and Maintaining a Good Credit Score

Now that you understand the importance of your credit score, here are some strategies to build and maintain a healthy financial profile:

1. Pay bills on time, every time: Set up automatic payments or reminders to ensure you never miss a due date.

2. Keep credit card balances low: Aim to use no more than 30% of your available credit limit.

3. Don't close old credit accounts: The length of your credit history matters, so keep old accounts open even if you're not using them regularly.

4. Limit new credit applications: Each application can result in a hard inquiry on your credit report, potentially lowering your score.

5. Regularly check your credit report: You're entitled to one free credit report from each of the three major credit bureaus every year through AnnualCreditReport.com. Review these reports for errors and dispute any inaccuracies.

Remember, building good credit takes time and consistency. It's a long-term process that requires patience and diligence.

Your credit score and report are powerful tools that can open doors to financial opportunities or create obstacles in your path. By understanding how they work and taking steps to maintain a healthy credit profile, you're setting yourself up for a brighter financial future. Take control of your financial foundation by monitoring your credit, making informed decisions, and consistently practicing good financial habits.

16. Understanding Credit Scores and Reports

I. Key Terms

1. Credit Score: _____

2. Credit Report: _____

II. Main Concept Overview

A credit score is a _____-digit number, typically ranging from _____ to _____, that represents your _____. It acts as a financial _____ indicator – the _____ the number, the more _____ you appear to potential lenders.

III. Credit Score Factors
Fill in the percentage that each factor contributes to your credit score:

1. Payment history: _____%

2. Credit utilization: _____%

3. Length of credit history: _____%

4. Types of credit accounts: _____%

5. Recent credit inquiries: _____%

IV. Credit Report Contents
List five components included in a credit report:

1. _____

2. _____

3. _____

4. _____

5. _____

V. Matching
Match each term with its correct description:

_____ Equifax   A. Detailed record of your credit history

_____ Credit Score   B. One of the three major credit bureaus

_____ Credit Report   C. Three-digit number representing creditworthiness

_____ TransUnion   D. Another major credit bureau

VI. True/False

_____ Credit scores only affect loan approvals and interest rates.

_____ Checking your own credit report is considered a "soft inquiry" and doesn't affect your score.

_____ It's a good idea to keep old credit accounts open even if you're not using them regularly.

_____ Your payment history has the most significant impact on your credit score.

_____ Credit reports are compiled by three major credit bureaus.

VII. Application Question

Describe three specific actions you can take to improve or maintain a good credit score:

1. _____

2. _____

3. _____

VIII. Reflection/Summary

In your own words, explain why understanding credit scores and reports is important for your financial future:

_____

_____

_____

How might your credit score affect your life in the next 5-10 years? List two potential impacts:

1. _____

2. _____

1

How might your current spending habits affect your future credit score?

Think about how you manage your money now. Do you pay bills on time? How often do you borrow money from friends or family? How might these habits translate to managing credit cards or loans in the future?

2

Why should you check your credit report, even if you don't have any credit cards or loans?

What if there's a mistake on your report? How could identity theft affect your credit? How might understanding your credit report now help you in the future?

3

If you found a mistake on your credit report, what would you do?

Who would you need to contact? What proof might you need? Why is it important to fix errors quickly?

The Forgotten Bill

Alex just moved into their first apartment after high school. They set up utilities but forgot about a $50 internet bill during the chaos of moving. Six months later, Alex applies for their first credit card and is surprised to be rejected.

Questions:

a) How might the forgotten bill have affected Alex's credit score?

b) What steps should Alex take to address this situation?

c) How could Alex have prevented this issue?

The Credit Card Spree

Casey gets their first credit card with a $1,000 limit. Excited by the prospect of "free money," Casey maxes out the card buying new clothes and electronics. When the bill comes, Casey can only afford to make the minimum payment.

Questions:

How might Casey's spending spree affect their credit score?

What are the potential long-term consequences of only making minimum payments?

What strategies could Casey use to improve their financial situation?

TERM	DEFINITION
Credit Score	
Credit Report	
Credit Bureau	
Creditworthiness	
Credit Utilization	

TERM	DEFINITION
Payment History	
Credit Limit	
Interest Rate	
Soft Inquiry	
Credit History	

Credit Scores and Reports

```
F O M W Z L C R E D I T W O R T H I N E S S W O
W M C T N O W F O V D C S T W D O H S P G G T H
Q U G I T R O O V Q R U R O O M U T C Y A F D V
J Y A I L B E V J V H L W E F K M I G U N U M K
C X I G D K R M K G I V O E D T F G C I Q P G C
R G W O G X P V C D Q T D V V I I V K Q K S Y O
E R Y L F B E A Y M V A A I N H T N C U R Q Z O
D X X Z J U J F X Q G C I J L Y B S Q K Q T M Q
I I G M L R C Q F W J G L E N O S H C U C Q Z M
T W V C R E D I T H I S T O R Y I E M O I G G T
B E C R E D I T U T I L I Z A T I O N M R R G O
U P A Y M E N T H I S T O R Y Y G J T J D E Y V
R S N Z B Y Z F F B B C F C G O M C I C A Q R A
E J X T S R Y B X M X R G V F K A K N R O K F X
A V M E T S I C L T P E R M M J N H T H H U I Y
U O F V N V W E E B D R Y U V A B E O Q L W F
O R R T U A C T M T P I U P W K N G R I C K T G
F H C E B P P I J H J T Y C H F T X E B K V J I
U Q D U E J A N L A Z L S S X K Y A S L M R B P
N H G N Z Z E M X V K I X B Z A S C T Z P L A R
M K F G E X X X K I B M U H Z B F I R E N P H Y
P R V K C R O N E T J I D V I V A A N J Y J K
G U K Y M H Q R N N Q T U G T H J O T Q F P F U
Q O B C R E D I T R E P O R T I P I E T T K V O
```

Credit Score	Credit Report	Credit Bureau
Credit Utilization	Payment History	Credit Limit
Interest Rate	Soft Inquiry	Credit History
Creditworthiness		

Credit Scores and Reports

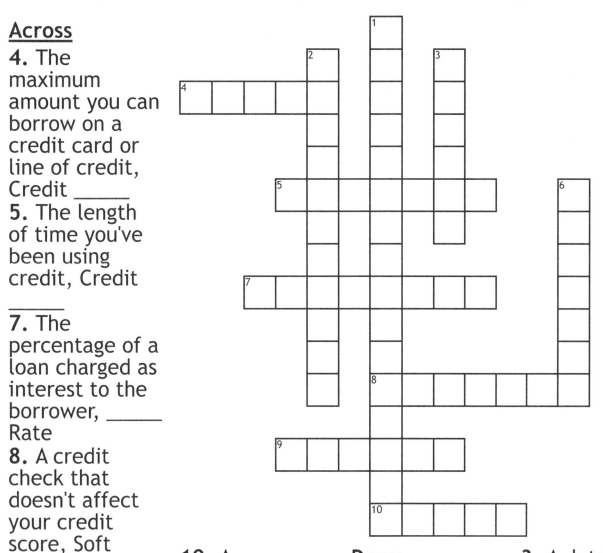

Across

4. The maximum amount you can borrow on a credit card or line of credit, Credit _____

5. The length of time you've been using credit, Credit _____

7. The percentage of a loan charged as interest to the borrower, _____ Rate

8. A credit check that doesn't affect your credit score, Soft _____

9. An agency that collects and maintains consumer credit information, Credit _____

10. A three-digit number representing an individual's creditworthiness, Credit _____

Down

1. A measure of how suitable an individual is to receive financial credit.

2. The amount of credit you're using compared to your credit limits, Credit _____

3. A detailed record of an individual's credit history, Credit _____

6. A record of whether you've paid your bills on time, Payment _____

Mastering the Plastic:
A Teen's Guide to Responsible Credit Card Use

In today's increasingly digital world, understanding credit cards is a crucial skill for your financial future. Whether you're about to make your first purchase or considering applying for a card, knowing how to use credit responsibly can set you up for financial success—or help you avoid a financial nightmare.

Credit Cards: More Than Just Plastic Money

Credit cards are powerful financial tools that, when used wisely, can help build your credit history, provide financial flexibility, and even earn rewards. However, they also come with significant responsibilities and potential pitfalls that every cardholder should be aware of.

At its core, a credit card allows you to borrow money from a financial institution to make purchases. You're expected to pay back this borrowed amount, typically on a monthly basis. While this concept might seem straightforward, it's the details that often trip up new credit card users.

When you receive your monthly statement, you have two options: pay the full balance or make a minimum payment. Here's where many people fall into a trap. If you don't pay the full amount, you'll be charged interest on the remaining balance. And trust us, that interest can add up faster than you might expect!

The Credit Card Balancing Act: Weighing Benefits and Risks

Using a credit card responsibly can offer several advantages:

1. Building Credit: Regular, on-time payments help establish a positive credit history, which is crucial for future loans, renting apartments, and even some job applications.

2. Convenience: Credit cards are widely accepted and eliminate the need to carry large amounts of cash.

3. Rewards: Many cards offer cash back, travel miles, or points on purchases, allowing you to earn while you spend.

4. Emergency Fund: In genuine emergencies, credit cards can provide a financial safety net when you need it most.

However, irresponsible use can lead to serious consequences:

1. Debt Accumulation: High-interest rates can cause small balances to balloon quickly, leading to a cycle of debt that's hard to break.

2. Credit Score Damage: Late payments or high credit utilization can negatively impact your credit score, affecting your financial opportunities for years to come.

3. Overspending: The "buy now, pay later" mentality can lead to purchasing beyond your means, causing financial stress and potential long-term debt.

Swipe Smart: Essential Tips for Responsible Credit Card Use

1. Pay in Full and On Time: Always aim to pay your entire balance each month to avoid interest charges. Setting up automatic payments can ensure you never miss a due date.

2. Stay Below 30% Utilization: Try to use less than 30% of your available credit limit. This shows lenders you can manage credit responsibly and can positively impact your credit score.

3. Monitor Your Statements: Regularly check your transactions for any errors or fraudulent charges. Quick detection can save you from financial headaches down the road.

4. Understand the Terms: Know your card's interest rate, fees, and reward structure. This knowledge will help you maximize benefits and minimize costs.

5. Avoid Cash Advances: Using your card for cash withdrawals often comes with high fees and interest rates. It's best to avoid this feature unless absolutely necessary.

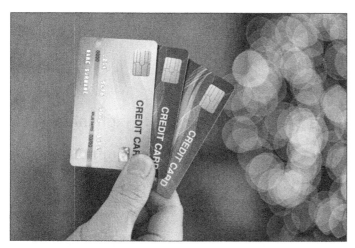

Credit cards are financial tools that allow individuals to borrow funds up to a certain limit for purchases, requiring repayment with interest if not paid in full by the due date.

6. Budget First, Swipe Second: Only use your credit card for planned purchases within your budget. This habit will help prevent overspending and potential debt accumulation.

Real-World Example: A Tale of Two Teens

Let's look at how responsible credit card use plays out in real life. Meet Alex and Jordan, both 18 and proud owners of their first credit cards with $1,000 limits.

Alex uses the card for occasional purchases, always paying the full balance each month. After a year, Alex has built a good credit score, has no debt, and has earned $50 in cash back rewards. This responsible use has set Alex up for better financial opportunities in the future.

Jordan, on the other hand, gets excited by the newfound "money" and maxes out the card on a shopping spree. Unable to pay the full balance, Jordan only makes minimum payments each month. After a year, Jordan owes over $1,200 due to accumulated interest, has a damaged credit score, and is stressed about mounting debt.

Your Credit, Your Future

Understanding responsible credit card use is more than just managing plastic—it's about shaping your financial future. By using credit wisely, you're not just avoiding debt; you're building a foundation for financial opportunities and stability.

As you embark on your credit journey, remember: the power of the card is in your hands. Use it wisely, and it can open doors to financial opportunities. Use it recklessly, and those doors might slam shut. Your future self will thank you for the smart choices you make today.

17. Responsible Use of Credit Cards
GUIDED NOTES

I. Key Terms

1. Credit Card: _____

2. Interest: _____

3. Credit Score: _____

II. Main Concept Overview

Credit cards allow you to _____ money from a financial

institution to make purchases. You're expected to pay back this amount

_____, typically on a _____ basis.

If you don't pay the full amount, you'll be charged _____ on the

remaining balance.

III. Benefits and Risks of Credit Cards

A. Benefits (Fill in the blank):

1. Building _____

2. C _____

3. R _____

4. Emergency _____

B. Risks (Match each risk with its description):

_____ Debt Accumulation   A. Purchasing beyond your means

_____ Credit Score Damage   B. Small balances growing quickly due to high interest

_____ Overspending   C. Negative impact from late payments or high utilization

IV. Tips for Responsible Credit Card Use (True/False)

_____ 1. It's okay to only make minimum payments each month.

_____ 2. You should aim to use less than 30% of your credit limit.

_____ 3. Regularly checking your transactions is important.

_____ 4. Understanding your card's terms and conditions isn't necessary.

_____ 5. Cash advances are a good way to use your credit card.

V. Application Question

Describe a real-world scenario where responsible credit card use could benefit a high school student. How might irresponsible use in the same scenario lead to problems?

_____

_____

_____

_____

VI. Reflection/Summary

Summarize the main points about responsible credit card use in your own words. How does this concept relate to your future financial decisions?

_____

_____

_____

_____

1

How might using a credit card responsibly now affect your life after high school?

Think about getting an apartment or buying a car. How might your credit score impact these? What about job applications? Consider the difference between having good credit versus poor credit.

2

What are some ways credit cards might tempt you to overspend?

When might you be tempted to buy something you haven't planned for? How easy is it to swipe a card compared to using cash? Think about how "buy now, pay later" might affect your budget.

3

If you found yourself in debt like Jordan, what would you do?

What immediate steps could you take to address the debt? How could you prevent it from happening again? Think about how this experience might change how you use credit cards in the future.

The Concert Ticket Temptation

Your favorite band announces a surprise concert in your city next month. Tickets are $200 each, which is more than you have in your savings. You've just received your first credit card with a $500 limit.

Questions:
a) What are the potential consequences of using your credit card to buy the ticket?
b) How might this purchase affect your credit utilization ratio?
c) What alternatives could you consider to attend the concert without risking your financial health?

_____

_____

_____

_____

_____

_____

_____

_____

_____

_____

The Roommate's Request

You're in college, and your roommate asks to borrow your credit card to buy textbooks, promising to pay you back before the bill is due. Your card has a $1,000 limit, and your roommate needs to charge $400.

Questions:
a) What are the risks of lending your credit card to someone else?
b How might this situation impact your credit score and history?
c) What alternative solutions could you suggest to your roommate?

_____

_____

_____

_____

_____

_____

_____

_____

_____

_____

TERM	DEFINITION
Credit Card	
Credit Score	
Interest	
Credit Limit	
Minimum Payment	

TERM	DEFINITION
Credit Utilization	
Annual Percentage Rate (APR)	
Cash Advance	
Credit History	
Rewards	

Responsible Credit Card Use

```
J C C A I W Q E I T L K W C W U E S B M X D Z P
J W R Z A R D X E A P Y H A R O B T F P H L J Z
F T K Z M N P F B F A V O R D E X I Y A K K D J
Q Q M S J S N B E O F N C F P P D W A Q T Z N K
W X C K K J R U I N T E R E S T N I G Z A C B T
X O C C R Q G U A O O M R S L K Y G T P M H P B
R E R H R S D K Q L Q T P R Y J F M Q L J D E H
O S E R F E S V I S P V T R R R S M K Q I G R D
P L D D T V D C V C R E D I T C A R D M Z M P V
N R I C R E D I T S C O R E X P L H Z U Y R I M
M G T Y P U I J T Q Y J U C O H D K N D X U A T
L G U J Z X C O K H L C C R E J M X P O V K Q F
S G T Y V S E C I V I A G M J N V J P V V P E P
C T I R V I M D W D S M S P Q T Q W X I N S M
A O L C E X Q A W I K S T S S U C A L A Y C W C
S J I L W O A P R S M X N O W S G Z G F G Z Z A
H P Z E A C P R W A A Q N F R A B J Z E O C U U
A M A R R B N K S Z Q X I F S Y N U L B R L H J
D N T S D H M K Z Q I X E L Q U P T B C G A G A
V Q I Z S D F T S N T X X C D L Y A J T F Y F T B
A G O R S R M I N I M U M P A Y M E N T G Z X E
N I N S J I I Q Z M K F W J S J V N L Y K R Q T
C S H J Q D T S F K V U R T X V U I K N K N X J
E M B D M U V P C G C O J I K F I E K I R Z N S
```

Credit Score

Credit Utilization

Credit History

Interest

Credit Limit

Annual Percentage Rate

Rewards

Credit Card

Minimum Payment

Cash Advance

APR

Responsible Credit Card Use

Across

5. The cost of borrowing money, typically expressed as a percentage of the amount borrowed.

8. A record of a person's ability to repay debts and demonstrated responsibility in repaying them, Credit _____

9. The yearly interest rate charged on outstanding credit card balances. (Abbrv.)

10. When you use your credit card to withdraw cash or transfer money to your checking account, Cash _____

Down

1. The maximum amount a financial institution will allow you to borrow on a credit card, Credit _____

2. The ratio of your credit card balance to your credit limit, expressed as a percentage, Credit ———

3. A financial tool that allows you to borrow money from a financial institution to make purchases. (2 words)

4. Incentives offered by credit card companies, such as cash back or travel miles, for using their card.

6. A numerical representation of a person's creditworthiness, based on their credit history, Credit _____

7. The smallest amount of money that you are required to pay on your credit card bill each month, _____ Payment

Financing Your Future:
Mastering Student, Auto, and Mortgage Loans

Life's major milestones often come with significant price tags. Whether pursuing higher education, buying a first car, or owning a home, these achievements frequently require financial assistance. This is where loans enter the picture, offering a pathway to turn aspirations into reality. Let's explore three common types of loans: student loans, auto loans, and mortgage loans. Understanding these financial tools is crucial for making informed decisions that align with personal goals and financial well-being.

The Basics of Loans

A loan is a sum of money borrowed from a lender, such as a bank or credit union, that the borrower agrees to repay over time, typically with interest. The interest represents the cost of borrowing money, expressed as a percentage of the loan amount. Loans enable significant purchases or investments while spreading the cost over time.

Key components of loans include:
• Principal: The original amount borrowed
• Interest Rate: The percentage charged on the borrowed amount
• Term: The length of time for loan repayment
• Monthly Payment: The amount paid each month, including both principal and interest

Student Loans:
Investing in Education

Student loans are designed to cover the costs of higher education, including tuition, books, and living expenses. They come in two main types: federal and private.

Federal Student Loans:
• Offered by the government
• Generally have lower, fixed interest rates
• Provide more flexible repayment options
• May offer forgiveness programs for certain professions

Private Student Loans:
• Offered by banks, credit unions, and online lenders
• Interest rates can be fixed or variable, often higher than federal loans
• May require a co-signer if the borrower has limited credit history
• Typically have fewer repayment options

According to the Federal Reserve, the average student loan debt in the United States is around $30,000 per borrower.

Auto Loans:
Financing Vehicle Purchases

Auto loans help finance the purchase of a vehicle, whether new or used. These loans are typically secured, meaning the vehicle serves as collateral.

Key features of auto loans:
• Term lengths usually range from 36 to 72 months
• Interest rates can be fixed or variable
• The loan amount is based on the vehicle's price minus any down payment
• Monthly payments are fixed, making budgeting easier

When shopping for an auto loan, it's advisable to compare offers from different lenders, including banks, credit unions, and dealerships. A larger down payment can lower monthly payments and potentially secure a better interest rate.

Mortgage Loans: Building Home Equity

A mortgage is a loan used to purchase real estate, typically a home. It's often the largest loan most people will take in their lifetime.

Types of mortgages include:
1. Fixed-Rate Mortgages: Interest rate remains the same for the entire loan term
2. Adjustable-Rate Mortgages (ARMs): Interest rate can change periodically
3. FHA Loans: Government-backed loans with more lenient requirements
4. VA Loans: For eligible veterans and service members

Mortgage terms typically range from 15 to 30 years. The interest rate received depends on factors like credit score, down payment, and current market conditions.

Making Informed Borrowing Decisions

Before taking out any loan, it's important to:
1. Assess the financial situation and determine affordable borrowing amounts
2. Shop around and compare offers from multiple lenders
3. Understand all terms and conditions, including fees and penalties
4. Consider the long-term impact on financial health

While loans can open doors to opportunities, they also represent a serious financial commitment. Responsible borrowing and a solid repayment plan are essential.

The Impact of Loans on Financial Health

Loans can have significant long-term effects on personal finances. Positive impacts include building credit history and enabling important life goals. However, excessive borrowing can lead to financial stress and limit future opportunities.

Student loans can provide access to education that may increase earning potential, but high debt levels can delay other financial milestones. Auto loans allow for reliable transportation, potentially improving job prospects and quality of life. Mortgages offer a path to homeownership and building equity, but they also represent a long-term financial obligation.

It's crucial to consider how loan payments will fit into overall financial plans. This includes budgeting for monthly payments, understanding how loans affect debt-to-income ratios, and planning for potential changes in income or expenses.

Student loans, auto loans, and mortgages are powerful financial tools that can help achieve significant life goals. Understanding how these loans work and carefully considering options enables informed decisions that support future success. As individuals navigate the world of loans, knowledge remains their greatest asset. Staying informed, asking questions, and seeking advice from financial professionals when needed are key strategies. Each financial journey is unique, and with the right approach, loans can serve as stepping stones to build the envisioned future.

Comparing Loan Types: A Quick Overview

Loan Type	Typical Term	Interest Rates	Collateral
Student	10-25 years	Lower (federal), Higher (private)	None
Auto	3-6 years	Moderate	The vehicle
Mortgage	15-30 years	Varies	The property

18. Types of Loans (Student, Auto, Mortgage)
GUIDED NOTES

I. Key Terms

1. Loan: _____

2. Principal: _____

3. Interest Rate: _____

4. Term: _____

5. Monthly Payment: _____

II. Main Concept Overview

A loan is a sum of money _____ from a _____

that the borrower agrees to _____ over time, typically with

_____. Loans enable significant _____ or

_____ while spreading the cost over time.

III. Matching Section

Match the loan type with its characteristic:

_____ Student Loans   A. Vehicle serves as collateral

_____ Auto Loans   B. Often the largest loan in a person's lifetime

_____ Mortgage Loans   C. Come in federal and private types

_____ Federal Loans   D. Usually have terms of 3-6 years

_____ Private Loans   E. May offer forgiveness programs for certain professions

IV. Fill in the Table

Complete the table with information about different loan types:

Loan Type	Typical Term	Interest Rates	Collateral
Student			
Auto			
Mortgage			

V. True/False

_____ Federal student loans generally have lower interest rates than private student loans.

_____ Auto loans typically have longer terms than mortgage loans.

_____ The interest rate on a fixed-rate mortgage remains the same for the entire loan term.

_____ FHA loans are government-backed loans with more lenient requirements.

_____ A larger down payment on an auto loan can potentially secure a better interest rate.

VI. Application Question

Before taking out any loan, the article mentions four important steps to consider. List three of these steps and explain why each is important.

Step 1: _____

Importance: _____

Step 2: _____

Importance: _____

Step 3: _____

Importance: _____

VII. Reflection/Summary

Based on the information in the article, summarize how student loans, auto loans, and mortgage loans can impact a person's financial health. Consider both positive and negative effects mentioned in the article.

_____

_____

_____

_____

1

How might your career goals affect your decision to take out student loans?

Think about the cost of education for your chosen career. Consider how much you might earn in that career. How long would it take to repay the loans based on your expected salary?

2

What are the pros and cons of taking out an auto loan for your first car?

How could having a car impact your job opportunities? What are the total costs of car ownership beyond the loan? How might monthly car payments affect your ability to save money?

3

How do you think your approach to loans might change as you get older?

How might your income and expenses change over time? How could your credit score affect your future loan options? How might your financial goals shift as you move through different life stages?

College Choice and Student Loans

Sarah has been accepted to two colleges: a private university that would require her to take out larger student loans, and a public state university with smaller loan requirements. Both schools offer programs in her chosen field.

Questions:
a) What factors beyond the loan amounts should Sarah consider when making her decision?
b) How might Sarah's choice impact her financial situation after graduation?
c) What steps could Sarah take to minimize her student loan debt, regardless of which school she chooses?

_____
_____
_____
_____
_____
_____
_____
_____
_____
_____

Auto Loan Decisions

John needs a car for his new part-time job. He's considering either a new car with a longer-term loan or a used car with a shorter-term loan. The new car is more expensive but has lower interest rates.

Questions:
a) What are the potential advantages and disadvantages of each option?
b) Besides the loan terms, what other costs should John consider for each car?
c) How might each choice affect John's overall financial health while he's in school and after graduation?

_____
_____
_____
_____
_____
_____
_____
_____
_____
_____

TERM	DEFINITION
Loan	
Interest Rate	
Principal	
Term	
Collateral	

TERM	DEFINITION
Federal Student Loan	
Private Student Loan	
Mortgage	
Fixed-Rate Loan	
Down Payment	

Financing Your Future - Student, Auto, and Mortgage Loans

```
G J R M B F S C O K I G W I Z O R J B W S Z X J
S V H X I C P I F J V I H M F X L W Q U F F X V
F E D E R A L S T U D E N T L O A N E L O V M I
M C W P R W G V X V R Y I C X Z K J O I J P A C
K V P P K H C Z L F K J D I V D M L Y Q C W Y J
D J R H M K E G J E A R K U O V S N G F O V I B
Z S I F N U D V A U I M J E M M E R P C L Z D F
A Q V L R D O U W O X T I P V C I D O N L B M A
T I A X J H J N J O N M M O R T G A G E A Q T W
I R T R L L I F E H F D U Q V I X S F Z T T R I
Q K E F W O T O W B V E G B U X N G T M E Z S J
Q P S A I I B L V K I Q Y C I Y P C Z L R X E K
W E T L M X N I X H N A S W J Z H T I N A N D C
W W U C Y Q E T Y A R F L L L S E L E P L H Z Q
L R D D Y W R D E X X H O L U L Z O H R A N K L
L K E J M F G Z R R R H S X M T M L A Y M L Z D
I M N P S B B A Z A E V U K W M R L V G E Y V N
B D T A N G G A Q Q T S H T S Q U V O G K I Z P
G M L A U O L I P M G E T B R S K D K A S D Y Q
X L O L U X X F G L O Y L R Z H D S I P N S I N
Z Z A Y B S Q L B Q D G K O A N F P F Q P K L Q
I M N J P C O H A Y D G R C A T G F H V V R U B
V X E Z K L W D B H S B C Q I N E G S O U A Z X
V W E Y D Y V R R O Q H M E U K Q T T S D L H C
```

Interest Rate	Federal Student Loan	Private Student Loan
Fixed-Rate Loan	Mortgage	Collateral
Term	Principal	Loan

Financing Your Future - Student, Auto, and Mortgage Loans

Across

4. The original amount borrowed in a loan.

5. An asset that a borrower offers as security for a loan, which can be seized by the lender if the borrower fails to repay the loan.

8. A loan used to purchase real estate, typically a home, where the property serves as collateral.

9. A loan for education expenses offered by banks, credit unions, and online lenders, often with higher interest rates than federal loans, _____ Student Loan

Down

1. A loan for education expenses provided by the government, generally with lower interest rates and more flexible repayment options, _____ Student Loan

2. A loan where the interest rate remains the same for the entire loan term, _____-_____ Loan

3. The percentage charged on the borrowed amount of a loan, _____ Rate

6. A sum of money borrowed from a lender that the borrower agrees to repay over time, typically with interest.

7. The length of time for loan repayment.

Taking Control: Smart Strategies for Managing and Reducing Debt

In today's world, understanding how to manage and reduce debt is a crucial life skill. As you prepare to enter adulthood, learning about debt management will equip you with the knowledge to make smart financial decisions and secure a stable financial future. This article explores effective strategies for managing and reducing debt, providing you with practical tools to navigate the complex world of personal finance.

Understanding Debt and Its Impact

Debt is money owed to another person or institution. It can take various forms, such as student loans, credit card balances, or personal loans. While debt can sometimes be useful, like when obtaining an education or buying a home, unmanaged debt can quickly become a burden that affects your daily life and future opportunities.

The impact of debt extends beyond just owing money. High levels of debt can limit your ability to save for important goals, negatively impact your credit score, cause stress, affect your mental health, and restrict your career and lifestyle choices. It's like carrying a heavy backpack – the more debt you accumulate, the harder it becomes to move forward financially.

Reducing debt requires a strategic approach to prioritize payments, cut unnecessary expenses, and increase income to achieve financial freedom.

Strategies for Managing Debt

1. Know What You Owe
The first step in managing debt is to get a clear picture of your financial situation. Make a comprehensive list of all your debts, including the creditor, total amount owed, interest rate, and minimum monthly payment. This overview will help you prioritize your debts and create an effective plan of action.

2. Create a Budget
A budget serves as your financial roadmap. It helps you understand your income and expenses, allowing you to allocate money for debt repayment. To create a budget, list all sources of income, track all expenses for a month, categorize expenses as needs (like food and housing) and wants (like entertainment), and look for areas where you can cut back to free up money for debt repayment.

3. Pay More Than the Minimum
Paying only the minimum on your debts, especially credit cards, can keep you in debt for years. Try to pay more than the minimum whenever possible. Even small extra payments can make a significant difference over time, reducing both the total amount you'll pay and the time it takes to become debt-free.

4. Use the Debt Snowball or Avalanche Method

These are two popular strategies for tackling multiple debts:

• **Debt Snowball:** Pay off the smallest debt first while making minimum payments on others. This method provides quick wins and motivation.
• **Debt Avalanche:** Focus on the debt with the highest interest rate first. This approach saves you money on interest in the long run.
Choose the method that works best for your situation and personality.

Strategies for Reducing Debt

1. Negotiate with Creditors

Don't be afraid to communicate with your creditors. Many are willing to work with you, especially if you're proactive. You might be able to lower your interest rate, set up a more manageable payment plan, or in extreme cases, settle for less than you owe. Remember, creditors would rather receive some money than no money at all.

2. Consider Debt Consolidation

Debt consolidation involves combining multiple debts into a single loan, often with a lower interest rate. This can make your debt more manageable by simplifying your payments, potentially lowering your overall interest rate, and providing a clear payoff date. However, be cautious and read the fine print before consolidating. Ensure it actually saves you money in the long run.

3. Increase Your Income

Finding ways to earn extra money can accelerate your debt repayment. Consider taking on part-time jobs or freelance work, selling items you no longer need, or turning a hobby into a side business. Every extra dollar you earn can go towards paying off your debt faster, bringing you closer to financial freedom.

4. Avoid Taking on New Debt

While working to pay off existing debt, it's crucial to avoid accumulating new debt. This might mean using cash or a debit card instead of credit cards, postponing major purchases, and finding free or low-cost alternatives for entertainment. By stopping the inflow of new debt, you can focus all your efforts on eliminating existing obligations.

Creating Your Debt Management Plan

Now that you understand these strategies, it's time to create your own debt management plan:

1. List all your debts
2. Create a budget
3. Choose a debt repayment strategy (snowball or avalanche)
4. Look for ways to reduce interest rates or consolidate debt
5. Find opportunities to increase income
6. Track your progress and celebrate milestones

Remember, managing and reducing debt is a journey that takes time and commitment. The financial freedom you'll gain is worth the effort. As you move forward, continue educating yourself about personal finance. The skills you learn now will serve you well throughout your life, helping you make informed decisions about credit, saving, and investing.

By understanding and implementing these strategies for managing and reducing debt, you're taking a crucial step towards financial independence. You're not just learning about money – you're learning how to take control of your financial future. The path to a debt-free life may seem challenging, but with persistence and the right strategies, it's an achievable goal that will set you up for long-term financial success.

19. Strategies for Managing and Reducing Debt
GUIDED NOTES

I. Key Terms

1. Debt: _____

2. Budget: _____

3. Debt Snowball: _____

4. Debt Avalanche: _____

5. Creditor: _____

II. Main Concept Overview

Debt management is crucial because high levels of debt can limit your

ability to _____ for important goals, negatively impact your

_____ score, cause _____ and affect your mental

health, and restrict your _____ and _____ choices.

III. Matching Section

Match the strategy with its description:

_____ Know What You Owe   A. List all debts, amounts, and interest rates

_____ Create a Budget   B. Track income and expenses

_____ Debt Snowball   C. Pay off the smallest debt first

_____ Debt Avalanche   D. Focus on the debt with the highest interest rate

_____ Negotiate with Creditors   E. Ask for lower interest rates or payment plans

IV. True/False

_____ Paying only the minimum on your debts can keep you in debt for years.

_____ Creditors are never willing to work with you on your debt.

_____ Increasing your income can accelerate your debt repayment.

_____ It's crucial to avoid accumulating new debt while paying off existing debt.

_____ A budget helps you understand your income and expenses.

V. Fill in the Table

Complete the table with strategies for managing and reducing debt:

Managing Debt	Reducing Debt

VI. Application Question

Explain how the debt snowball method works and why it might be motivating for someone trying to pay off multiple debts.

_____

_____

_____

_____

_____

VII. Reflection/Summary

List the six steps for creating your own debt management plan, as outlined in the article. How might these steps be relevant to your life now or in the future?

_____

_____

_____

_____

1

How might having debt affect your daily life and future plans?

Think about your current spending habits. How would they change if you had debt? Consider how debt might influence your education or career choices.

2

Why do you think creating a budget is important for managing debt?

What information does a budget provide? How can this information help in paying off debt? Think about how a budget might help in other areas of life.

3

How could you increase your income to pay off debt faster?

What skills do you have that could earn money? Are there items you could sell? Think about how you might balance extra work with your other responsibilities.

Sarah's Debt Dilemma

Sarah, a recent high school graduate, has accumulated $3,000 in credit card debt from buying textbooks and a laptop for college. She also has a part-time job that pays $800 per month. Sarah wants to pay off her debt before starting college in 8 months.

Questions:
a) What strategy could Sarah use to tackle her debt efficiently?
b) How might creating a budget help Sarah in this situation?
c) What are some ways Sarah could increase her income to pay off the debt faster?

Emily's Future Student Loan Concerns

Emily is about to start her senior year of high school and is planning for college. She expects to need student loans to cover some of her education costs. Emily wants to minimize her debt and have a plan for repayment after graduation.

Questions:
a) What steps can Emily take now to minimize the amount of student loan debt she'll need?
b) How could understanding different debt repayment strategies help Emily plan for her future?
c) Why is it important for Emily to avoid taking on additional debt (like credit cards) while in college?

TERM	DEFINITION
Debt	
Budget	
Credit Score	
Creditor	
Debt Snowball	

TERM	DEFINITION
Debt Avalanche	
Debt Consolidation	
Interest Rate	
Minimum Payment	
Financial Freedom	

Strategies for Managing and Reducing Debt

```
S  N  I  H  N  S  D  B  B  L  T  W  W  V  N  R  N  O  M  T  M  G  F  T
F  R  G  F  Y  A  X  C  D  V  V  N  I  H  D  G  F  Q  R  J  H  W  T  J
K  Z  K  O  Z  Z  R  H  W  F  H  T  L  W  G  Y  J  B  I  J  C  F  X  F
W  Y  I  E  Q  X  T  M  L  X  R  F  T  Z  W  Y  K  M  W  C  R  W  W  I
M  P  X  I  O  E  C  D  I  B  E  M  G  J  Z  A  S  T  D  O  E  M  G  N
W  R  F  F  Y  W  R  L  J  N  H  B  V  N  E  P  U  R  W  N  D  Q  D  A
P  C  V  W  O  I  E  D  C  O  I  D  K  O  J  V  V  W  H  S  I  X  S  N
R  U  V  L  Y  N  D  R  F  E  W  M  A  N  Y  H  L  Z  D  O  T  X  U  C
E  J  I  L  Y  T  I  Y  P  R  V  N  U  Q  Y  G  L  Q  G  L  S  D  D  I
M  R  P  N  H  E  T  Y  E  A  E  E  T  M  C  J  U  Z  C  I  C  G  Q  A
S  V  V  X  K  R  O  K  G  P  H  L  X  F  P  B  X  O  P  D  O  G  O  L
W  M  Z  Y  N  E  R  D  W  M  R  S  K  K  C  A  O  G  H  A  R  J  W  F
Z  Z  B  A  E  S  A  Y  N  X  P  P  P  W  K  H  Y  Y  G  T  E  M  I  R
S  Y  H  N  J  T  D  K  A  I  X  U  B  Q  Q  L  P  M  Q  I  J  I  S  E
F  F  O  S  X  R  S  A  D  O  U  J  W  A  Z  N  S  O  E  O  N  I  X  E
Q  U  T  G  I  A  N  L  I  U  K  O  F  D  N  G  I  G  T  N  B  O  H  D
N  A  A  B  X  T  D  E  B  T  A  V  A  L  A  N  C  H  E  P  T  V  Y  O
Q  O  Y  F  O  E  X  X  F  H  L  Z  N  B  T  O  A  J  Z  C  B  L  V  M
D  E  B  T  C  O  N  S  O  L  I  D  A  T  I  O  N  K  Z  K  Y  A  E  I
M  I  F  Y  D  U  C  A  V  G  O  W  S  D  G  Q  U  J  O  C  I  M  R  T
L  M  Q  Z  I  Q  Z  W  W  I  E  D  E  B  T  S  N  O  W  B  A  L  L  M
M  T  P  Y  I  B  N  W  V  R  D  P  O  V  Q  K  M  F  K  P  W  H  O  N
T  W  B  E  E  U  U  L  G  E  B  U  D  G  E  T  N  A  Y  H  Q  B  E  F
L  G  X  S  L  V  A  T  I  W  S  G  Q  C  U  E  Q  C  Q  I  A  V  L  L
```

Debt Snowball	Debt Avalanche	Debt Consolidation
Minimum Payment	Financial Freedom	Interest Rate
Consolidation	Creditor	Credit Score
Budget		

Strategies for Managing and Reducing Debt

Across

2. The person or institution to whom money is owed.

7. A numerical representation of a person's creditworthiness, affected by their debt management practices. (2 words)

9. The percentage of a loan that a lender charges as interest to the borrower. (2 words)

10. The smallest amount of money that must be paid on a debt each month to keep the account in good standing, _____ Payment

Down

1. The process of combining multiple debts into a single loan, often with a lower interest rate, Debt _____

3. A debt repayment strategy where you focus on paying off the debt with the highest interest rate first, Debt _____

4. A financial plan that helps you understand and manage your income and expenses.

5. Money owed to another person or institution.

6. The state of having sufficient personal wealth to live without having to work actively for basic necessities, Financial _____

8. A debt repayment strategy where you pay off the smallest debt first while making minimum payments on others, Debt _____

Safeguarding Your Financial Future: Unmasking Predatory Lending and Financial Scams

In today's complex financial landscape, knowledge is your most powerful shield. As you step into adulthood and start making independent financial decisions, you'll encounter a world of opportunities—and unfortunately, a fair share of pitfalls. Two significant threats to your financial well-being are predatory lending and financial scams. But don't worry! By the end of this article, you'll be equipped with the tools to identify, avoid, and protect yourself from these deceptive practices.

The Cunning World of Predatory Lending

Imagine you're in urgent need of money. You come across a lender offering quick cash with "easy" terms. Sounds great, right? Not so fast. This might be the bait of a predatory lender.

Predatory lending refers to unfair, deceptive, or fraudulent practices of some lenders during the loan origination process. These lenders prey on financially vulnerable individuals, often targeting specific communities, the elderly, or those with limited financial literacy.

Red Flags of Predatory Lending:

1. Excessive Interest Rates: While payday loans averaging 400% APR might seem extreme, even rates above 36% for personal loans can be predatory.

2. Pressure Tactics: If a lender rushes you to sign without fully understanding the terms, walk away.

3. Balloon Payments: Beware of loans with low initial payments that suddenly skyrocket.

4. Prepayment Penalties: Some predatory lenders charge hefty fees for paying off your loan early.

5. No Credit Check: While this might seem appealing, it often masks sky-high interest rates.

The Real-World Impact

Let's consider Sarah, a college freshman who needed $500 for textbooks. She took out a payday loan with a two-week term and a $15 fee per $100 borrowed. This 391% APR loan spiraled into a cycle of debt, with Sarah eventually owing over $1,500 on her initial $500 loan.

Unraveling Financial Scams

While predatory lending operates in a legal gray area, financial scams are outright criminal. These schemes aim to trick you into parting with your money or personal information.

Common Types of Financial Scams:

1. Phishing: Fake emails or websites posing as legitimate institutions to steal your data.

2. Ponzi Schemes: Investment frauds promising high returns, paid using money from new investors.

3. Identity Theft: Criminals use your personal information to open accounts or make purchases in your name.

4. Advance Fee Frauds: Scammers ask for upfront payments for prizes or services that never materialize.

Protecting Yourself

1. Be Skeptical: If an offer sounds too good to be true, it probably is.

2. Guard Your Information: Never share personal or financial details unless you've verified the recipient.

3. Research: Before engaging with any financial institution, check their credentials and reviews.

4. Take Your Time: Don't let anyone pressure you into making immediate financial decisions.

Your Financial Armor

Knowledge and vigilance are your best defenses against predatory lending and financial scams. Here's a simple activity to reinforce your understanding:

Create a "Financial Red Flags" list. Write down five warning signs each for predatory lending and financial scams. Keep this list handy when making financial decisions or encountering offers.

Empowering Your Financial Future

As you navigate the financial world, remember that you have the power to protect yourself. By staying informed, asking questions, and trusting your

instincts, you can avoid the traps set by predatory lenders and scammers.

Understanding these risks isn't just about self-protection—it's about building a foundation for a secure financial future. As you make wise choices and share your knowledge with friends and family, you contribute to a more financially literate and scam-resistant community.

Legitimate financial institutions and opportunities will welcome your questions and give you time to make informed decisions. Your financial journey is a marathon, not a sprint. Take it one step at a time, and don't hesitate to seek advice from trusted sources when in doubt.

By mastering the art of identifying and avoiding predatory lending and financial scams, you're not just safeguarding your wallet—you're paving the way for a lifetime of financial success and peace of mind.

To avoid falling victim to predatory lending and financial scams, individuals should stay informed, thoroughly research lenders, read all terms and conditions, and be cautious of offers that seem too good to be true.

I. Key Terms

1. Predatory Lending: _____

2. Balloon Payments: _____

3. Phishing: _____

4. Ponzi Scheme: _____

5. Identity Theft: _____

II. Main Concept Overview

Predatory lending and financial scams are significant threats to financial

well-being. They operate by _____ and often target

_____.

The two main categories discussed in the article are:

1. _____

2. _____

III. Predatory Lending

Fill in the table with the red flags of predatory lending:

Red Flag	Description
Excessive Interest Rates	
Pressure Tactics	
Balloon Payments	
Prepayment Penalties	
No Credit Check	

IV. Financial Scams

Match each type of financial scam with its description:

_____ Phishing   A. Investment frauds promising high returns

_____ Ponzi Scheme   B. Criminals use your information to open accounts or make
                                        purchases

_____ Identity Theft   C. Fake emails or websites posing as legitimate institutions

_____ Advance Fee Fraud   D. Scammers ask for upfront payments for prizes or
                                        services that never materialize

V. True or False

_____ Legitimate financial institutions will always give you time to make informed decisions.

_____ If an offer sounds too good to be true, it's still worth considering.

_____ Sharing personal or financial details is safe as long as you're dealing with a bank.

_____ Creating a "Financial Red Flags" list can help protect you from scams.

_____ Predatory lending operates in a legal gray area.

VI. Protecting Yourself

List four ways to protect yourself from predatory lending and financial scams:

1. _____ 2. _____

3. _____ 4. _____

VII. Reflection

How might understanding predatory lending and financial scams impact your future financial decisions?

_____

_____

_____

Remember, your financial journey is a _____. Take it one step at a

time, and don't hesitate to seek advice from _____ when in doubt.

1

How might understanding predatory lending change the way you approach borrowing money in the future?

Think about the red flags of predatory lending from the article. How could you use this knowledge when looking at loan offers? Consider steps you might take to research and compare different loan options.

2

In what ways could knowing about financial scams change your online behavior?

Reflect on how you currently handle personal information online. What might you do differently to protect yourself from phishing or identity theft? Think about how you could verify if a financial opportunity is legitimate.

3

If a friend was thinking about taking a loan that seemed predatory, how would you advise them?

What key points from the article would be most helpful to share? How could you guide them towards finding better financial options? Think about how to be supportive while providing useful information.

The Tempting Loan Offer

Alex, a high school senior, needs $500 for a new smartphone. A website offers "instant approval" loans with no credit check. The loan terms state "low bi-weekly payments" but don't specify the interest rate or total repayment amount.

Questions:
a) What red flags can you identify in this loan offer?
b) How could Alex determine if this is a fair loan?
c) What alternatives could Alex explore instead of this online loan?

_____
_____
_____
_____
_____
_____
_____
_____
_____
_____

The Scholarship Scam

Emma receives a text message congratulating her on winning a $5,000 scholarship. The message asks her to click a link and enter her social security number and bank details to "claim her prize."

Questions:
a) What elements of this scenario suggest it might be a scam?
b) How should Emma respond to this text message?
c) If Emma wants to verify the scholarship, what steps should she take?

_____
_____
_____
_____
_____
_____
_____
_____
_____

TERM	DEFINITION
Predatory Lending	
Financial Scam	
Interest Rate	
Credit Score	
Phishing	

TERM	DEFINITION
Identity Theft	
Balloon Payment	
Annual Percentage Rate (APR)	
Ponzi Scheme	
Financial Literacy	

Safeguarding Your Financial Future

```
L I O U Y K U I P R E D A T O R Y L E N D I N G
Q U N I R Y P M K R N G Z A U B B B I E E C H K F
C U F I N A N C I A L L I T E R A C Y M R H Q P
L N F U C H X W K X C A J P X F N S W H E L U D
A Z C P N Q A O F H T M W F S U O V I I D P P S
N M M V Z B Z P E I N V T I X Y L I S Z I O W O
N F A S M J W P R G L T A M N V D D C M T N U G
U Q F J I N N A R J K Y P S N E J F G M S Z J C
A V D F I N A N C I A L S C A M Y X C O C I T H
L Y S M O L Z K A H I Y V G K P S Y U Q O S W S
P B U A A L B V U Y N X X I Z I P Q S P R C O A
E O Y R I N J W W D T T X J O X I U F L E H U Y
R L U I T J I G A A E S R U L C M U Z V L E E U
C X N Y R B X O U M R C N O F X A B V U V M U Q
E Q Q T O B V M Q Q E G J B N A Z N F K R E H K
N X Q P Y X O Q L O S A H Z V P P D Q P J I T I
T O M W Q L T D K V T O Y U R I Z H W M H U K X
A I O E Q X R I S K R D W A Q U S F I N F M F U
G Z B A Z L B N U V A X C A M I Y O J S K X F J
E N S D K K U R U Z T P G H P K G S P H S A U
R B V A H W N C J J E J Q D P D M X W J E I P D
A B A L L O O N P A Y M E N T G Z K Z Y F K N W
T T Z H V M Y I Z Q F Q J U K I V U K Q B A J G
E Q I D E N T I T Y T H E F T X X O M O W S B S
```

Predatory Lending	Financial Scam	Interest Rate
Identity Theft	Balloon Payment	Annual Percentage Rate
Ponzi Scheme	Financial Literacy	APR
Phishing	Credit Score	

Safeguarding Your Financial Future

Across

4. The fraudulent acquisition and use of a person's private identifying information, usually for financial gain, _____ Theft

6. The yearly cost of a loan, including interest and fees, expressed as a percentage. (Abbrv.)

7. A fraudulent investing scam promising high rates of return with little risk to investors, _____ Scheme

8. The fraudulent practice of sending emails or messages purporting to be from reputable companies to induce individuals to reveal personal information.

9. Fraudulent schemes designed to trick people into parting with their money or personal information, Financial _____

10. Unfair, deceptive, or fraudulent practices of some lenders during the loan origination process, _____ Lending

Down

1. A numerical expression based on a statistical analysis of a person's credit files, representing their creditworthiness. (2 words)

2. The percentage of a loan amount that a lender charges for borrowing money, _____ Rate

3. A large payment due at the end of a loan term, much larger than the regular payments, _____ Payment

5. The possession of skills and knowledge that allows an individual to make informed and effective decisions with their financial resources, Financial _____

Securing Your Future:
The Basics of Retirement Planning

Imagine yourself at 65, ready to embark on a new chapter of life. Will you be financially prepared for retirement? For many high school students, retirement seems like a distant concern. However, understanding the basics of retirement planning now can set you up for a secure and comfortable future. In this article, we'll explore the fundamental concepts of retirement planning, why it's crucial to start early, and how you can take the first steps towards financial independence in your golden years.

What is Retirement Planning?

Retirement planning is the process of determining retirement income goals and the actions and decisions necessary to achieve those goals. It involves making strategic financial decisions today that will impact your quality of life in the future. The key components of retirement planning include:

1. Setting retirement goals
2. Estimating future expenses
3. Calculating how much you need to save
4. Choosing appropriate investment vehicles
5. Managing risks and adjusting your plan over time

Retirement planning involves setting financial goals for the future, assessing current savings, and investing wisely to ensure sufficient funds are available to maintain a desired lifestyle after leaving the workforce.

The Power of Compound Interest

One of the most compelling reasons to start retirement planning early is the power of compound interest. This financial principle allows your money to grow exponentially over time. When you invest, you earn returns not just on your initial investment, but also on the accumulated interest from previous periods. The earlier you start, the more time your money has to grow.

For example, if you start investing $200 per month at age 20, assuming an average annual return of 7%, you could have over $600,000 by age 65. If you wait until age 30 to start, you'd have less than half that amount, around $290,000, by age 65.

Retirement Savings Vehicles

There are several types of accounts designed specifically for retirement savings. Each has its own benefits and considerations:

1. 401(k) Plans: Employer-sponsored retirement accounts that allow you to contribute pre-tax dollars from your paycheck. Many employers offer matching contributions, essentially providing free money for your retirement.

2. Individual Retirement Accounts (IRAs):
Personal retirement savings accounts that come in two main types:
• Traditional IRA: Contributions may be tax-deductible, and you pay taxes on withdrawals in retirement.
•Roth IRA: Contributions are made with after-tax dollars, but withdrawals in retirement are tax-free.

3. Social Security: A government program that provides a basic level of income in retirement, based on your work history and the amount you've paid into the system over your career.

Creating a Retirement Plan

Developing a retirement plan involves several steps:

1. *Assess your current financial situation:* Take stock of your assets, debts, and current savings rate.

2. *Set retirement goals:* Consider what kind of lifestyle you want in retirement and estimate how much it will cost.

3. *Calculate your retirement needs:* Use online calculators or consult with a financial advisor to determine how much you need to save.

4. *Choose appropriate investments:* Select a mix of stocks, bonds, and other assets based on your risk tolerance and time horizon.

5. *Make regular contributions:* Consistently save a portion of your income for retirement, taking advantage of any employer matches.

6. *Review and adjust your plan:* Regularly reassess your retirement strategy and make changes as needed.

Challenges and Considerations

While retirement planning is crucial, it's not without challenges. Some key considerations include:

1. *Inflation:* The rising cost of goods and services over time can erode the purchasing power of your savings.

2. *Healthcare costs:* Medical expenses often increase as we age and can significantly impact retirement savings.

3. *Longevity risk:* With increasing life expectancies, you need to plan for a potentially longer retirement period.

4. *Market volatility:* Investment returns can fluctuate, impacting the growth of your retirement savings.

Retirement planning may seem overwhelming, but starting early and understanding the basics can set you on the path to financial security. By taking advantage of compound interest, utilizing retirement savings vehicles, and creating a solid plan, you can work towards a comfortable retirement. The choices you make today will shape your financial future.

Did You Know?

• The concept of retirement is relatively new. It became widespread in the United States only after the introduction of Social Security in 1935.
• According to a 2022 survey by the Employee Benefit Research Institute, only 7 in 10 American workers feel confident about having enough money for a comfortable retirement.

---

21. Basics of Retirement Planning
GUIDED NOTES

I. Key Terms

1. Retirement Planning: _____

2. Compound Interest: _____

3. 401(k): _____

4. Individual Retirement Account (IRA): _____

5. Social Security: _____

II. Main Concept Overview

Retirement planning is the process of _____ retirement income

goals and the _____ and _____ necessary to

achieve those goals. It involves making _____ financial decisions

today that will impact your _____ of life in the future.

III. Matching Section

Match each term with its correct description:

_____ Traditional IRA   A. Contributions are made with after-tax dollars, but
                              withdrawals in retirement are tax-free

_____ Roth IRA   B. Employer-sponsored retirement account that allows
                              pre-tax contributions

_____ 401(k)   C. Government program providing basic retirement
                              income based on work history

_____ Social Security   D. Personal retirement account where contributions may
                              be tax-deductible

_____ Compound Interest   E. Financial principle allowing money to grow
                              exponentially over time

IV. Fill in the Table

Complete the table with information about the steps involved in creating a retirement plan:

Step	Description
1	
2	
3	
4	
5	
6	

V. True/False

_____ Retirement planning is only necessary for people nearing retirement age.

_____ The power of compound interest means that starting to save early can result in significantly more savings.

_____ 401(k) plans are personal retirement accounts that are not connected to your employer.

_____ Inflation can erode the purchasing power of your retirement savings over time.

_____ Once you create a retirement plan, you don't need to review or adjust it.

VI. Reflection/Summary

Summarize the main points of retirement planning in your own words. How does this concept relate to your life or other financial ideas you've learned?

_____

_____

_____

_____

1

How might your retirement goals differ from those of your parents or grandparents?

Think about changes in technology, work environments, and lifestyles. How might these affect your retirement plans compared to older generations? Consider both financial goals and lifestyle expectations.

2

Why is starting to save for retirement early so important?

Use the concept of compound interest in your explanation. Compare two scenarios: starting to save at age 20 vs. age 30. How much difference could ten years make? Think about how compound interest grows your money over time.

3

How do you think technology might change retirement planning for your generation?

Reflect on how technology affects jobs and investing today. How might future tech innovations impact how we save, invest, or even think about retirement? Consider both potential benefits and challenges.

The Early Starter

Sarah, age 22, just started her first job after college. Her employer offers a 401(k) plan with a match. Sarah is considering whether to start contributing to her 401(k) now or wait until she's older and earning more.

Questions:
a) What are the potential benefits of Sarah starting to contribute to her 401(k) now?
b) How might the principle of compound interest affect Sarah's decision?
c) What factors should Sarah consider when deciding how much to contribute to her 401(k)?

_____

_____

_____

_____

_____

_____

_____

_____

_____

_____

The College Planning Duo

Best friends Jamie and Casey, both 17, are discussing their college plans. Jamie is considering taking on student loans to attend an expensive out-of-state university. Casey is thinking about attending a local community college for two years before transferring to a state university to save money.

Questions:
a) How might Jamie and Casey's college decisions impact their ability to save for retirement in the future?
b) What are some strategies Jamie could use to minimize the impact of student loans on their long-term financial goals?
c) How could Casey's choice to attend community college first affect their long-term financial outlook, including retirement savings?

_____

_____

_____

_____

_____

_____

_____

_____

_____

TERM	DEFINITION
Retirement Planning	
Compound Interest	
401(k) Plan	
Individual Retirement Account (IRA)	
Social Security	

TERM	DEFINITION
Inflation	
Diversification	
Risk Tolerance	
Employer Match	
Longevity Risk	

Basics of Retirement Planning

```
S O H E U R I Y V R I S K T O L E R A N C E G E
M C R Y D E 0 Y C C K K 4 A E H T I L U F M K I
H K L P C T 1 O C A U G T S 1 4 N 1 S E U D U D
I O R R D I V E R S I F I C A T I O N F F E G G
1 1 0 0 C R 0 M L 1 4 G A E D V L H C C T H R G
C D T P 1 E C P Y D M M E F H O T O A L R R N C
4 T Y U Y M O 1 L P K S C T N I L R E E Y F N M
L Y K A U E M K M P D L M V 4 Y N P H O K O D G
H R D U G N P M L 4 P L C 4 G F Y A M C 1 4 V R
M G F S G T O E K O U 1 S 0 0 U A H 4 I R R G 4
L R Y O D P U P M Y N M 0 C V G D G A E 4 I 1 C
F Y Y C V L N N C C E G R F U S 4 G F 0 0 T D C
4 H E I D A D K V G M K E C M I I N L D 1 E O D
4 N O A E N I K E P P D R V L 4 0 P 0 C K 0 M M
C M U L D N N T I E L H Y O I 4 K 4 0 A P M 1 N
D I S S U I T S 4 V O V O R K T N M E G L T V L
A N P E L N E Y I 0 Y U R S C R Y S C Y A I G I
O F 4 C P G R O S 1 E E Y P E 4 0 R C O N M G R
E L S U H C E G Y S R F F T M 0 H 0 I 0 K U S A
M A 0 R A 1 S E U E M L C H L N O A C S E M T P
T T D I U O T C C L A M D P F Y O U L 0 K H 4 Y
P I 4 T A S D V Y 1 T D C R M I C A T C O N K O
F O Y Y F P Y D F N C 4 4 C M H O 4 D G O P E 4
M N 1 V R L C E 0 K H C C 4 M H Y L V 1 M H 1 T
```

Retirement Planning	Compound Interest	401(k) Plan
Risk Tolerance	Employer Match	Longevity Risk
Diversification	Inflation	Social Security
IRA		

Basics of Retirement Planning

Across

2. The process of determining retirement income goals and the actions and decisions necessary to achieve those goals, _____ Planning

3. A government program that provides a basic level of income in retirement, based on your work history and the amount you've paid into the system over your career. (2 words)

7. An employer-sponsored retirement account that allows you to contribute pre-tax dollars from your paycheck, 401(k) _____

8. A personal retirement savings account that comes in two main types: Traditional and Roth, (Abbrv.)

9. The degree of variability in investment returns that an investor is willing to withstand, Risk _____

10. The risk of outliving one's savings in retirement due to increased life expectancy, _____ Risk

Down

1. The practice of spreading your investments across various financial instruments to minimize risk.

4. A financial principle that allows your money to grow exponentially over time, _____ Interest

5. The rising cost of goods and services over time, which can erode the purchasing power of your savings.

6. A contribution made by an employer to an employee's retirement account, typically a percentage of the employee's contribution, Employer _____

Navigating the World of Banking:
Your Guide to Smart Financial Choices

You've just received your first paycheck from your new part-time job. The thrill of earning your own money is exciting, but now comes the crucial question: what do you do with it? This is where understanding banking services becomes essential. In this guide, we'll explore the world of banking, helping you make informed decisions about managing your hard-earned money.

The Basics of Banking Services

Banking services are financial products and tools offered by banks and credit unions to help individuals and businesses manage their money effectively. These services go beyond just storing your cash; they include a range of options designed to help you save, spend, borrow, and grow your money efficiently.

At the heart of banking services are checking and savings accounts. A checking account serves as your financial command center, allowing you to deposit money, write checks, and use debit cards for everyday transactions and bill payments. On the other hand, a savings account is the foundation of your financial future, helping you set aside money and earn interest. It's ideal for emergency funds and short-term savings goals.

As technology advances, online and mobile banking have become increasingly popular. These services offer the convenience of managing your accounts, paying bills, and transferring money from your smartphone or computer, providing 24/7 access to your finances.

For those looking to maximize their savings, Certificates of Deposit (CDs) offer an opportunity to lock in higher interest rates. By depositing money for a fixed term, you can earn more interest than a traditional savings account, making CDs useful for medium to long-term savings goals.

Credit cards and personal loans fall into the borrowing category of banking services. Credit cards allow you to make purchases on credit, which can help build your credit history when used responsibly. Personal loans provide financing for larger expenses, such as education costs or home improvements, by allowing you to borrow a lump sum to be repaid over time.

The Importance of
Banking Services in Your Life

As a high school student, you're at the perfect age to start building good financial habits, and understanding banking services is crucial for managing your money effectively. Learning to manage your own money is a key step towards financial independence and adulthood.

Starting with a checking account can lead to responsible credit card use, helping you build

Comparing banking services entails assessing fees, interest rates, account features, and customer service to find the best fit for individual needs.

a good credit score for the future. This credit history will be invaluable when you apply for loans, rent an apartment, or even apply for certain jobs after graduation.

Banking services also play a vital role in helping you save for your goals. Whether you're saving for college, a car, or the latest tech gadget, the right combination of banking products can help you save efficiently and track your progress.

Banks offer security for your money that you simply can't get by keeping cash under your mattress. Federal deposit insurance protects your money up to certain limits, giving you peace of mind about the safety of your funds.

Comparing Banking Services: Making Informed Choices

When it comes to choosing banking services, it's essential to compare options and understand how they align with your specific needs. Let's look at a real-world example of comparing checking accounts from two different banks.

Bank A offers a student-friendly checking account with no mini mum balance requirement, a free debit card, and a mobile app with check deposit functionality. It has a $5 monthly fee, but this fee is waived for students. Bank B, on the other hand, requires a $100 minimum balance but offers a free debit card and checks, along with a mobile app that includes budgeting tools. It has no monthly fee but charges $2 for out-of-network ATM usage.

Choosing between these options depends on your specific situation. If you're starting with a small amount of money and value no fees, Bank A might be the better choice. However, if you can maintain a $100 balance and rarely use ATMs outside your bank's network, Bank B could save you money in the long run and provide helpful budgeting tools.

This example illustrates the importance of looking beyond just the basics when comparing banking services. Consider factors such as minimum balance requirements, fees (including hidden ones), interest rates, online and mobile banking features, ATM access, and any special perks or discounts for students.

Putting Your Knowledge into Action

Now that you understand the basics of banking services, it's time to put your knowledge into action. Start by researching three local banks or credit unions in your area. Compare their checking account offerings, noting fees, minimum balances, and special features. Then, based on your personal financial situation and needs, decide which account would be best for you and explain your reasoning.

This exercise will give you practical experience in comparing banking services and making informed financial decisions. It's a skill that will serve you well throughout your life, helping you manage your money more effectively and build a solid financial foundation for your future.

Remember, the right banking services can do more than just store your money – they can help you develop good financial habits, save for your goals, and set you on the path to long-term financial success. By starting to understand and use these services now, you're taking an important step towards financial literacy and independence.

As you continue your journey into the world of banking and personal finance, don't hesitate to ask questions. Financial institutions often have resources specifically designed for young adults, and many offer financial literacy programs that can further enhance your understanding. Your smart financial choices today will pave the way for a secure and prosperous financial future.

I. Key Terms

1. Banking Services: _____

2. Checking Account: _____

3. Savings Account: _____

4. Online and Mobile Banking: _____

5. Credit Card: _____

II. Main Concept Overview

Banking services are financial products and tools offered by _____

and _____ to help individuals and businesses _____

their money. These services go beyond just storing cash; they include options to

help you _____, _____, _____, and

_____ your money efficiently.

III. Importance of Banking Services

1. Financial Independence: _____

2. Building Credit: _____

3. Saving for Goals: _____

4. Security: _____

IV. True or False

_____ 1. Banking services only include storing your cash.

_____ 2. A checking account serves as your financial command center.

_____ 3. Credit cards always help build a good credit history, regardless of how
they're used.

_____ 4. Online banking allows you to manage your accounts 24/7.

_____ 5. When comparing banking services, you should only consider the
minimum balance requirements.

V. Comparing Banking Services

When comparing banking services, it's important to consider:

1. _____

2. _____

3. _____

4. _____

5. _____

VI. Application Question

The article provides an example comparing two banks. Based on this example, answer the following:

If you're starting with a small amount of money and value no fees, which bank might be better for you? Explain why.

_____

_____

_____

VII. Reflection/Summary

Summarize two ways that understanding banking services can benefit you as a high school student:

_____

_____

_____

How can comparing banking services help you make informed financial decisions?

_____

_____

_____

1

How might using banking services change your current money habits?

Think about how you handle money now. Consider how a checking or savings account could affect your spending and saving. How might budgeting tools in banking apps help you?

2

Why is it important to compare different banks instead of assuming they're all the same?

Consider the differences in fees, interest rates, and minimum balances between banks. Think about special features some banks offer. How could choosing the right bank save you money?

3

How do you think your banking needs might change after high school?

Think about how your income and expenses might be different in college or when you start working. Consider what new banking services might become important to you then.

First Job, First Bank Account

You've just gotten your first part-time job at a local cafe. Your parents suggest it's time to open your first bank account. You visit two local banks to compare their student checking accounts.

Questions:
a) What features of the checking accounts would be most important for your needs?
b) How might having a bank account change how you manage your earnings?
c) What questions would you ask the bank representatives to help you make your decision?

Online Banking Security Concerns

Your friend Alex is hesitant to use online banking because he is worried about the security of his personal information. He would prefer to do all his banking in person at his local branch.

Questions:
a) What security features of online banking would you explain to Alex to address his concerns?
b) How might Alex's banking experience differ from someone who uses online and mobile banking regularly?
c) What situations might make online banking particularly useful for a high school student?

TERM	DEFINITION
Banking Services	
Checking Account	
Savings Account	
Online Banking	
Mobile Banking	

TERM	DEFINITION
Interest Rate	
Minimum Balance	
Debit Card	
Credit Card	
Certificate of Deposit (CD)	

Understanding and Comparing Banking Service

```
J Z C E R T I F I C A T E O F D E P O S I T B L
V I C U O S Y R N I N T E R E S T R A T E Q A A
S H H O P G L U E R V L H D Y O O I K M Y S N H
J A E P F V E K O G D X E I O E V S D O V D K N
T Q C X T C B X R A P J K D U U W V S B N K I N
R E K N G R B V B S W G G L O G N J Q I Z T N B
M N I Q V E P G N O A M S H K N R C N L W D G B
I B N Z A D T M G L T V X L Q S E K U E U S S U
N R G P T I A Y X J D R I O W A P J D B U P E Z
I L A P C T F A J T F D M N B X Y K W A X N R B
M Z C J G C E G O Y F I W O G J Q G H N C X V Q
U W C O E A J D I N Z H I D G S K A G K E O I J
M L O J Z R C D K F L Z W J Z B A E M I Q W C X
B F U S V D I I I R C I O N Z M I C V N N V E E
A B N J P F P T J S L M N W K S X Y C G G M S U
L O T C L X C O D H S Y M E K F H U W O Y B M D
A Y I S O Z I B X V S S W Q B B I O V K U B U G
N V U V A L K R Z P W C O E U A Q E W K N N F T
C D Z X C H U K C Y I K A D R A N X F Q C H T N
E D E B I T C A R D W E O Y X H M K B W V C P U
W R I K A C J F V X Y L W C W G W Q I T E D W Y
Q Z E B P H Y C J N O S G F M D M A F N W Z J A
X B D X C K H Q F K D A S U N H L M A G G X T A
Y K L T L B O Q I B S T Q Y L M B B O W I H T V
```

Banking Services	Checking Account	Savings Account
Online Banking	Mobile Banking	Minimum Balance
Debit Card	Credit Card	Certificate of Deposit
CD	Interest Rate	

Understanding and Comparing Banking Service

Across

2. An account that allows you to deposit money, write checks, and use debit cards for everyday transactions and bill payments, _____ Account

6. A service that allows you to manage your accounts, pay bills, and transfer money through the internet, _____ Banking

7. A payment card that allows the cardholder to borrow funds to pay for goods and services, _____ Card

9. An account that helps you set aside money and earn interest, ideal for emergency funds and short-term savings goals, _____ Account

10. A service that enables you to perform banking activities through a smartphone or tablet app, _____ Banking

Down

1. The percentage of an amount of money that is paid for its use, typically expressed as an annual percentage of the principal amount. (2 words)

3. A savings account that holds a fixed amount of money for a fixed period of time, typically offering higher interest rates than regular savings accounts. (Abbrv.)

4. Financial products and tools offered by banks and credit unions to help individuals and businesses manage their money, _____ Services

5. A payment card that deducts money directly from a checking account to pay for purchases, _____ Card

8. The lowest amount of money required to keep an account open or avoid fees, as specified by a financial institution, _____ Balance

Consumer Rights and Responsibilities: Empowering Smart Shoppers

Have you ever felt frustrated after making a purchase, wishing you knew more about your rights as a consumer? Whether you're buying a new smartphone, signing up for a gym membership, or ordering food online, understanding your consumer rights and responsibilities is crucial. Let's explore how these concepts can help you become a savvier shopper and make more informed financial decisions.

What Are Consumer Rights?

Consumer rights are legal protections designed to ensure fair and ethical treatment of customers in the marketplace. These rights empower you to make informed choices, receive quality products and services, and seek redress when things go wrong. In the United States, consumer rights are primarily based on the Consumer Bill of Rights, introduced by President John F. Kennedy in 1962.

The four fundamental consumer rights include:

1. The right to safety: Products and services should not pose unnecessary risks to your health or well-being.

2. The right to be informed: You should have access to accurate information about products and services, including prices, terms, and conditions.

3. The right to choose: You should have the freedom to select from a variety of options in the marketplace without undue pressure or manipulation.

4. The right to be heard: You should have the ability to voice complaints and seek resolution for legitimate grievances.

Consumer rights protect individuals from unfair business practices, ensuring access to safe products, truthful advertising, and the right to seek redress for grievances.

Consumer Responsibilities: The Other Side of the Coin

While consumer rights protect you, consumer responsibilities ensure that you play your part in maintaining a fair and efficient marketplace. These responsibilities include:

1. Being an informed consumer: Research products and services before making purchases.

2. Reading and understanding contracts: Take the time to review terms and conditions before agreeing to them.

3. Using products and services as intended: Follow instructions and safety guidelines to prevent accidents or damage.

4. Reporting fraudulent or deceptive practices: Help protect others by reporting suspicious business activities to the appropriate authorities.

Real-World Application: The Smartphone Purchase

Imagine you're in the market for a new smartphone. Here's how consumer rights and responsibilities come into play:

1. Right to safety: You can expect that the phone won't overheat or explode during normal use.
2. Right to be informed: The store must provide accurate information about the phone's features, warranty, and return policy.
3. Right to choose: You should be able to compare different models and brands without pressure from salespeople.
4. Right to be heard: If the phone is defective, you have the right to complain and seek a resolution.

Your responsibilities in this scenario include:
• Researching different phone models and reading reviews before making a decision.
• Understanding the terms of your phone plan and any financing agreements.
• Using the phone as intended and following the manufacturer's guidelines.
• Reporting any suspicious or deceptive practices you encounter during the purchasing process.

The Impact of Consumer Rights and Responsibilities

Understanding and exercising your consumer rights and responsibilities can have a significant impact on your financial well-being:

1. Better financial decisions: Being an informed consumer helps you make smarter choices with your money.
2. Increased confidence: Knowing your rights empowers you to stand up for yourself in the marketplace.
3. Improved product quality: When consumers exercise their rights and fulfill their responsibilities, it encourages businesses to maintain high standards.
4. Fraud prevention: Awareness of your rights and responsibilities can help you identify and avoid scams and fraudulent practices.

Putting Knowledge into Action

To become a more empowered consumer, consider taking these steps:

1. Stay informed: Keep up with consumer protection laws and your rights in different industries.
2. Read the fine print: Always review contracts and agreements carefully before signing.
3. Ask questions: Don't hesitate to seek clarification on products, services, or policies.
4. Document everything: Keep records of purchases, warranties, and any communication with businesses.
5. Know where to turn: Familiarize yourself with consumer protection agencies and resources in your area.

Being a responsible consumer isn't just about protecting yourself—it's about contributing to a fair and ethical marketplace for everyone. By understanding and exercising your consumer rights and responsibilities, you're not only making smarter financial decisions but also helping to shape a better economic environment for all.

Did You Know?

• The Better Business Bureau (BBB) receives over 1 million consumer complaints annually, highlighting the importance of consumer advocacy.
• Many countries have adopted and expanded upon the original Consumer Bill of Rights.

23. Consumer Rights and Responsibilities
GUIDED NOTES

I. Key Terms

1. Consumer Rights: _____

2. Consumer Responsibilities: _____

3. Consumer Bill of Rights: _____

II. Main Concept Overview

Consumer rights and responsibilities are crucial for _____ in the

marketplace. They help ensure _____ treatment of customers and

promote _____ financial decisions.

III. Matching Section

Match each term with its correct description:

_____ Right to safety   A. Freedom to select from various options

_____ Right to be informed   B. Products should not pose unnecessary risks

_____ Right to choose   C. Access to accurate information about products

_____ Right to be heard   D. Ability to voice complaints and seek resolution

_____ Informed consumer   E. Researching before making purchases

IV. Four Fundamental Consumer Rights

1. _____   2. _____

3. _____   4. _____

V. True or False

_____ Consumer responsibilities include using products as intended.

_____ The right to safety means products should not pose unnecessary risks to
   health or well-being.

_____ Consumers have a responsibility to report fraudulent or deceptive practices.

_____ Understanding contracts is a consumer responsibility.

_____ Consumer rights apply to various types of purchases, including buying a
   smartphone.

VI. Fill in the Table

Complete the table with examples of how consumer rights and responsibilities apply when purchasing a smartphone:

Consumer Right/ Responsibility	Example for Smartphone Purchase
Right to safety	
Right to be informed	
Consumer responsibility	
Right to be heard	

VII. Application Question

Based on the article, list three steps you can take to become a more empowered consumer. How might these steps help you make better financial decisions?

_____

_____

_____

_____

VIII. Reflection/Summary

Summarize the main points about consumer rights and responsibilities in your own words. How do these concepts contribute to a fair and ethical marketplace for everyone?

_____

_____

_____

_____

1

How might knowing your consumer rights change your next big purchase?

Think about something expensive you want to buy. How could understanding your rights to safety, information, and choice affect your decision? Consider how you might approach the seller differently.

2

How has online shopping changed consumer rights and responsibilities?

Reflect on your online shopping experiences. How easy is it to find product information or return items? Think about how digital platforms have changed the way we shop and share feedback about products.

3

How do consumer rights and responsibilities connect to your personal finances?

Consider your spending habits. How might being an informed consumer help you make better financial choices? Think about how responsible consuming could affect your long-term financial goals.

Faulty Smartphone

You bought a new smartphone last week. Today, you notice that the battery drains completely within two hours of normal use, much faster than advertised. The store refuses to exchange the phone, claiming all sales are final.

Questions:
a) Which consumer right is most relevant in this situation?
b) What steps could you take to address this issue?
c) How might being an informed consumer have prevented this problem?

Misleading Advertisement

A local gym is advertising a "no-commitment" membership with "easy cancellation." After signing up, you discover there's a six-month minimum contract and a complicated cancellation process with fees.

Questions:
a) Which consumer right has potentially been violated here?
b) What responsibilities did you have as a consumer before signing up?
c) How could this situation impact consumer trust in fitness industry advertising?

TERM	DEFINITION
Consumer Rights	
Consumer Responsibilities	
Consumer Bill of Rights	
Right to Safety	
Right to Be Informed	

TERM	DEFINITION
Right to Choose	
Right to Be Heard	
Informed Consumer	
Consumer Protection Agency	
Marketplace	

Consumer Rights and Responsibilities

```
C O N S U M E R P R O T E C T I O N A G E N C Y
O I F S A E L B O Q L J J X K P D S L Q O Q Q D
N Z U H K O W Z L M W R Y J M Y N B X M N T C G
S R I G H T T O B E H E A R D L E Y K I T T S M
U L Q N X P H B I N R C K C S L E K Y Z A V I A
M E E O F O M P Z K Y I W Z L X W A P H Y N D R
E N E B A O N D A I C R G I O D B V R S P S L K
R Q H E L X R T R L R O L H Y X G V V Z O C D E
R G Z T I S I M I P J K N D T G J Z F Z Z V I T
E W Y R Y L D J E Y C Q Q S M T Q N B T S Y G P
S Z C C B V O B C D V X N R U K O A I Q J L J L
P G E F Q Q K Z M O C M E W E M A S J X T H X A
O P N L N Y F G F D Q O Y V M Q E A A E X S E C
N P N R P G B H M H V X N I P L B R Q F M Q J E
S B K H W V L R O D K N C S W P O F R D E F J Z
I I D S P I R H O K O U P A U X B M E I L T J O
B V N L C O G X G C V C G S N M V Y B J G U Y C
I U S H V Y R N W J S A U J C W E V I W Z H T A
L M T M Z I O F B G X A B D O B P R H D E Z T A
I H O C O N S U M E R B I L L O F R I G H T S S
T R I G H T T O B E I N F O R M E D X L P L J Z
I U I G O J F C D J J Z Q B P M I G D K X A A R
E J S F D A O K R I G H T T O C H O O S E F D S
S Q S C L T J D N V P Y J Y P X A Q A N B I M V
```

Consumer Rights

Consumer Responsibilities

Consumer Bill of Rights

Right to Safety

Right to Be Informed

Right to Choose

Right to Be Heard

Informed Consumer

Consumer Protection Agency

Marketplace

Consumer Rights and Responsibilities

Across

3. Legal protections designed to ensure fair and ethical treatment of customers in the marketplace, Consumer _____

5. The consumer protection ensuring freedom to select from a variety of options in the marketplace without undue pressure or manipulation, Right to _____

8. The arena, physical or digital, where goods and services are bought and sold.

10. Actions and obligations of consumers to maintain a fair and efficient marketplace, Consumer _____

Down

1. A set of principles introduced by President John F. Kennedy in 1962, forming the basis for consumer protections in the United States, Consumer _____ __ _____

2. Government organizations responsible for protecting consumer interests and enforcing consumer rights, Consumer _____ Agency

4. The consumer protection ensuring that products and services do not pose unnecessary risks to health or well-being, Right to _____

6. The consumer protection providing the ability to voice complaints and seek resolution for legitimate grievances, Right to Be _____

7. A shopper who researches products and services before making purchases, _____ Consumer

9. The consumer protection guaranteeing access to accurate information about products and services, including prices, terms, and conditions, Right to Be _____

Navigating the Financial Maze:
How to Evaluate Financial Information and Advice

In today's information-rich world, financial advice is everywhere – from social media influencers to traditional financial advisors. But how do you know which advice to trust? Learning to evaluate financial information and advice is a crucial skill that can save you from costly mistakes and help you make informed decisions about your money.

Understanding the Landscape of Financial Advice

Financial advice comes in many forms and from various sources. Some common sources include:

1. Professional financial advisors
2. Bank representatives
3. Online financial blogs and websites
4. Social media influencers
5. Friends and family
6. Books and educational materials

Each of these sources can offer valuable insights, but they also come with potential biases and limitations. The key is to approach all financial advice with a critical eye and a healthy dose of skepticism.

Evaluating financial information involves analyzing data to assess an organization's performance, make informed decisions, and identify areas for improvement.

Key Factors in Evaluating Financial Information

When assessing financial information or advice, consider the following factors:

1. Credentials and Qualifications

Look for advisors with recognized financial certifications such as Certified Financial Planner (CFP), Chartered Financial Analyst (CFA), or Certified Public Accountant (CPA). These credentials indicate a certain level of education and expertise in financial matters.

2. Experience and Track Record

Consider the advisor's experience in the field. How long have they been providing financial advice? What is their track record? While past performance doesn't guarantee future results, it can give you an idea of their expertise.

3. Potential Conflicts of Interest

Be aware of how financial advisors are compensated. Some earn commissions on products they sell, which could influence their recommendations. Fee-only advisors, who charge a flat rate or percentage of assets managed, may have fewer conflicts of interest.

4. Transparency and Communication

A good financial advisor should be able to explain complex concepts in terms you can understand. They should also be transparent about their fees, investment strategies, and potential risks.

Red Flags to Watch Out For

As you navigate the world of financial advice, be on the lookout for these warning signs:

1. Promises of guaranteed high returns with little or no risk
2. Pressure to make quick decisions without time for research
3. Lack of transparency about fees or how the advisor is compensated
4. Reluctance to provide references or credentials
5. Advice that seems too good to be true

Remember, if something sounds too good to be true, it probably is. Trust your instincts and don't be afraid to ask questions or seek a second opinion.

The Importance of Personal Research

While expert advice can be valuable, it's crucial to do your own research as well. Here are some steps you can take:

1. Use reputable financial websites and government resources for information
2. Compare advice from multiple sources to get a balanced perspective

3. Stay informed about current financial news and trends
4. Learn basic financial concepts to better understand the advice you receive

By combining expert advice with your own research, you'll be better equipped to make informed financial decisions.

Applying Financial Advice to Your Situation

Remember that even good financial advice may not be right for everyone. Your financial situation, goals, and risk tolerance are unique. When evaluating advice, consider how it applies to your specific circumstances. What works for a friend or a social media influencer might not be the best choice for you.

Evaluating financial information and advice is a critical skill in today's complex financial world. By considering the source, looking for red flags, doing your own research, and applying advice to your unique situation, you can make more informed financial decisions. Remember, the goal is not to find perfect advice, but to gather enough reliable information to make confident choices about your financial future.

Did You Know?

According to a 2022 survey by the National Financial Educators Council, financial illiteracy costs the average American $1,819 per year. By learning to evaluate financial advice effectively, you can potentially save thousands of dollars over your lifetime!

24. Evaluating Financial Information and Advice
GUIDED NOTES

I. Key Terms

1. Financial Advisor: _____

2. Credentials: _____

3. Conflict of Interest: _____

4. Fee-only Advisor: _____

5. Red Flags: _____

II. Main Concept Overview

Evaluating financial information and advice is crucial because _____

_____.

The goal of evaluating financial advice is not to find _____ advice, but to

gather enough _____ information to make _____ choices

about your financial future.

III. Matching Section

Match each term with its correct description:

_____ Certified Financial Planner (CFP)   A. Indicates a certain level of education and expertise

_____ Chartered Financial Analyst (CFA) B. Another credential mentioned in the article

_____ Credentials   C. How financial advisors are compensated

_____ Transparency   D. Ability to explain complex concepts clearly

_____ Compensation   E. Being open about fees and strategies

IV. True or False

_____ Professional financial advisors are the only reliable source of financial information.

_____ It's important to approach all financial advice with a critical eye and healthy skepticism.

_____ Doing your own research is unnecessary if you have a certified financial advisor.

_____ Even good financial advice may not be right for everyone's specific situation.

_____ Promises of guaranteed high returns with little or no risk are a common red flag.

V. Fill in the Table: Key Factors in Evaluating Financial Information

Factor	Example from the article
Credentials and Qualifications	
Experience and Track Record	
Potential Conflicts of Interest	
Transparency and Communication	

VI. Application Question

You come across a social media post from a popular influencer promoting a "guaranteed" investment opportunity with high returns and no risk. Using what you've learned about evaluating financial information, how would you approach this situation? What steps would you take to verify the credibility of this advice?

_____

_____

_____

VII. Reflection/Summary

Summarize three key points you've learned about evaluating financial information and advice:

1. _____

2. _____

3. _____

How might these skills impact your financial decision-making in the future?

_____

_____

1

How might you use what you've learned about evaluating financial advice in your own life?

Think about any financial decisions you or your family have made recently. How could the evaluation techniques you've learned have helped? What might you do differently next time you receive financial advice?

2

Why is it important to be cautious of financial advice that promises high returns with no risk?

Have you ever seen ads or social media posts promising easy money? How do these compare to what you've learned about realistic financial expectations? Why might someone make unrealistic promises about money?

3

How does understanding conflicts of interest change how you view financial advice?

Why might a financial advisor recommend one product over another? How could their pay (like commissions) affect their advice? How can knowing this help you make better decisions?

Social Media Investment Tip

Your favorite social media influencer, who usually posts about fashion and lifestyle, starts promoting a new investment app. They claim it's an easy way to make money quickly and that they've personally made thousands of dollars in just a few weeks. The influencer provides a special link where their followers can sign up and get a bonus.

Questions:
a) What potential red flags do you see in this scenario?
b) How would you go about evaluating the credibility of this financial advice?
c) What steps would you take before deciding whether to use the app or not?

_____
_____
_____
_____
_____
_____
_____
_____
_____
_____

Online Financial Course

You come across an online advertisement for a financial education course. The ad promises to teach you "secret" investing strategies that will make you rich. The course is expensive, but the ad claims that the knowledge you'll gain will be worth much more than the cost. They offer testimonials from people who say they've made a lot of money after taking the course.

Questions:
a) What elements of this advertisement might be concerning?
b) How would you go about verifying the claims made in the ad?
c) What alternatives might you consider for learning about investing?

_____
_____
_____
_____
_____
_____
_____
_____
_____
_____

TERM	DEFINITION
Financial Advisor	
Credentials	
Certified Financial Planner (CFP)	
Conflict of Interest	
Fee-only Advisor	

TERM	DEFINITION
Transparency	
Risk Tolerance	
Diversification	
Financial Literacy	
Red Flags	

Evaluating Financial Information and Advice

```
Z Y A Y S Y Q V O X Y D V T L G Z C N R X F D T
N I X Q O C L J N A G Q L Z J P E K W I V A M R
Q W T M M S T B J Q U L Z C K K E V E S I D S A
C F M W I A B J T Z W U N C E A C Q W K U I B N
E O V O W O H U X J W C J I P S N D F T K Y C S
Y X N D T Y C P L F P D W P L V T O E O N Y M P
F Z F F U B Q R V V Q V D P O R K P E L C U F A
I X I I L W R H E V J J R P O X K T O E Z O R R
N S N B J I A K V D E B D A Q B A X N R N M L E
A R A R M E C Y D P E Z E H V D F H L A D O R N
N O N S H G C T K B H N N N H H R M Y N M Z O C
C J C R N M F J O B Q V T I V O L L A C R C Z Y
I P I E E Z P Q J F H S U I F M A C D E U O I A
A M A D V D Q F R H I E P H A V O C V H B W O G
L F L D Z B F L S Q T N Z O I L D Q I H H H U R
A M L A V R M L O C R I T G L L S I S E U P O E
D I I S N N G Y A K M U W E A M Y G O X R Q K T
V Z T P Y R H D H G C J N Z R D I T R Q F X L T
I W E X O I N L X Y S C R J Q E B S I I T R V J
S S R S X J E Y Z W Z H L N B H S E N Z L Q F U
O B A C W K O L S M V D G A J I C T U M N P I L
R R C A E U X S Q D L V T P M O D U K H Q P E O
X B Y X D I V E R S I F I C A T I O N P J H E K
H A X K J U T C O E W T F Y S Q K X M N G X T V
```

Financial Literacy	Financial Advisor	Conflict of Interest
Fee-only Advisor	Risk Tolerance	Red Flags
Diversification	Transparency	CFP
Credentials		

Evaluating Financial Information and Advice

Across

3. A financial advisor who is compensated solely by fees paid by clients, rather than commissions on financial products sold, ___-_____

4. The quality of being open, clear, and honest in communication and business practices.

6. A situation where a person's personal interest might interfere with their professional responsibilities, _____ of Interest

7. Warning signs or indicators of potential problems or issues, particularly in financial advice or investments. (2 words)

9. The degree of variability in investment returns that an individual is willing to withstand, _____ Tolerance

10. The practice of spreading investments among different financial instruments to reduce risk.

Down

1. The ability to understand and effectively use various financial skills, including personal financial management and investing, Financial _____

2. Professional qualifications or achievements that demonstrate a person's expertise in a particular field.

5. A professional certification for financial advisors who have met specific education and experience requirements. (Abbrv.)

8. A professional who provides guidance and advice on managing finances and investments, Financial _____

Charting Your Financial Future:
The Power of a Comprehensive Financial Plan

Imagine standing at the edge of a vast, unexplored forest. Without a map or compass, the journey ahead seems daunting and uncertain. Now, picture yourself with a detailed map, marking clear paths and highlighting potential obstacles. Suddenly, the forest becomes an exciting adventure waiting to be experienced. This is the essence of a comprehensive financial plan – a powerful tool that transforms the complex landscape of personal finance into a navigable journey towards your financial goals.

Understanding Comprehensive Financial Planning

What is a Comprehensive Financial Plan?
A comprehensive financial plan is a detailed strategy that outlines your current financial situation, defines your financial goals, and charts a course to achieve those goals. It's like a roadmap for your financial life, encompassing various aspects such as budgeting, saving, investing, insurance, and retirement planning.

Key Components of a Financial Plan

1. Financial Goals: These are the destinations on your financial journey. They can be short-term (like saving for a vacation), medium-term (buying a house), or long-term (retiring comfortably).

2. Net Worth Statement: This is a snapshot of your current financial position, listing all your assets (what you own) and liabilities (what you owe).

3. Budget: A detailed plan of your income and expenses, helping you understand and control your cash flow.

4. Savings and Investment Strategy: This outlines how you'll grow your wealth over time, considering factors like risk tolerance and time horizons.

5. Risk Management: This includes insurance policies to protect you and your assets from unforeseen events.

6. Retirement Planning: A strategy to ensure you have enough funds to maintain your desired lifestyle after you stop working.

7. Estate Planning: This involves planning for the transfer of your assets after your death, including wills and trusts.

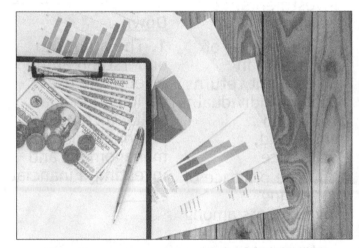

Creating a comprehensive financial plan involves assessing current financial status, setting goals, budgeting, investing wisely, and regularly reviewing progress to ensure long-term financial stability.

The Process of Creating a Financial Plan

Step 1: Assess Your Current Financial Situation

Start by gathering all your financial information. This includes bank statements, investment accounts, debts, and recurring expenses. Calculate your net worth and analyze your spending patterns.

Step 2: Define Your Financial Goals

What do you want to achieve financially? Whether it's buying a home, starting a business, or retiring early, clearly define your goals and prioritize them.

Step 3: Develop Strategies to Achieve Your Goals

Based on your current situation and goals, create specific strategies. This might involve increasing your savings rate, adjusting your investment portfolio, or finding ways to increase your income.

Step 4: Implement Your Plan

Put your strategies into action. This could mean setting up automatic savings transfers, opening new investment accounts, or purchasing insurance policies.

Step 5: Monitor and Adjust

Regularly review your plan and adjust as needed. Life changes, and your financial plan should evolve with it.

The Benefits of a Comprehensive Financial Plan

1. Clarity and Direction: A financial plan provides a clear picture of your finances and a roadmap to follow.

2. Improved Decision Making: With a plan in place, you can make informed decisions that align with your long-term goals.

3. Reduced Financial Stress: Understanding your financial situation and having a plan to improve it can significantly reduce anxiety about money.

4. Increased Savings: A good plan often leads to increased savings as you become more intentional about your finances.

5. Better Preparedness: A comprehensive plan helps you prepare for both expected life events and unexpected emergencies.

Real-World Application

Meet Sarah, a 28-year-old marketing professional. After creating her comprehensive financial plan, she realized she was spending too much on discretionary items and not saving enough for her goal of buying a house. By adjusting her budget and setting up automatic savings, she was able to save $20,000 for a down payment in just two years. Moreover, her plan helped her start contributing to her retirement account early, putting her on track for a comfortable retirement.

Creating a comprehensive financial plan is a powerful step towards taking control of your financial future. It provides clarity, direction, and peace of mind. Remember, financial planning is not a one-time event but an ongoing process. As you navigate through life's financial forest, your comprehensive financial plan will be your trusted guide, helping you make informed decisions and stay on track towards your goals.

Whether you're just starting your career or nearing retirement, it's never too early or too late to create a comprehensive financial plan. Take the first step today – your future self will thank you.

25. Creating a Comprehensive Financial Plan
GUIDED NOTES

I. Key Terms

1. Comprehensive Financial Plan: _____

2. Net Worth: _____

3. Budget: _____

4. Financial Goals: _____

II. Main Concept Overview

A comprehensive financial plan is a _____ that outlines your

_____ financial situation, defines your _____ goals,

and charts a course to _____ those goals.

III. Matching Section

Match each component of a financial plan with its description:

_____ Financial Goals   A. A detailed plan of income and expenses

_____ Net Worth Statement   B. Strategy to grow wealth over time

_____ Budget   C. Destinations on your financial journey

_____ Savings and Investment Strategy   D. Snapshot of current financial position

_____ Retirement Planning   E. Ensuring funds for life after work

IV. True or False

_____ A comprehensive financial plan is a one-time document that never needs to be
updated.

_____ The net worth statement lists all your assets and liabilities.

_____ Budgeting is not an important part of a comprehensive financial plan.

_____ Risk management includes insurance policies to protect you and your assets.

_____ A good financial plan often leads to increased savings.

V. Application Question

Sarah, a 28-year-old marketing professional, created a comprehensive financial plan. How did this plan help her achieve her financial goals? Provide at least two specific examples from the article.

_____

_____

_____

_____

_____

VI. Reflection/Summary

Summarize the main benefits of having a comprehensive financial plan in your own words. How might creating such a plan impact your own financial decisions?

_____

_____

_____

_____

_____

1

How might having a financial plan change the way you spend your money?

Think about your recent purchases. Would a financial plan have changed your decisions? How might it affect your spending on things like snacks, clothes, or entertainment?

2

Why do you think creating a financial plan could be important for your future?

Imagine your life 10 years from now. What financial goals might you have? How could planning now help you achieve those goals?

3

In what ways could a financial plan help reduce stress about money in your life?

Have you ever worried about money? How might having a plan make you feel more secure? Think about how it could help you prepare for unexpected expenses.

The Part-Time Job

Chris, a high school junior, just got his first part-time job at a local store. He'll be earning $200 per week and wants to save for a car.

Questions:
a) What parts of a financial plan would be most helpful for Chris right now?
b) How could Chris balance saving for a car with having money for other expenses?
c) What might Chris include in his budget based on this scenario?

_____
_____
_____
_____
_____
_____
_____
_____
_____
_____

The Summer Plan

Miguel has three options for the summer: take unpaid classes to get ahead in school, work full-time to save money, or do a mix of both with part-time work and some classes.

Questions:
a) How could a financial plan help Miguel evaluate these options?
b) What short-term and long-term effects should Miguel consider for each option?
c) Besides money, what other factors might Miguel include in his decision-making process?

_____
_____
_____
_____
_____
_____
_____
_____
_____

TERM	DEFINITION
Financial Plan	
Budget	
Net Worth	
Financial Goals	
Risk Management	

TERM	DEFINITION
Asset	
Liability	
Retirement Planning	
Estate Planning	
Investment Strategy	

Creating a Comprehensive Financial Plan

```
L C B R J N T I O G H X X K B J O H Z R A I F S
R O V U O X N Q L I A B I L I T Y S M C K N D R
R I O X D C X I A O A C K Y J K D H X W B D Y K
B E S B G G S D U L B O F H N G A C G P F B P S
W K J K Z Z E I E C O C A N V A A X R Z F R Z J
F A E K M G D T B Q Q X D R V P A D L Y X E O C
V F C C O A I Y Y L K Z S R X F T N X S D T Z X
D W Z Y Y X N F I N A N C I A L P L A N E I N H
Q Q S U M T V A N I J V T E S E F Q U Q Z R R C
B Z N F W P E A G D T K Z W W S I D E G B E J W
R X H X K B S S X E B Z S W B J N P S M F M J X
W Y G Z L E T S L T M X C N Z S A J T O Q E Y Y
M U Y U U O M E L Y R E U L Y B N B A N Y N I M
T A W A D S E T O V K J N K M C C Q T X M T K R
A V K F A V N Y X R L F H T M M I D E R L P N M
X I T K Z R T N S X M N U I C Y A G P L I L A N
H H T K O J S G I U N V Z U U S L X L Q B A Y E
H G C W P F T M D K Y E F U L C G S A M O N O T
K P N I M Q R C C E P F Q O K D O M N D L N C W
G L D H O T A Q I N V R Z R I S A C N Y B I G O
L K X Z R G T N E P S F I M C J L W I O K N C R
I Y G K J T E W X S Y T A G B Y S H N D T G V T
N E H R O J G L P B W R H E O V H S G T G O O H
V Y L Q X F Y S Z A H S P O N K K K J L K Y A Y
```

Financial Plan

Financial Goals

Risk Management

Retirement Planning

Estate Planning

Investment Strategy

Liability

Asset

Net Worth

Budget

Creating a Comprehensive Financial Plan

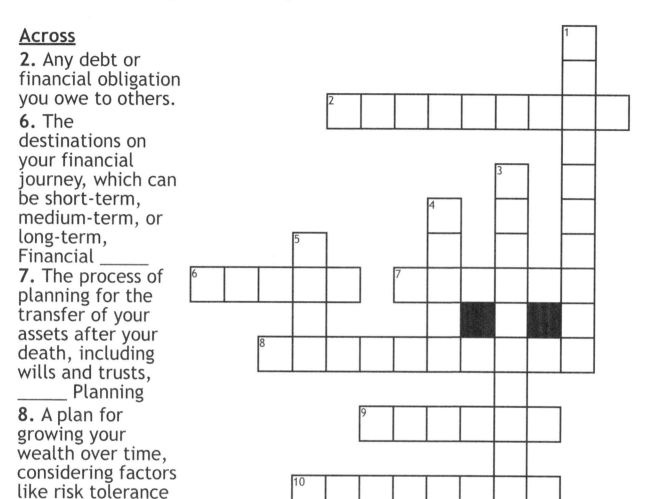

Across

2. Any debt or financial obligation you owe to others.

6. The destinations on your financial journey, which can be short-term, medium-term, or long-term, Financial _____

7. The process of planning for the transfer of your assets after your death, including wills and trusts, _____ Planning

8. A plan for growing your wealth over time, considering factors like risk tolerance and time horizons, _____ Strategy

9. A detailed plan of your income and expenses, helping you understand and control your cash flow.

10. A snapshot of your current financial position, listing all your assets (what you own) and liabilities (what you owe). (2 words)

Down

1. A strategy to ensure you have enough funds to maintain your desired lifestyle after you stop working, _____ Planning

3. The process of identifying potential financial risks and taking steps to minimize their impact, often through insurance, Risk _____

4. Anything of value that you own, such as cash, investments, or property.

5. A detailed strategy that outlines your current financial situation, defines your financial goals, and charts a course to achieve those goals, Financial _____

Your greatest superpower is your ability to choose one thought over another.

Choose positive thoughts over negative to live your very best life.

Our Lessons On:
TeachersPayTeachers (TPT)
https://www.teacherspayteachers.com/store/3andb

Our Workbooks On:
Amazon
https://amzn.to/3ygpsvk

Answer Keys

I. Key Terms

1. Personal Finance: The art and science of managing your money to achieve your goals and dreams
2. Budgeting: Creating a spending roadmap
3. Investing: Making your money work for you

II. Main Concept Overview

Personal finance is the art and science of managing your money to achieve your goals and dreams. It involves making smart decisions with your money that align with your values and goals.

III. Components of Personal Finance

C Budgeting   A. Protecting you from unexpected financial setbacks
D Saving   B. Making your money work for you
B Investing   C. Creating a spending roadmap
E Debt   D. Putting money aside for future you
A Insurance   E. Keeping loans under control

IV. Importance of Personal Finance

1. Empowers you to make informed decisions about:
   a) Education
   b) Career
   c) Lifestyle
2. Helps you avoid financial stress by: giving you tools to manage your money effectively
3. Allows you to start: saving and investing early

V. True or False

F   Personal finance is only about numbers and spreadsheets.
T   Understanding personal finance can help you choose a college or career path.
F   Personal finance is mainly about restricting your life and saying "no" to everything.
T   The financial habits you develop today will shape your future in significant ways.
F   It's best to wait until after high school before learning about personal finance.

VI. Real-World Application

Fill in the table below based on the example of Alex buying a car:

Personal Finance Action	Description
Set a realistic budget	Based on their part-time job income
Researched costs	Researched total cost of car ownership
Shopped around	For the best auto loan rates
Made a wise choice	Decided to buy a reliable used car
Set up savings plan	For future car expenses

VII. Reflection/Summary

1. Answers will vary, but should reflect understanding of how personal finance skills can help make informed decisions about education, career, and lifestyle, as well as avoid financial stress in the future.

2. Two small steps mentioned in the article to start your personal finance journey:
a) Begin by tracking your spending for a month
b) Set a small savings goal

Part 1: Example Lecture

Introduction
- Define personal finance: managing one's money to achieve goals and dreams
- Explain its importance in everyday life and future decision-making

Key Components of Personal Finance
- Budgeting: Creating a spending plan
- Saving: Setting money aside for future use
- Investing: Making money grow over time
- Managing debt: Controlling borrowing and repayment
- Insurance: Protecting against financial risks

Real-World Applications
- Discuss how personal finance applies to:
  - Choosing a college or career path
  - Buying a car or other major purchases
  - Planning for future financial security

Impact and Implications
- Explain how personal finance knowledge can:
  - Reduce financial stress
  - Improve decision-making
  - Increase financial security and freedom

Conclusion
- Reinforce the importance of starting personal finance journey early
- Encourage students to apply concepts to their own lives

Interesting Insights

1. The concept of compound interest is so powerful that Albert Einstein allegedly called it the "eighth wonder of the world."
2. April is designated as Financial Literacy Month in the United States, highlighting the importance of personal finance education.

Part 2: Class Schedule

1. Introduction to Personal Finance
   - Brief lecture using the outline from Part 1

2. Article Reading
   - Students read the "What is Personal Finance?" article

3. Guided Notes Completion
   - Students fill out guided notes while discussing key points
   - Facilitate class discussion on responses

4. Reflection Questions
   - Students answer 2-3 selected reflection questions
   - Facilitate brief class discussion on responses

5. Hypothetical Scenarios
   - Present 2 "what-if" scenarios
   - Group discussion on potential outcomes

6. Vocabulary Review
   - Review key vocabulary words as a class

Part 3: Discussion Prompts and Further Exploration

Class Discussion Prompts:
1. How do you currently make decisions about money?
2. What financial goals do you have for the next year? Five years?
3. How do you think personal finance knowledge could change your daily life?

Further Exploration:
1. The Psychology of Money: Explore how emotions and behavior affect financial decisions.
2. Technology and Personal Finance: Discuss how apps and online tools can help with budgeting and financial planning.
3. Cultural Influences on Personal Finance: Examine how different cultures approach money management and financial decisions.

Additional Notes

- Encourage students to share their own experiences and thoughts throughout the lesson
- Use the hypothetical scenarios as opportunities for group work or role-playing exercises
- Consider inviting a local financial professional as a guest speaker for a future class
- Assess student understanding through their participation in discussions and completion of guided notes

Remember, the goal is to introduce students to the basics of personal finance and spark their interest in the subject. Emphasize the relevance of these concepts to their current and future lives.

What is Personal Finance?

```
S Z A H A E V C A N I C B S U G F T E B B F I Y
J O W R Z Q N J V Y C W M U K G G U P J R I V X
P S A V I N G Z W N M C A G T M K Z W V N N S N
B G N G E P H M Z L V T E J V A B G L I M A K A
J P Z Z U L C I B P E M Y C V M G N R P K N Q G
J N E C O Q N F L E N K K V W H F L Y D C V P
E S D R H Y F C R S V U F F N I W M J H E I G F
Y O P V S H J C S M U Z M Y T X T J R U B A W H
L C K A M O H S K I X R R Q H Q S E Z X T L Y S
W O V L N U N D E Y Z W A P J G S D U X F L Q B
G M M L W E C A F Z H C W N B V S N D V L I P V
E P V L O S R H L G P Q E B C F Z D K C C T W R
M O L V E J E U T F F G Y A A E U U V R E B U
S U S D G T D F Q H I H U O B V X B F W X R E S
B N C R O R I N L F W N H G I O D U O C R A I C
E D R X A U T E O J M I A C G O B D T P R C N F
O I M K L N I N V E S T I N G G Z G S O W Y Q U
J N U J S V H K K E P X U I C W F E G X B U L X
N T O I N Q B X P B Q C K S C E A T X H Q W X Y
B E N Y S F A K J T H T Q T J U S Z H U D X M A
P R F I R H L F Q N N G X M C U E Q B G G C J A
S E N S E D G S I C F H W H P P G Q L E D Q X C
W S C W L G K Z V K W Z G W R Y J W R F H U G I
W T R X F I N A N C I A L G O A L S Y B Z N O W
```

Financial Goals	Financial Literacy	Compound Interest
Credit	Insurance	Debt
Investing	Saving	Budget
Personal Finance		

What is Personal Finance?

Across

5. A form of risk management primarily used to protect against the risk of potential financial loss.

6. Interest calculated on the initial principal and the accumulated interest from previous periods, _____ Interest

7. The ability to understand and effectively use various financial skills, including personal financial management and budgeting, Financial _____

8. A plan for managing income and expenses over a specific period.

9. The act of setting aside money for future use rather than spending it immediately.

10. Money owed or due to another party.

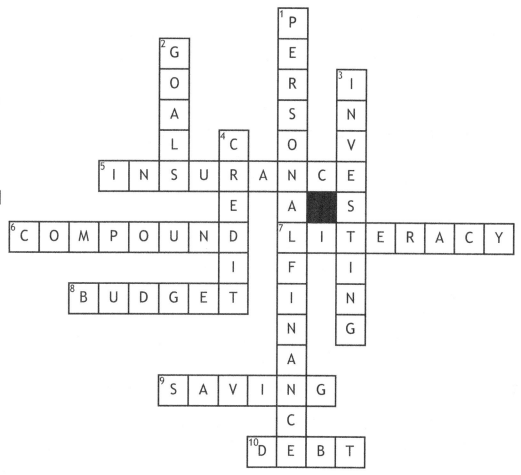

Down

1. The practice of managing one's money, including earning, spending, saving, investing, and protecting financial resources. (2 words)

2. Specific, measurable objectives related to money management and future financial well-being, Financial _____

3. Putting money into financial schemes, shares, property, or other ventures with the expectation of achieving profit.

4. The ability to borrow money or access goods or services with the understanding that payment will be made in the future.

I. Key Terms

1. Personal Values: The fundamental beliefs and principles that shape your identity and guide your actions
2. Spending Priorities: What you consider worth spending money on
3. Risk Tolerance: Your attitude towards financial risk

II. Main Concept Overview

Personal values are like an internal compass that guides our actions and decisions, including how we handle money. They influence our spending priorities, saving habits, financial goals, and attitude towards financial risk.

III. Matching Section

C. Family: Prioritizing relationships and family well-being
D. Freedom: Valuing independence and personal autonomy
B. Security: Emphasizing stability and safety
A. Adventure: Seeking new experiences and excitement
E. Achievement: Striving for success and personal growth

IV. The Value-Money Connection

Aspect of Finance	How Values Influence It
Spending Priorities	Values determine what you consider worth spending money on
Saving Habits	Values like security might lead to prioritizing saving and investing, while values like spontaneity might make you more likely to spend in the moment
Financial Goals	Long-term financial objectives are often a direct reflection of your values
Risk Tolerance	If you value security, you might prefer low-risk investments, while someone who values growth might be more comfortable with higher-risk options
Career Choices	The career path you choose is often aligned with your values, which in turn affects your earning potential and financial decisions

V. True or False

False: Personal values remain constant throughout a person's life. (The "Did You Know?" section mentions that values can change over time)

True: Values like security might lead to prioritizing saving and investing.

True: People who align their spending with their values report higher levels of financial satisfaction.

False: It's impossible to balance multiple values when making financial decisions. (The article mentions it's possible and often necessary to balance multiple values)

True: Your attitude towards financial risk is influenced by your personal values.

VI. Real-World Application

1. Alex prioritizes adventure. This affects her spending by leading her to spend money on concert tickets, trying new restaurants, or saving for a summer road trip.

2. Jordan prioritizes security and future success. This affects his financial behavior by leading him to save most of his earnings from his weekend job, investing in a savings account for college, and being careful with his spending.

3. According to the article, neither approach is inherently right or wrong – they simply reflect different values. The article states that understanding these differences can help both friends make more intentional decisions and find a balance that works for them.

VII. Reflection/Summary

(Answers will vary, but should reflect understanding of the connection between personal values and financial decisions)

Steps for aligning your money with your values:
1. Identify Your Values
2. Examine Your Spending
3. Set Value-Based Goals
4. Make Mindful Decisions
5. Seek Balance

Chapter 1: Lecture, Schedule, Discussion & Exploration

Part 1: Example Lecture

I. Introduction
- Define personal values as fundamental beliefs guiding actions and decisions
- Explain the connection between personal values and financial choices

II. Key Components of Personal Values and Financial Decisions
A. Types of Personal Values
- Family, Freedom, Security, Adventure, Achievement
- How these values manifest in financial behaviors

B. The Value-Money Connection
- Spending priorities
- Saving habits
- Financial goals
- Risk tolerance
- Career choices

C. Real-World Example: Alex and Jordan
- Contrasting financial behaviors based on different values

III. Aligning Money with Values
- Identifying personal values
- Examining spending habits
- Setting value-based goals
- Making mindful decisions
- Seeking balance between multiple values

IV. Impact and Implications
- How understanding values leads to better financial decisions
- Long-term effects on financial satisfaction and well-being

V. Conclusion
- Recap the importance of aligning financial decisions with personal values
- Encourage ongoing reflection on values and financial choices

Interesting Insights

- Studies show higher financial satisfaction when spending aligns with values
- Values can change over time, necessitating periodic reassessment of financial goals

Part 2: Class Schedule

1. Introduction to Personal Values and Finance
   - Brief lecture using the outline from Part 1
2. Article Reading
   - Students read the article on personal values and financial decisions
3. Guided Notes Completion
   - Students fill out guided notes while discussing key points
   - Facilitate class discussion on responses
4. Reflection Questions
   - Students answer reflection questions
   - Facilitate class discussion on responses
5. Hypothetical Scenarios
   - Present "what-if" scenarios
   - Group discussion on potential outcomes
6. Vocabulary Reinforcement
   - Students complete crossword puzzle
   - Review answers as a class

Part 3: Discussion Prompts and Further Exploration

1. Class Discussion Prompts:
   - How do you think your current financial habits reflect your personal values?
   - Can you think of a time when your financial decision conflicted with your values? What happened?
   - How might understanding your values help you make better financial decisions in the future?
2. Further Exploration:
   - Cultural influences on financial values: Explore how different cultures prioritize various financial values and how this impacts economic behaviors.
   - Changing values over time: Investigate how personal values might shift from adolescence to adulthood and the implications for financial planning.
   - Values in marketing: Analyze how advertisers appeal to personal values to influence consumer spending habits.

Additional Notes

- Encourage students to share personal experiences throughout the lesson, fostering engagement and relevance.
- Use the hypothetical scenarios as group activities, allowing students to discuss and debate different approaches.
- Consider assigning a personal reflection journal entry as homework, where students examine their own values and financial habits.
- Adapt the schedule as needed for different class lengths. For shorter classes, prioritize the article reading, guided notes, and one or two reflection questions.
- Assess understanding through class participation, completion of guided notes, and thoughtful responses to reflection questions and scenarios.

Remember, the goal is to help students recognize the connection between their personal values and financial decisions, encouraging more mindful and satisfying financial choices in the future.

Personal Values and Their Impact on Financial Decisions

```
F L X G Y T S P E N D I N G P R I O R I T I E S
I I S E U M J Y H T P E R S O N A L V A L U E S
R G N T V M O S M J A W S G E L E Q D P L J H U
Z L O A R A M K R I U D P F X C S M D E H I S W
J Z Y V N Q L H C Y N R L F T A E S V N P F Q F
N M P S C C X U U W A D H A O E U N A S I O L I
P L C G E M I R E V K M F H U P K E W I Q S U N
C J M P E B S A Y B P G D U U X O I U A U F T A
O T D Y S V D A L V A A A X L M I F V O M T E N
Q G B Y P V R K V S V S A X X S R Q F L Z M Z C
R G Y H F K I Y A I A P E Q R J P O W T V J H I
M F W R I E S M R O N T O D Y C I E S T D B O A
R N E V N I K I P G C G I D B Q D A N J L C V L
L C I Z A R T W P U D V H S S U L I N D R T P D
M W H A N U O S D R L Z V A F N D R M N I Y N E
Z A D Q C S L K V E Z S D J B A J G D M V N K C
D M J O I R E L F X V N E Y Z I C V E R W E G I
L B U V A F R J I K U G J B Z Y T T K T P V K S
L K U X L Y A M D H M M B I U Z E S I V I C U I
R S Z E G I N Q K I P W F G F Y C L I O Z N D O
P F G U O J C U I W E U N P F I O B N N C G N
A T U P A V E J E M X B P V U S U N W R Q N L S
R D C X L X G B S O O V B Q N K H L G Z T S G Z
Y V F A S O T S M U S K J U W X F D Y B H G N A
```

Value-Based Budgeting   Financial Satisfaction   Mindful Spending

Impulse Buying   Risk Tolerance   Financial Goals

Saving Habits   Spending Priorities   Financial Decisions

Personal Values

Personal Values and Their Impact on Financial Decisions

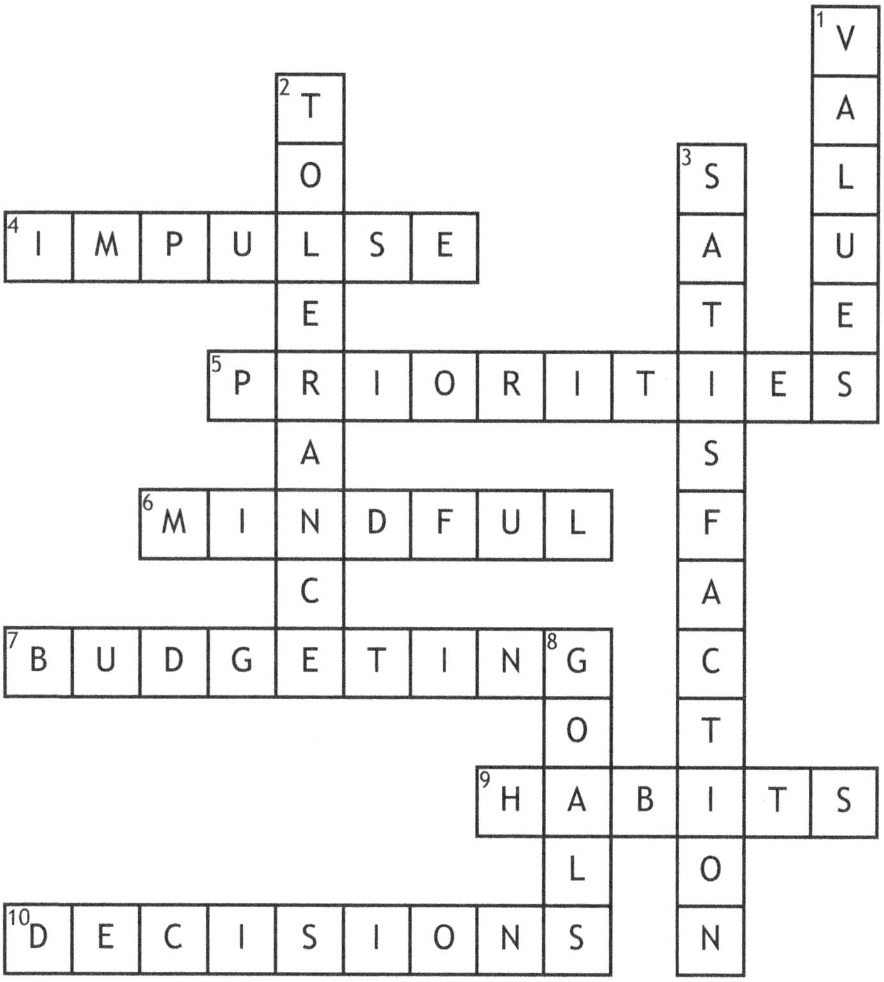

1 V A L U E S
2 T O L E R A N C E
3 S A T I S F A C T I O N
4 I M P U L S E
5 P R I O R I T I E S
6 M I N D F U L
7 B U D G E T I N G
8 G O A L S
9 H A B I T S
10 D E C I S I O N S

Across

4. Making unplanned purchases based on sudden desires rather than thoughtful consideration, _____ Buying

5. The items or experiences on which an individual chooses to spend their money, based on personal preferences and values, Spending _____

6. The practice of making conscious, deliberate decisions about purchases that align with personal values and financial goals, _____ Spending

7. A method of creating a spending plan that prioritizes allocating money to areas that align with personal values and goals, Value-Based _____

9. Regular patterns of setting aside money for future use or goals, Savings _____

10. Choices made regarding money management, including earning, spending, saving, and investing, Financial _____

Down

1. These core beliefs act as your internal compass for decision-making, Personal _____

2. The degree of variability in investment returns that an individual is willing to withstand, often influenced by personal values, Risk _____

3. A sense of contentment and fulfillment derived from one's financial situation and decisions, Financial _____

8. Specific objectives related to money management, often reflecting personal values and life aspirations, Financial _____

I. Key Terms

1. SMART Goals: An acronym for Specific, Measurable, Achievable, Relevant, and Time-bound goals
2. Financial landscape: The realm of financial opportunities and challenges
3. Financial literacy: Understanding of budgeting, saving, and managing money

II. Main Concept Overview

SMART is an acronym that stands for:

S: Specific
M: Measurable
A: Achievable
R: Relevant
T: Time-bound

These components help create clear and attainable financial goals.

III. Matching Section

C. Specific   A. You can track your progress
A. Measurable   B. Aligns with your values and long-term objectives
E. Achievable   C. Clear and well-defined
B. Relevant   D. Has a deadline
D. Time-bound   E. Realistic given your current situation

IV. True or False

T - SMART financial goals are like having a GPS for your money.
T - Setting a deadline for your goal creates a sense of urgency.
F - It's better to set vague goals to allow for flexibility.
T - SMART goals can help with decision-making about purchases.
F - You should only set ambitious, large-scale financial goals.

V. Fill in the Table

Goal Description	Total Amount	Time Frame	Monthly Savings
College textbooks	$600	6 months	$100

VI. Application Question

(Answers may vary, but should follow the SMART framework. Example:)

Specific: Save $500 for a new smartphone
Measurable: Track savings in a dedicated account
Achievable: Save a realistic amount each month based on income and expenses
Relevant: Explain why the smartphone is important (e.g., for school or work)
Time-bound: Set a deadline, e.g., "in 5 months"

VII. Reflection/Summary

Three reasons why SMART financial goals matter (any three from the article):
1. They give you direction, helping you focus your efforts and resources.
2. They provide motivation and help resist impulsive spending.
3. They aid in decision-making about purchases.
4. They help improve financial literacy.
5. They provide a sense of achievement upon completion.

How to apply the process of setting SMART financial goals (based on the article's suggestions):
Identify a financial goal, use the SMART criteria to refine it, write it down and make it visible, create a simple action plan with specific steps, and track progress regularly, adjusting as needed. Start with small goals and work up to more ambitious ones as you build the habit of setting and achieving SMART financial goals.

Part 1: Example Lecture

Introduction
- Define SMART financial goals: Specific, Measurable, Achievable, Relevant, Time-bound goals for managing money
- Explain importance: Provides direction, motivation, and a framework for financial decision-making

Key Components of SMART Financial Goals
1. Specific
   - Clear, well-defined objectives
   - Example: "Save $500 for a new smartphone" vs. "Save money"

2. Measurable
   - Quantifiable progress
   - Example: Track savings growth towards $500 goal

3. Achievable
   - Realistic given current circumstances
   - Example: Saving $500 over several months vs. $10,000 in a month

4. Relevant
   - Aligns with values and long-term objectives
   - Example: Saving for college textbooks aligns with educational goals

5. Time-bound
   - Set deadline creates urgency and focus
   - Example: "Save $500 for a new smartphone in 5 months"

Real-World Applications
- Provide Sarah's example from the article: Saving $600 for college textbooks in 6 months
- Walk through how each SMART component applies to this goal

Impact and Implications
- Discuss how SMART goals improve financial decision-making
- Explain how achieving SMART goals builds confidence and financial literacy

Conclusion
- Summarize the SMART framework
- Encourage students to start with small, achievable goals

Interesting Insights

1. SMART goals act like a GPS for your money, providing direction and helping you navigate financial decisions.
2. Achieving small SMART goals can create a positive feedback loop, motivating you to set and achieve larger financial goals in the future.

Part 2: Class Schedule

1. Introduction to SMART Financial Goals
   - Brief lecture using the outline from Part 1
   - Encourage questions and discussion throughout

2. Article Reading
   - Students read the article on Setting SMART Financial Goals
   - Suggest students highlight or underline key points as they read

3. Guided Notes Completion
   - Students fill out guided notes while discussing key points
   - Facilitate class discussion on each section of the notes

4. Reflection Questions
   - Students answer reflection questions individually
   - Pair students to share and discuss their responses

5. Hypothetical Scenarios
   - Present "what-if" scenarios to small groups
   - Groups discuss and share their solutions with the class

6. Vocabulary Review
   - Quick review of key vocabulary words
   - Clarify any terms students find confusing

Part 3: Discussion Prompts and Further Exploration

Class Discussion Prompts:
1. How might setting SMART financial goals now impact your future financial decisions?
2. What challenges do you foresee in setting and achieving SMART financial goals?
3. How could you use the SMART framework for non-financial goals in your life?

Further Exploration:
1. Budgeting Techniques: Explore different budgeting methods that can support SMART financial goals. This connects to SMART goals by providing tools to track progress and make goals achievable.

2. Long-term Financial Planning: Investigate how SMART goals can be applied to long-term financial objectives like saving for college or retirement. This extends the concept of SMART goals to larger, more complex financial decisions.

Additional Notes

- Encourage active participation throughout the lesson
- Use real-life examples relevant to high school students to maintain engagement
- Adapt the schedule as needed based on class size and student engagement levels
- Consider using a mix of individual, pair, and group activities to cater to different learning styles
- Assess understanding through observation of discussions and completion of guided notes

Setting SMART Financial Goals

```
H N L K O I N L V B Y C T I H C B M A R W Z N M
F G C I M P U L S E S P E N D I N G E P A S N R
I Z G H T Q N F I N A N C I A L P L A N N I N G
N Q G G Z E A R I P I H I X G U Q Y N B C A W X
A K E W M J W B Z N G W R P O Y V X P E L Z J W
N S I L F B U B K P A I J A N Y W H F I F Y J A
C Z M Q M J A H R X H N X G Y Q E U D P I P Q B
I P O A E X D D D P P W C I C T E I L I N C H U
A P F X R V X L H N A S E I U M Z E N Y A R A D
L Y Y F W T I I S Q K G A M A C U Y L V N C G G
D Z I X F X G E D R Z Y O W G L E I W U C M H E
E J G S Z Y Z O O S I Z R L V Z L S C T I E K T
C G C H B Y E A A Z K R P J I Q R I S F A O U Z
I B G O H V R A S L N Z Z N O M E I T G L U W H
S Z R R U K C U J I S Y H P X U O C E E P K Z V
I Y N T F E E P G J W Q U V N O K I U U R I Q S
O R S T H D J B J N B D G D W S C R L A I A O N
N C A T W E K O V V U W L O O C U F K P O K C C
M V V R D W E S O E H Z T P W L E J U T R B B Y
A F I M N Y W O T C X G K T Q R N E D A I M Q E
K V N G T Y K J V R C M D N T L A F D Y T C X E
I K G O O L O N G T E R M G O A L E X Z I K N I
N E S A V U B N I M I W A C K J P O J Z E M U M
G L B L S R V O Q H E H J B W E Z A M D S W J L
```

SMART Goals

Short-term Goal

Impulse Spending

Budget

Financial Literacy

Long-term Goal

Financial Priorities

Financial Decision-making

Financial Planning

Savings

Setting SMART Financial Goals

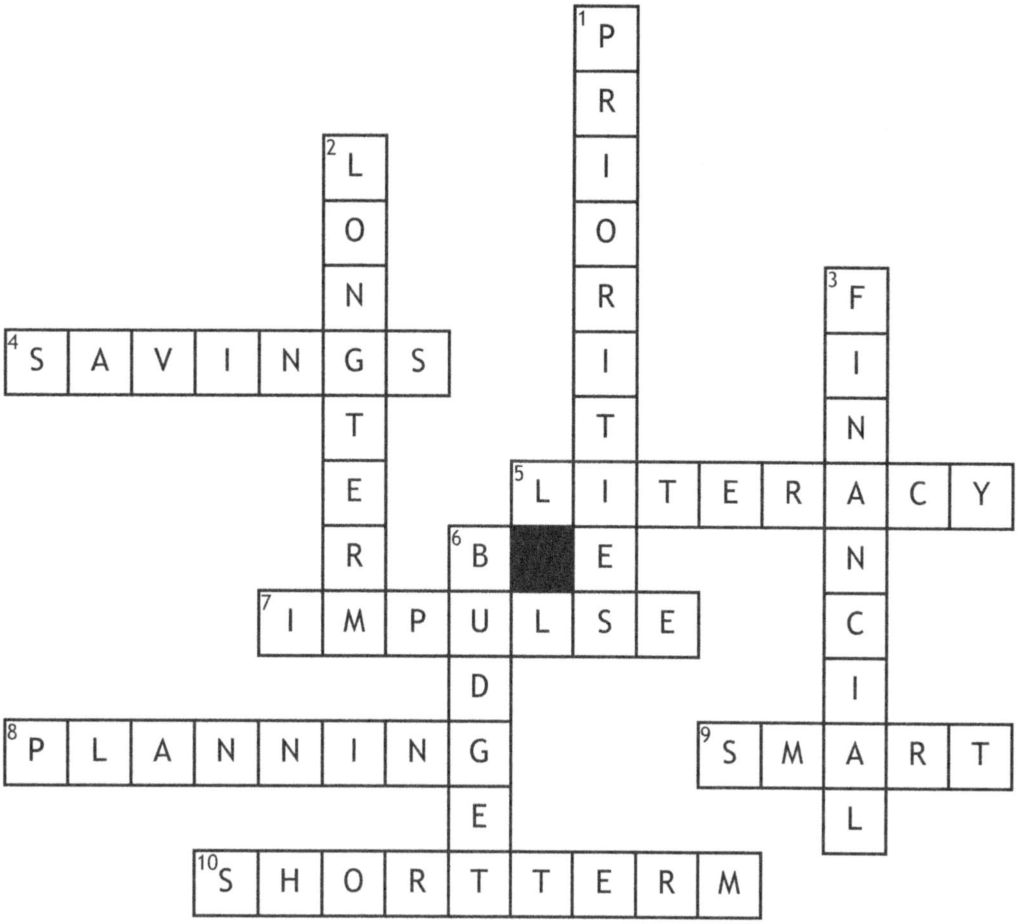
1 PRIORITIES
2 LONGTERM
3 FINANCIAL
4 SAVINGS
5 LITERACY
6 BUDGET
7 IMPULSE
8 PLANNING
9 SMART
10 SHORTTERM

Across

4. Money set aside for future use rather than spent immediately.

5. The ability to understand and effectively use various financial skills, including personal financial management, budgeting, and investing, Financial _____

7. Unplanned or unnecessary purchases made without careful consideration of financial consequences, _____ Spending

8. The process of managing your money to achieve personal economic satisfaction and meet life goals, Financial _____

9. An acronym for Specific, Measurable, Achievable, Relevant, and Time-bound goals used to guide goal setting, _____ Goals

10. A financial objective that can be achieved in a relatively short period, typically less than a year, ____-____ Goal

Down

1. The order of importance assigned to various financial goals or expenses based on personal values and circumstances, Financial _____

2. A financial objective that requires more time to achieve, often several years or more. ____-____ Goal

3. The process of making choices about how to manage money and financial resources, _____ Decision-Making

6. A financial plan for a defined period, typically a month or a year, that outlines estimated income and expenses.

I. Key Terms

1. Personal Budget: A plan for managing your money over a specific period, usually a month.
2. Income: All the money you receive, including allowances, part-time job earnings, or gifts.
3. Expenses: Your costs, divided into fixed (like a phone plan) and variable (like entertainment) categories.
4. Savings: The money you set aside for future goals or emergencies.

II. Main Concept Overview

A personal budget is a plan for managing your money over a specific period, usually a month. It helps you track your income, plan your expenses, and make informed decisions about your spending and saving habits.

III. Matching Section

D Fixed Expenses   A. Money set aside for future goals or emergencies
C Variable Expenses   B. All money received, including allowances, part-time job earnings, or gifts

B Income   C. Costs that change, like entertainment
A Savings   D. Regular costs that stay the same, like a phone plan

IV. True/False Questions

T 1. A personal budget is about making conscious choices that align with your values and goals.
T 2. The 50/30/20 rule suggests allocating 50% of your income to needs.
T 3. Tracking your expenses for a month is an important step in creating a budget.
T 4. A budget is a living document that needs to be adjusted as your income, expenses, and goals change.
T 5. Using cash envelopes can help limit overspending in certain categories.

V. Fill in the Table

Complete the table below with the steps for creating a personal budget:

Step	Description
1	Track Your Income and Expenses
2	Categorize Your Expenses
3	Set Financial Goals
4	Create Your Budget Plan
5	Implement and Adjust

VI. Application Question

The "Coffee Shop Conundrum" refers to a scenario where someone spends $4 on a latte every day, totaling $120 a month. Using a budget reveals that this habit is impacting savings goals. The budget helps make an informed decision by presenting options:
1. Cut out lattes entirely (saving $120)
2. Reduce to twice a week (saving $80)
3. Learn to make lattes at home (potentially saving $100)
The budget allows for an informed decision that aligns with financial goals without completely giving up something enjoyable.

VII. Reflection/Summary

(Answers will vary, but should touch on these main points:)
- A personal budget is a tool for managing money, tracking income and expenses.
- It helps in setting and achieving financial goals.
- Creating a budget involves tracking income/expenses, categorizing expenses, setting goals, creating a plan, and implementing/adjusting.
- Budgets help in making informed financial decisions.
- Budgeting develops skills like discipline, planning, and delayed gratification.
- Personal benefits might include better control of money, reduced financial stress, ability to save for specific goals, etc.

Example Lecture

1. Introduction to Personal Budgeting
   - Define personal budget
   - Explain its importance in financial decision-making

2. Key Components of a Budget
   - Income: Money received (allowance, part-time job, gifts)
   - Expenses: Fixed (phone plan) and variable (entertainment) costs
   - Savings: Money set aside for future goals or emergencies
   - Debt Payments: If applicable (e.g., credit card bills)

3. Steps to Create a Personal Budget
   - Track income and expenses
   - Categorize expenses
   - Set financial goals
   - Create a budget plan (introduce 50/30/20 rule)
   - Implement and adjust as needed

4. Using Your Budget Effectively
   - Review regularly
   - Use tools like cash envelopes or budgeting apps
   - Find ways to increase income or cut unnecessary expenses

5. Real-World Application
   - Discuss "Coffee Shop Conundrum" example
   - Emphasize making informed financial decisions

6. Conclusion
   - Recap key points
   - Emphasize long-term benefits of budgeting

Interesting Insights

- Budgeting skills can lead to better financial health in adulthood
- Many successful people, including billionaires, still budget their money

Class Schedule

1. Introduction to Personal Budgeting
   - Brief lecture using the outline above
   - Engage students with questions about their current money management practices

2. Article Reading
   - Students read the article on personal budgeting
   - Encourage highlighting or note-taking

3. Guided Notes Completion
   - Students fill out guided notes
   - Discuss key points as a class

4. Reflection Questions
   - Students answer 2-3 reflection questions
   - Facilitate brief class discussion on responses

5. Hypothetical Scenarios
   - Present 1-2 "what-if" scenarios
   - Small group discussions on potential solutions
   - Share group insights with the class

6. Vocabulary Reinforcement
   - Quick review of key terms
   - Consider using a matching game or flashcards

Discussion Prompts

1. How do you currently manage your money? Do you think a budget could help you?
2. What financial goals do you have? How might a budget help you achieve them?
3. What challenges do you think you might face in creating and sticking to a budget?

Further Exploration

1. Budgeting Tools and Apps: Explore various budgeting apps and their features
2. Cultural Perspectives on Money Management: Discuss how different cultures approach saving and spending
3. Psychology of Spending: Investigate how emotions and marketing influence our spending decisions

Additional Notes

- Encourage students to start tracking their expenses for a week as a take-home activity
- Consider inviting a guest speaker (e.g., local bank representative) to discuss real-world budgeting
- Use all activities as opportunities for class discussion to keep students engaged
- Be sensitive to varying financial situations among students; focus on principles rather than specific amounts

Creating and Using a Personal Budget

```
S M Z B U B J L U R O R K V Z B I M K I U H R F
T S G J M U A P B Y Q H B O G G M X G B D E B T
H Z P D H Y U F I M K T E D S Z F R X V S G S Q
S D Q M I B V A M Y P N Z N W S K S L B Z Y V J
G X O C O S O Z J S B W K U D U J E E R K B A S
B Z L D A Q C D S B G C H Y A O Y R N Y E G R E
J V F A M S P R I J Z F C L R T H B J Q K S I W
R B K P P F H D E G G Y I I Z D Q V P Z F V A M
D J B S K I C F I T U U F X L Z C F M V N H B S
X N S U C N M U L S I Q B K E G H C G E R M L F
T P A R N A J E D O C O G Z V D R D T M Z R E R
Y S A V I N G S M M W R N K C C E X S E B O E Q
A A O O R C G C T E Q Y E A U X Z X O Z I H X M
M C Q R P I J B T O J A P T R D O A P P G C P O
M D H Y U A L I J C P I T C I Y P Z X E Z G E M
G D F D W L P P H G F A N T W O I P G S N D N T
E B L Q B G D T A I O J U C I J N N W Y J S S V
P A C J P O X Z I S V L U D O G R A C E F A E Y
C V G H F A T E D D J U K B B M T V R O I K S S
V P M X K L C T M U Q I U N E C E U Q Y M R F F
Q A R V H S G H B T E B S M Y H V F Y F V E B Z
A E X P E N S E S R N V L J B U D G E T Z C H D
H P Q J O N C W W I L R R Y X B B O L C W V O X
E S P R H M L W B R G P J S L H A Q Z B H L L C
```

Discretionary Income	Financial Goals	Variable Expenses
Fixed Expenses	Debt	Cash Flow
Savings	Expenses	Income
Budget		

Creating and Using a Personal Budget

Across

5. Money set aside for future use or for unexpected costs.

6. Money received, especially on a regular basis, for work or through investments.

8. A plan for managing money during a given period of time.

9. Regular expenses that generally remain the same each month, such as rent or a phone plan, _____ Expenses

10. Expenses that change from month to month, such as entertainment or groceries, _____ Expenses

Down

1. Specific, measurable objectives related to money management, _____ Goals

2. The movement of money into and out of a budget. (2 words)

3. Money left over after paying for necessities, available for spending or saving as desired, _____ Income

4. The amount of money that is spent on goods and services.

7. Money owed to another person or institution.

I. Key Terms

1. Income: Money that comes into your possession
2. Expenses: Ways you spend your money
3. Financial tracking: The process of recording all income and expenses

II. Main Concept Overview

Financial tracking is the process of recording all the money that comes into your possession and all the ways you spend it.

III. Importance of Tracking (Fill in the blanks)

1. Awareness: Makes all expenses visible
2. Goal Setting: Helps set realistic financial goals and timelines
3. Budgeting: First step in creating a financial plan
4. Financial Responsibility: Builds important lifelong habits
5. Identifying Patterns: Helps spot areas of overspending

IV. Methods of Tracking (Match each method with its description)

B Pen and Paper   A. Offers features like category sorting and visual reports
C Spreadsheets   B. Simple and straightforward method using a notebook
A Mobile Apps   C. Programs like Excel or Google Sheets for detailed analysis

V. Steps to Effective Tracking (True/False)

F   You only need to record large expenses when tracking.
T   Categorizing expenses helps you see where most of your money is going.
F   It's enough to review your tracker once a month.
T   Consistency is key to successful financial tracking.
F   You should start by tracking all categories of expenses at once.

VI. Real-World Application (Fill in the table)

Monthly Fast Food Spending	Annual Cost	Potential Savings
$100	$1,200	Hundreds of dollars could be saved by packing lunch more often

VII. Overcoming Challenges (Match the challenge with its solution)

C Forgetting to Record

A Losing Receipts

D Feeling Overwhelmed

B Lack of Motivation

A. Take pictures of receipts or request digital ones

B. Set small, achievable financial goals

C. Keep tracking tool easily accessible, set reminders

D. Start with one category, then gradually add more

VIII. Reflection/Summary

(Answers will vary, but should reflect understanding of the article's content)

1. How might tracking your income and expenses benefit you in the future?
Possible answer: Tracking income and expenses can help me manage larger financial responsibilities in the future, such as student loans, rent, or mortgage payments. It can also help me make informed decisions about my career path and income needs.

2. What method of tracking do you think would work best for you, and why?
Possible answer: A mobile app might work best for me because I always have my phone with me, making it easy to record expenses immediately. The features like category sorting and visual reports would help me understand my spending patterns better.

Part 1: Example Lecture

Introduction
- Define financial tracking as the process of recording all income and expenses
- Explain its importance in personal finance management

Key Components of Financial Tracking
1. Income Tracking
    - Identify various sources of income (jobs, allowances, gifts)
    - Emphasize the importance of recording all income, no matter how small

2. Expense Tracking
    - Categorize expenses (food, entertainment, transportation, etc.)
    - Stress the need to record all expenses, including small purchases

3. Regular Review and Analysis
    - Set aside time weekly to review financial records
    - Look for patterns in spending and income

Real-World Applications
- Saving for large purchases (e.g., car, college tuition)
- Identifying areas of overspending
- Making informed financial decisions

Impact and Implications
- Develops lifelong financial management skills
- Aids in setting and achieving financial goals
- Increases overall financial literacy and confidence

Conclusion
- Reinforce the importance of consistent tracking
- Encourage students to start tracking their finances immediately

Interesting Insights

1. Many adults who struggle with finances never learned proper tracking skills in their youth.
2. Studies show that people who track their expenses tend to save more money and reach their financial goals faster.

Part 2: Class Schedule

1. Introduction to Financial Tracking
   - Brief lecture using the outline from Part 1

2. Article Reading
   - Students read the article on tracking income and expenses

3. Guided Notes Completion
   - Students fill out guided notes while discussing key points

4. Reflection Questions
   - Students answer reflection questions
   - Facilitate class discussion on responses

5. Hypothetical Scenarios
   - Present "what-if" scenarios
   - Group discussion on potential outcomes

6. Vocabulary Reinforcement
   - Students complete crossword puzzle
   - Review answers as a class

Part 3: Discussion Prompts and Further Exploration

Class Discussion Prompts:
1. What surprised you most about the importance of tracking income and expenses?
2. How do you think your spending habits might change if you tracked every dollar?
3. What challenges do you foresee in consistently tracking your finances?
4. How might the skill of financial tracking benefit you in your future career?

Further Exploration:
1. Budgeting: Explore how tracking leads to effective budget creation and management.
2. Financial Goal Setting: Discuss how tracking can help in setting and achieving both short-term and long-term financial goals.
3. Digital Tools for Financial Tracking: Investigate various apps and software designed for personal finance management.

Additional Notes

- Encourage students to share their own experiences with managing money throughout the lesson.
- Consider having students start a simple tracking exercise during class using a provided template.
- Adapt the schedule as needed for different class lengths or student engagement levels.
- Use the hypothetical scenarios as group work opportunities to promote collaborative problem-solving.
- Emphasize the real-world applications of financial tracking to maintain student interest and motivation.

Tracking Income and Expenses

```
V N Y L T T Z D A G U J E B D N C A S H F L O W
S B N R J Z A X U J Y B T C B B E F V M N Y G D
C Z O A F L Z Z A M K J V N G F I L P Q D F V U
P K A Z Y F J D Z R W H N I F R A N W G Z J M W
S L M C T X I T T L E Q Z K I G V S C Q H X E I
J L K Q G W U A P Z N E R S H N G S D O L H S B
P S G F U C B H F T X I X D P R A X J H M S B M
S R P T W C P P I R E R C P Z F Z X T Y V E C C
T E Y S A F S F N Y Z I M W E I H D H K A Y A D
Z F I N A N C I A L R E S P O N S I B I L I T Y
T P G X G Q L H N B E J W H E A S B T C S A E C
O T H Q T Z V M C K H Y R D P N O E V S S O G Q
O K K M I O U R I K F R D N Y C D H S Q P K O P
S V Y K Y F I N A N C I A L L I T E R A C Y R S
C Y E L O E V P L Q F K U U N A B G R W N Q I R
Z D Z R W X D Y G I H V X A Y L S P N Y K E Z W
Q C S X S U T E O O P V R W B T C B R I S J A S
O S Y V R P X B A S P F Y Y C R X M A Q B B T R
C F Z I J B E B L O K J U L B A A X B E I H I M
Y V G E B Q U N S I E R X G M C F E T P U J O A
Z T C L Q J B D D V I U K C X K R E I B Y N N H
M X N V C H M S G I T C H C R I B P O G X D U F
Q E P J M M D G G E N E F B K N D P Z K W C A C
K N G W E E V O F S T G M T S G N U I S T U Y D
```

Financial Tracking	Financial Goals	Financial Responsibility
Financial Literacy	Categorization	Overspending
Cash Flow	Budget	Expenses
Income		

Tracking Income and Expenses

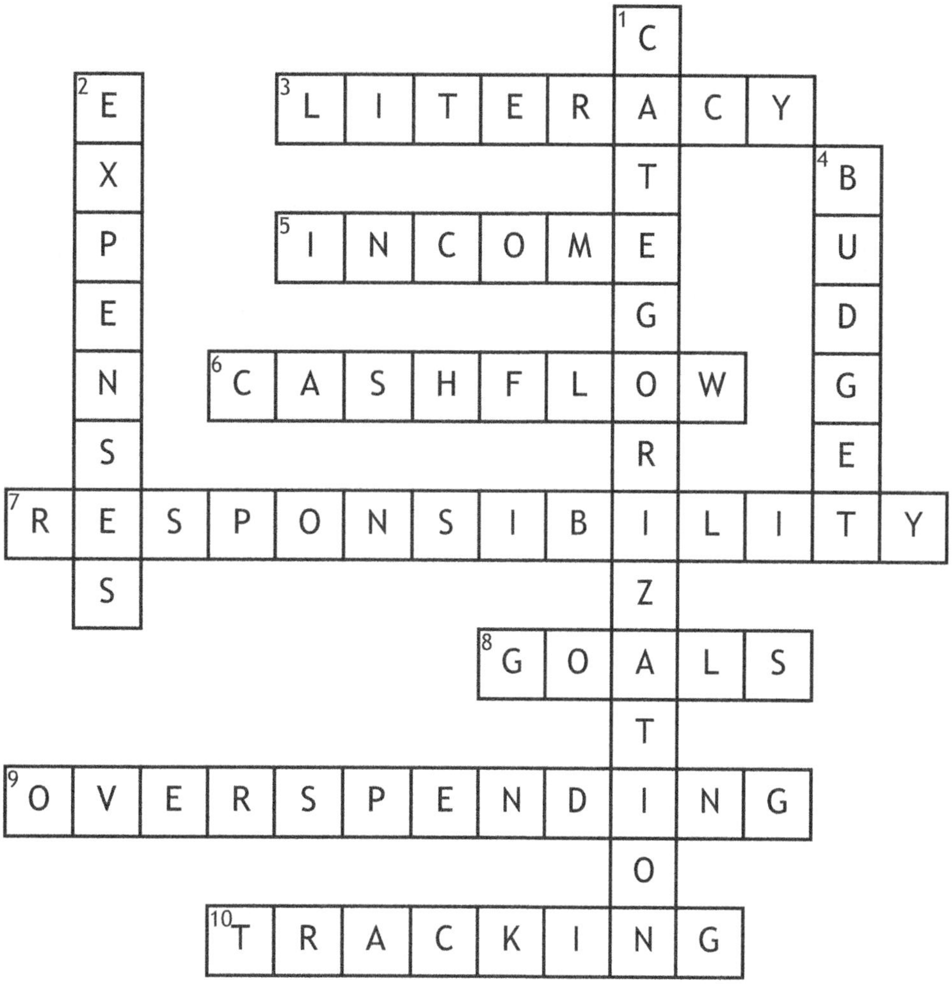

LITERACY
INCOME
CASHFLOW
RESPONSIBILITY
GOALS
OVERSPENDING
TRACKING
CATEGORIZATION
EXPENSES
BUDGET

Across

3. The ability to understand and effectively use various financial skills, Financial _____

5. This term refers to all the funds you receive, whether from a job, allowance, or gifts.

6. The movement of money into and out of your possession. (2 words)

7. The practice of managing money and financial decisions effectively, Financial _____

8. Specific objectives you aim to achieve with your money, Financial _____

9. The act of spending more money than planned or available.

10. This practice involves keeping a detailed record of your money's inflow and outflow, Financial _____

Down

1. The process of grouping expenses into specific types or classes.

2. These are the costs you incur in your daily life, from buying lunch to paying for a movie ticket.

4. This financial tool helps you allocate your money to different categories of spending and saving.

I. Key Terms

1. Opportunity Cost: The value of the best alternative you give up when making a choice
2. Financial Awareness: Becoming more conscious of your money habits
3. Long-Term Thinking: Considering the future impact of your choices

II. Main Concept Overview

Opportunity cost is the value of the best alternative you give up when making a choice. It's the "road not taken" in your financial journey.

III. Matching Section

B Budgeting Skills   A. Considering future impact of choices

C Resource Management   B. Prioritizing spending and saving effectively

A Long-Term Thinking   C. Allocating limited resources efficiently

D Time Management   D. Considering opportunity costs of how you spend time

E Financial Awareness   E. Being conscious of your money habits

IV. Fill in the Table

Decision	Chosen Option	Opportunity Cost
Buying a $5 latte	$5 latte	$5 saved towards a new bike
Working a part-time job	Part-time job	Athletic experience and skills from sports
Saving for college	Saving for college	Immediate fun and memories from concert

V. True/False

False Opportunity costs only apply to monetary decisions.

True Understanding opportunity costs can lead to better decision making.

True The formula for calculating opportunity cost is: Value of Next Best Alternative - Value of Chosen Option.

True Opportunity costs encourage considering both immediate and future consequences of financial decisions.

True Time should be considered when evaluating opportunity costs.

VI. Application Question

The article mentions a scenario about a summer job offer that pays $2,000 but means missing a family vacation. The opportunity costs involved in this decision include:

- Missing out on family experiences and memories
- Potential lost networking opportunities and work experience if the job is declined

This example illustrates that opportunity costs aren't always purely monetary. They can include intangible factors like experiences, skills, and relationships. It shows how we often have to weigh multiple factors when making decisions.

VII. Reflection/Summary

Understanding opportunity costs can help make smarter financial choices and achieve long-term goals by:

- Encouraging consideration of all alternatives before making a decision
- Promoting long-term thinking over immediate gratification
- Helping to align spending with personal values and goals
- Improving overall financial awareness and decision-making skills
- Assisting in more effective budgeting and resource management

This understanding allows you to see beyond the surface of your choices and make decisions that truly serve your best interests, leading to a stronger and more secure financial future.

Chapter 5: Lecture, Schedule, Discussion & Exploration

Example Lecture

1. Introduction
   - Define opportunity cost: The value of the best alternative given up when making a choice
   - Explain its importance in financial decision-making

2. Key Components of Opportunity Costs
   - Trade-offs in financial decisions
     - Every choice means giving up something else
     - Examples from daily life (buying latte vs. saving for a bike)
   - Short-term vs. long-term considerations
     - Immediate gratification vs. future benefits
     - How opportunity costs affect long-term goals
   - Non-monetary factors
     - Time, experiences, and personal growth as part of opportunity costs

3. Calculating Opportunity Costs
   - Basic formula: Value of Next Best Alternative - Value of Chosen Option
   - Example calculation (savings account vs. stocks scenario)

4. Real-World Applications
   - Education and career choices
   - Spending vs. saving decisions
   - Time management considerations

5. Impact on Financial Decision-Making
   - Improved budgeting and resource management
   - Better alignment with personal goals and values
   - Enhanced financial awareness and literacy

6. Conclusion
   - Recap the importance of considering opportunity costs
   - Encourage application in daily financial decisions

Interesting Insights

- Opportunity costs apply to non-financial decisions too, like time management
- Understanding opportunity costs can lead to more satisfying long-term outcomes, even if short-term sacrifices are needed

Class Schedule

1. Introduction to Opportunity Costs
   - Brief lecture using the outline above
2. Article Reading
   - Students read the article on Opportunity Costs
3. Guided Notes Completion
   - Students fill out guided notes while discussing key points
4. Reflection Questions
   - Students answer reflection questions
   - Facilitate brief class discussion on responses
5. Hypothetical Scenarios
   - Present "what-if" scenarios
   - Group discussion on potential outcomes
6. Vocabulary Reinforcement
   - Quick review of key terms

Discussion Prompts and Further Exploration

1. Class Discussion Prompts:
   - How might understanding opportunity costs change your daily financial decisions?
   - Can you think of a time when you didn't consider opportunity costs and regretted a decision?
   - How could applying the concept of opportunity costs help you achieve your long-term goals?

2. Further Exploration:
   - Behavioral economics: How emotions and cognitive biases affect our perception of opportunity costs
   - Opportunity costs in business decisions: How companies weigh alternatives when making investments
   - Global economics: How nations consider opportunity costs in policy-making and resource allocation

Additional Notes for Instructors

- Encourage students to share personal examples of opportunity costs they've encountered
- Use real-time examples or current events to illustrate opportunity costs in action
- Consider having students keep a "decision journal" for a week, noting the opportunity costs of their choices
- Emphasize that there's often no "right" answer, but understanding opportunity costs leads to more informed decisions
- Adapt the lesson timing as needed, potentially extending the hypothetical scenarios or reflection questions if students are highly engaged

Remember to use all activities as opportunities for class discussion and to assess student understanding throughout the lesson. Be prepared to offer additional examples or clarifications as needed, especially when discussing the calculation of opportunity costs.

Opportunity Costs in Financial Decisions

```
N F V Y R I X L T E H V Y J D I R Y W W N N K P A
N N I H C T R F Q A P Y W V W J I A O I F G G I
O V Z N T R R Y M Z T A U D U C B X P D Y L E J
P X V S A D Z N Z V P C I H Y U V Z T M Z R H D
P F J O J N C H N J T V X P S K E S N M B W U S
O B I Q F H C X O R W R H I K A S E K Z K U C B
R V M N M H L I X C U W A K A H V N L G S N I U
T T Y S A X X F A B T B G D K U P I O P P F B Q
U K N P Q N T G W L Y U P Q E T L C N Z E S W Y
N G I C T H C R D D D Q E Q B O U A G G N E C M
I P R V U N L I K Y F E Q P V R F B T F D S H W
T R E V T G R V A R Y V C X K K S F E D I F A J
Y Q J J L R U T O L X C H I L X N A R A N J W I
C K N B T C G C Z X A Q R X S W T P M M G S S M
O Y U U P J J F H Z L W J L Z I N Y G K C L S Y
S U S T N O O M I N E Z A E P E O Y O R H B V U
T W E N B F X N X Q F C W R I Y P N A W O F C X
L Y X X H N B Y J V X D P K E E P O L B I H Z I
V S U B B J Q N P B A F F P Z N G A Y A C O H O
B O Y R V R M C A Z U L P O C E X E F E O C X
N J H R E O O D X G U U U E O O I S M B D Q J S
B G Z L G G W O D R C W Z E Y J K O S P B P Z P
O T M S R N H S B A B U D G E T Y I H I S X D P
E N D U R E S O U R C E M A N A G E M E N T Q R
```

Financial Decision	Long-Term Goal	Resource Management
Financial Awareness	Spending Choice	Trade-off
Value	Saving	Budget
Opportunity Cost		

Opportunity Costs in Financial Decisions

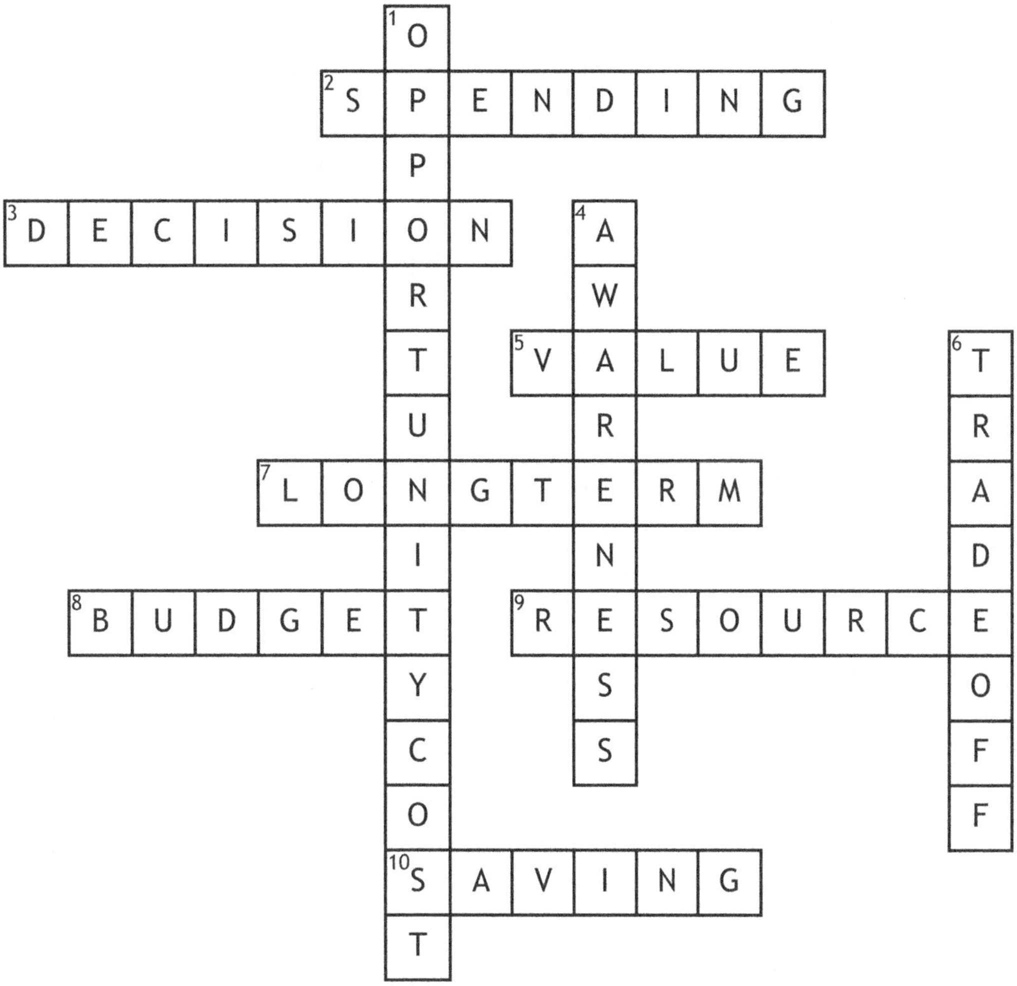
OPPORTUNITY COST
SPENDING
DECISION
AWARENESS
VALUE
TRADEOFF
LONGTERM
BUDGET
RESOURCE
SAVING
1
2
3
4
5
6
7
8
9
10

Across

2. Each of these involves an opportunity cost, _____ Choice

3. A choice made about money matters, Financial _____

5. The importance, worth, or usefulness of something.

7. An objective or desired result that requires time and planning to achieve, ____-____ Goal

8. A plan for saving and spending money.

9. The efficient and effective deployment of an organization's resources when they are needed, _____ Management

10. Setting aside money for future use.

Down

1. The value of the best alternative given up when making a choice. (2 words)

4. Being conscious and knowledgeable about one's money habits and financial situation, Financial _____

6. A balance achieved between two desirable but incompatible features. (2-words)

I. Introduction

A. Income is defined as: Money received, especially on a regular basis, for work or through investments.

B. Why is understanding different types of income important? (List two reasons)

   1. It's crucial for making informed financial decisions.

   2. It's important for planning for a secure financial future.

II. Types of Income

A. Earned Income

   1. Definition: Money you receive for providing services or selling products directly.

   2. Examples:

      a. Wages and Salaries

      b. Self-Employment Income

      c. Tips and Commissions

B. Passive Income

   1. Definition: Money earned with minimal ongoing effort.

   2. Examples:

      a. Rental Income

      b. Royalties

      c. Dividend Income

C. Portfolio Income

   1. Definition: Income derived from investments and the selling of investments.

   2. Examples:

      a. Interest Income

      b. Capital Gains

D. Residual Income

   1. Definition: Ongoing income from work done once.

   2. Examples:

      a. Network Marketing

      b. Online Courses or E-books

III. Impact of Income Types on Financial Planning

List four ways understanding income types impacts financial planning:

A. Tax Implications: Different types of income are taxed at different rates.

B. Financial Stability: Diversifying income sources can provide more financial security.

C. Retirement Planning: Building passive income streams can be an effective strategy for maintaining lifestyle in retirement.

D. Wealth Building: Some types of income have the potential to grow wealth more quickly than relying solely on earned income.

IV. Applying Knowledge

Scenario: Sarah's Income Diversification

1. Earned Income: Salary as a high school teacher
2. Residual Income: Creating and selling online lesson plans
3. Portfolio Income: Investing in dividend-paying stocks

V. True or False

T Different types of income are taxed at different rates.

T Passive income requires minimal ongoing effort.

T Diversifying income sources can provide more financial security.

T Portfolio and passive income have the potential to grow wealth more quickly than relying solely on earned income.

T Understanding different income types is crucial for effective financial planning.

VI. Matching

B Wages and Salaries   A. Portfolio Income

D Rental Income   B. Earned Income

A Interest   C. Residual Income

C Online Courses   D. Passive Income

E Capital Gains   E. Portfolio Income

VII. Reflection

1. What is the key to financial success according to the article?

The key to financial success often lies not just in how much you earn, but in how diversified and strategic your income sources are.

2. How does financial literacy relate to income diversification?

Financial literacy helps you identify new opportunities for income diversification and make more informed decisions about your financial future.

Example Lecture Outline

1. Introduction
   - Define income: Money received, especially on a regular basis, for work or through investments
   - Explain importance: Crucial for financial decisions and planning for a secure financial future

2. Key Components of Income Types
   a. Earned Income
      - Definition: Money received for providing services or selling products directly
      - Examples: Wages, salaries, self-employment income, tips, commissions

   b. Passive Income
      - Definition: Money earned with minimal ongoing effort
      - Examples: Rental income, royalties, dividend income

   c. Portfolio Income
      - Definition: Income derived from investments and selling investments
      - Examples: Interest income, capital gains

   d. Residual Income
      - Definition: Ongoing income from work done once
      - Examples: Network marketing, online courses, e-books

3. Real-World Applications
   - Discuss Sarah's example: Teacher (earned), online lesson plans (residual), stocks (portfolio)
   - Emphasize how different income types can work together

4. Impact and Implications
   - Tax implications: Different income types taxed at different rates
   - Financial stability: Diversification provides security
   - Retirement planning: Building passive income streams
   - Wealth building: Potential for faster growth with multiple income streams

5. Conclusion
   - Summarize key points about income types
   - Encourage exploration of diverse income streams

Interesting Insights
- The gig economy has created new opportunities for mixing income types
- Passive income often requires significant upfront effort but can provide long-term benefits

Class Schedule

1. Introduction to Income Types
   - Brief lecture using the outline from Part 1
   - Engage students with questions about their understanding of income
2. Article Reading
   - Students read the article on Understanding Different Types of Income
   - Encourage note-taking and highlighting key points
3. Guided Notes Completion
   - Students fill out guided notes while discussing key points
   - Teacher facilitates discussion and clarifies any confusion
4. Vocabulary Review
   - Quick review of the 10 key vocabulary terms
   - Students can create their own examples for each term
5. Reflection Questions
   - Students answer 2-3 reflection questions individually
   - Facilitate brief class discussion on responses
6. Hypothetical Scenarios
   - Present 1-2 "what-if" scenarios
   - Small group discussions on potential outcomes
   - Share group insights with the class

Additional Notes

- Encourage class discussion throughout all activities
- Adapt the schedule as needed for different class lengths or student needs
- Use real-world examples and current events to make the content more relatable
- Consider assigning the article reading as homework before class to allow more time for discussion and activities

Discussion Prompts

1. How might your future career choices be influenced by understanding different income types?
2. What are some creative ways you could potentially generate passive or residual income?
3. How do you think the rise of the digital economy has changed the landscape of income opportunities?

Further Exploration

1. Investment strategies for generating portfolio income
2. The impact of technology on creating new income streams
3. Balancing multiple income sources: case studies of successful entrepreneurs

Remember to assess student understanding throughout the lesson through questioning and observation of their engagement with the activities.

Understanding Different Types of Income

```
F X X J U U A U P F J W O B E C K J Z V Z M Y Z
I B D M T L F I N A N C I A L L I T E R A C Y G
G J Q W X G C I Q F K S A U T W P R L N C J H E
N Q U N L W S W D B D J F D S U O Z H Y S E M G
G R E S I D U A L I N C O M E T R A E B K R N J
W W V G G D N A E N V F M K L O T I A T V N Q P
Z T R I N P K O I A Z E P F E R F M P O D F T V
S V E B K A E J T J R N R G J Z O O Q H S O T F
I E T C H X H W A M J N C S M F L B S H Y D U R
G A I J Y K H E W E J K E I I H I Y I T I M R S
B G R I T L Y A N H I M X D T F O L Z T Q X U N
M P E A A Q B L N Z N P P B I B I B F H Y U K U
I J M P B U O T J N C B D L O N N C H P Z B I D
I G E N N D R H M V O M S V Y Y C U A T Y Z N C
Q D N A E X X B O J M E S M U V O O S T S M H R
M A T O Q Z Q U H H E Z X Y V W M K M L I C K G
O D P P A S S I V E I N C O M E E N Q E P O X R
A X L H E E D L R C Z T U Y F B F Y O K F K N I
G G A H E S D D V G H T D R F R W F T W U D P Z
Q K N V Y X Z I N K X N S E R R G Y O B Z P I M
F N N M C C E N M F M E X D M I R F Q S T D P O
K V I T H T P G G A D Q V T H I L T G Z U K K Y
A Y N G G F I N A N C I A L S T A B I L I T Y B
K N G S V E T F R Q X X E S J P N T R Q J V N Q
```

Earned Income	Passive Income	Portfolio Income
Residual Income	Financial Stability	Retirement Planning
Wealth Building	Financial Literacy	Diversification
Income		

Understanding Different Types of Income

Across

2. The ability to understand and effectively use various financial skills, including personal financial management, budgeting, and investing, Financial _____

5. The process of generating long-term income through multiple sources, often with a focus on creating assets that appreciate in value over time, _____ Building

8. Money received for providing services or selling products directly, such as wages, salaries, or self-employment income, _____ Income

9. The practice of varying income sources or investments to reduce risk and increase financial stability.

10. Money received, especially on a regular basis, for work or through investments.

Down

1. The state of having consistent income and manageable debts, allowing for financial security and the ability to meet financial obligations, Financial _____

3. The process of determining retirement income goals and the actions and decisions necessary to achieve those goals, _____ Planning

4. Ongoing income from work done once, such as royalties from books or revenues from online courses, _____ Income

6. Money earned with minimal ongoing effort, often from investments or business ventures that don't require active involvement, _____ Income

7. Income derived from investments and the selling of investments, including interest, dividends, and capital gains, _____ Income

Solution grid:

- 1 Down: STABILITY
- 2 Across: LITERACY
- 3 Down: RETIREMENT
- 4 Down: RESIDUAL
- 5 Across: WEALTH
- 6 Down: PASSIVE
- 7 Down: PORTFOLIO
- 8 Across: EARNED
- 9 Across: DIVERSIFICATION
- 10 Across: INCOME

I. Main Concept Overview

The choice of career significantly impacts your FINANCIAL future. It affects not just your job responsibilities, but also your EARNING potential, LIFESTYLE, and long-term financial HEALTH.

II. Matching Section

C Salary

A Benefits

B Student Loan Debt

D Entrepreneurship

A. Additional job perks beyond base pay

B. Money owed for educational expenses

C. Base monetary compensation for work

D. Starting and running your own business

III. The Salary Spectrum

Career	Average Annual Salary
Software Developer	$107,510
Teacher	$61,730
Nurse Practitioner	$117,670

IV. True or False

FALSE The highest paying job is always the best financial choice.

FALSE Location has no impact on career finances.

FALSE All high-paying careers require a four-year college degree.

TRUE Certifications can increase earning potential in some fields.

V. Beyond the Paycheck

List three examples of benefits that can boost overall compensation:

(Any three of the following)

1. Health insurance
2. Retirement plans (like 401(k)s with employer matching)
3. Paid time off
4. Stock options
5. Educational reimbursement

VI. Education and Training

1. The average student loan debt in the U.S. is about $37,574.
2. An electrician can earn a median salary of $56,900 after completing an apprenticeship program.
3. A Certified Information Systems Security Professional (CISSP) can earn an average of $116,900 annually.

VII. Career Progression and Financial Growth

List two ways career progression can lead to financial growth:
(Any two of the following)
1. Promotions
2. Specialization
3. Entrepreneurship

VIII. The Impact of Location

How does location affect career finances? Provide an example from the article:
Location can significantly affect career finances due to differences in salaries and cost of living. For example, a teacher in Mississippi might earn an average of $45,574, while the same position in New York could pay $87,543. However, the cost of living in New York is significantly higher, which could offset the salary difference.

IX. Application Question

The article mentions the importance of balancing passion and practicality in career choices. Explain why this balance is important and how it relates to both job satisfaction and financial considerations.
Answer may vary, but should include:
- While financial considerations are important, they shouldn't be the sole factor in career choice.
- Job satisfaction, work-life balance, and personal fulfillment play crucial roles in overall life satisfaction.
- The key is to find a balance between passions and financial realities.
- This balance can lead to both financial stability and personal fulfillment in a career.

X. Planning for Your Financial Future

List three steps the article suggests for planning your financial future as you explore career options:
(Any three of the following)
1. Research potential salaries and benefits for careers you're interested in.
2. Understand the education or training required and its associated costs.
3. Look into career progression opportunities within your chosen field.
4. Consider the impact of location on your career and finances.

Example Lecture

I. Introduction
- Define career choice as a critical life decision with long-term financial implications
- Explain the importance of understanding these implications for future financial well-being

II. Key Components of Career Financial Planning
A. Salary Considerations
   - Discuss salary ranges for different careers
   - Explain the concept of earning potential
B. Benefits Beyond Salary
   - List types of benefits (health insurance, retirement plans, etc.)
   - Discuss how benefits contribute to overall compensation
C. Education and Training Investments
   - Explain the costs associated with different educational paths
   - Discuss the concept of return on investment in education

III. Real-World Applications
- Provide examples of how career choices impact financial situations
  - Compare software developer ($107,510) vs. teacher ($61,730) salaries
  - Discuss how location affects salaries (e.g., teachers in Mississippi vs. New York)

IV. Impact and Implications
- Discuss how career choices affect long-term financial health
- Explain the importance of balancing passion with financial practicality

V. Conclusion
- Summarize key points about the financial implications of career choices
- Encourage students to research and consider financial aspects when exploring careers

Interesting Insights

- Share that some high-paying careers don't require a four-year degree (e.g., electricians)
- Discuss how certifications in fields like IT can significantly boost earning potential

Class Schedule

1. Introduction to Career Financial Planning
   - Brief lecture using the outline from Part 1
2. Article Reading
   - Students read the article on exploring career options and their financial implications
3. Guided Notes Completion
   - Students fill out guided notes while discussing key points
   - Facilitate class discussion on responses
4. Reflection Questions
   - Students answer 2-3 reflection questions
   - Facilitate class discussion on responses
5. Hypothetical Scenarios
   - Present 2 "what-if" scenarios
   - Group discussion on potential outcomes
6. Vocabulary Reinforcement
   - Students complete crossword puzzle
   - Review answers as a class

Class Discussion Prompts

1. How might your dream career affect your future finances?
2. Is pursuing additional education worth it financially for your chosen career?
3. How could where you choose to work impact your finances?

Further Exploration

1. Research salaries and job outlooks for specific careers using the Bureau of Labor Statistics website
2. Explore the concept of work-life balance and how it relates to career satisfaction and financial well-being
3. Investigate the gig economy and how it's changing traditional career paths

Additional Notes

- Encourage students to share personal experiences or aspirations related to career choices
- Use the hypothetical scenarios to spark debate and critical thinking
- Consider inviting a guest speaker (e.g., a career counselor or local professional) to share real-world insights
- Remind students that career paths can change over time and the importance of adaptability in the modern job market

Remember, the goal is to create an engaging, interactive lesson that helps students understand the crucial link between career choices and financial outcomes.

Exploring Career Options and Their Financial Implications

```
N M K P W U F O X P W P H P R M J K G K I Z M Y
N H R C S H O X P C E Z F P U Z Y F I B Q E N M
A W P B R H Y N V T F E Q J H Z W L I X K F J F
L R F I N A N C I A L I M P L I C A T I O N T G
B T Q V S X N H G C O M P E N S A T I O N G E E
Z E G W U X G J T B A C Z G J I Q U A M R Z B A
O N N E O H V D W E H O L E P N N L I M Z V V V
E I I E I G I G G N E S L A D I Q W L Y I K M B
N N I V F I O N H T F T B R A G D Q N O P R N
O S O N K I F F B R P O G N S J O I F V A W D A
D T M I V H T T J E E F J I O O K G P C R A R L
T U D E F E P S H P P L Q N E M C U X Z V X M H
S D S S R H S E A R K I C G I A V J A D K T H V
H E S C A H C T U E G V F P T C B B R Z Y V X B
Z N K R E L C W M N N I X O N U X G E H X C A F
Y T E K J N A N J E M N U T S U X W U D B Y G Y
T L C C N M V R Q U N G N E Q R X R K B X E G R
B O S W W T E R Y R P T I N J P T F S Y O B C X
R A G A O M T O Y S G P T T N W L Z U K T X A O
V N W Z C F L S V H M D P I K Y U L O Y D Q R J
J O X O X A D P X I G F O A J N S D W Q X K E H
B B S L P M X X D P J X V L T X E Z H P R B E C
L K G L J N I M C T Q K R X G W Z T A R D Z R J
D R X B Q Y Z S J J T B Q L E U O C O J E U S P
```

Student Loan	Cost of Living	Financial Implication
Earning Potential	Entrepreneurship	Compensation
Investment	Benefits	Salary
Career		

Exploring Career Options and Their Financial Implications

Across

4. The total amount of the monetary and non-monetary pay provided to an employee by an employer in return for work performed.

8. The action of investing money for future financial return.

9. The activity of setting up a business, taking financial risks in the hope of profit.

10. A fixed regular payment, typically paid on a monthly basis, made by an employer to an employee.

Down

1. A profession or occupation chosen as one's life's work.

2. The potential financial effect or consequence of a decision or action, Financial _____

3. Money borrowed to pay for educational expenses, Student _____

5. The amount of money a person has the ability to earn in their career over time, Earning _____

6. The amount of money needed to sustain a certain standard of living, including basic expenses such as housing, food, and healthcare, Cost of _____

7. Additional compensation provided to employees beyond salaries.

Crossword grid answers:

- 1 Down: CAREER
- 2 Down: IMPLICATIONS
- 3 Down: LOAN
- 4 Across: COMPENSATION
- 5 Down: POTENTIAL
- 6 Down: LIVING
- 7 Down: BENEFIT
- 8 Across: INVESTMENT
- 9 Across: ENTREPRENEURSHIP
- 10 Across: SALARY

I. Key Terms

1. Gross Pay: The total amount you've earned before any deductions
2. Net Pay: The amount that will be deposited into your bank account or given to you as a physical check after all deductions
3. FICA: Federal Insurance Contributions Act, which funds Social Security and Medicare

II. Main Concept Overview

Paychecks consist of several components, including gross pay, various deductions, and net pay. Understanding these elements is crucial for effective budgeting and financial planning.

III. Matching Section

C Federal Income Tax   A. Funds Social Security and Medicare
D State Income Tax   B. The amount you actually receive
A FICA   C. Percentage taken by the federal government
E Gross Pay   D. Varies depending on where you live and work
B Net Pay   E. Total amount earned before deductions

IV. True/False

FALSE	Gross pay is what ends up in your bank account.
FALSE	Understanding your paycheck is only important for budgeting purposes.
TRUE	FICA stands for Federal Insurance Contributions Act.
TRUE	Your pay stub includes Year-to-Date (YTD) totals.
FALSE	All states have income tax.

V. Application Question

Using the example from the article:

If you earn $12 per hour and work 20 hours a week:
a) What is your gross pay? $240
b) Assuming 20% in deductions, what is your approximate net pay? $192

How could you use this information for budgeting?
Possible answer: Knowing your net pay helps you plan your spending and saving accurately. You can create a realistic budget based on the actual amount you'll receive, not the gross pay. This helps ensure you don't overspend and can allocate funds for savings or specific goals.

VI. Reflection/Summary

1. List three reasons why understanding your paycheck is important, according to the article:
   a) Budgeting
   b) Tax Awareness
   c) Career Planning
   (Note: Financial Responsibility is also mentioned in the article as a fourth reason)

2. How might understanding your paycheck benefit you in future career decisions?
Possible answer: Understanding your paycheck can help you evaluate job offers more effectively. You'll be able to compare the true value of different compensation packages, considering not just the salary but also benefits and deductions. This knowledge allows you to make more informed decisions about which jobs to pursue or accept.

3. What are two questions you should consider when thinking critically about your paycheck?
Possible answers (any two of the following):
a) How do different deductions affect your take-home pay?
b) What steps can you take to maximize your earnings and minimize unnecessary deductions?
c) How might understanding your paycheck now benefit you in future career decisions?
d) If you're offered a job with benefits like health insurance or a 401(k), how will that impact your take-home pay? Is the trade-off worth it?

Example Lecture Outline

1. Introduction
   - Define a paycheck as a document that shows an employee's earnings and deductions
   - Explain the importance of understanding paychecks for personal financial management

2. Key Components of a Paycheck
   - Gross Pay
     - Definition: Total amount earned before deductions
     - Calculation methods: Hourly rate x Hours worked, or portion of annual salary
   - Deductions
     - Taxes: Federal Income Tax, State Income Tax, FICA (Social Security and Medicare)
     - Other possible deductions: Health insurance, retirement contributions
   - Net Pay
     - Definition: Take-home pay after all deductions
     - Importance for budgeting and financial planning

3. Understanding Your Pay Stub
   - Key information found on a pay stub: Pay period, YTD totals, personal information
   - Importance of reviewing your pay stub regularly

4. Real-World Applications
   - Budgeting based on net pay rather than gross pay
   - Evaluating job offers by considering total compensation package
   - Planning for taxes and other deductions

5. Impact and Implications
   - How understanding your paycheck contributes to overall financial literacy
   - Long-term benefits of managing your income effectively

6. Conclusion
   - Recap the importance of understanding your paycheck
   - Encourage students to apply this knowledge to their future jobs

Interesting Insights

- The design of modern paychecks dates back to the 1940s when the U.S. government mandated income tax withholding
- Some companies are moving towards paperless pay stubs to reduce environmental impact and increase security

Class Schedule

1. Introduction to Paychecks
   - Brief lecture using the outline from Part 1
   - Encourage questions and discussion
2. Article Reading
   - Students read the article on "Understanding Your Paycheck"
   - Instruct students to highlight or underline key points as they read
3. Guided Notes Completion
   - Students fill out guided notes while discussing key points
   - Facilitate class discussion on any confusing concepts
   - Tip: Use think-pair-share strategy for some questions to encourage peer learning
4. Reflection Questions
   - Students answer reflection questions individually
   - Facilitate brief class discussion on responses
   - Tip: Choose 1-2 questions for whole-class discussion if time is limited
5. Hypothetical Scenarios
   - Present "what-if" scenarios to the class
   - Divide class into small groups to discuss and answer questions
   - Have groups share their thoughts with the class
   - Tip: Assign different scenarios to different groups to cover all scenarios
6. Vocabulary Reinforcement
   - Students complete crossword puzzle individually or in pairs
   - Review answers as a class
   - Tip: If time is short, this activity can be assigned as homework

Discussion Prompts and Further Exploration

1. Class Discussion Prompts:
   - How might understanding your paycheck influence your career choices?
   - Why is it important to consider more than just the salary when evaluating a job offer?
   - How can understanding paycheck deductions help you make better financial decisions?

2. Further Exploration:
   - Tax brackets and how they affect income: Understand how earning more might change your tax obligations
   - Employee benefits: Explore different types of benefits and how they complement salary
   - Paycheck laws: Investigate federal and state laws that govern how and when employees must be paid

Additional Notes

- Encourage students to bring in pay stubs (with personal information blocked out) from their part-time jobs, if applicable, to make the lesson more relevant
- Consider inviting a local HR professional or accountant as a guest speaker to provide real-world insights
- Remind students that this knowledge will be immediately applicable as they enter the workforce
- Emphasize the connection between understanding paychecks and overall financial literacy

Understanding Your Paycheck

```
I  U  S  G  T  J  D  Z  G  T  H  X  J  Q  J  V  G  Q  M  O  R  V  J  X
I  N  A  X  M  U  G  D  Y  S  F  L  W  O  Z  I  Z  R  P  C  P  Y  R  C
I  F  H  T  O  C  R  X  S  P  X  F  I  C  A  S  A  F  O  H  E  K  Z  V
B  O  F  V  W  F  L  E  W  D  N  V  Q  V  R  J  J  D  Q  S  T  L  T  G
W  G  Y  F  N  M  A  I  A  I  W  X  G  T  R  L  Z  Z  I  D  S  H  R  X
H  U  P  E  T  K  E  Q  C  J  T  Y  Z  I  G  N  U  F  R  U  F  P  P  C
K  F  Y  U  A  W  P  L  M  F  X  H  O  T  P  L  K  N  H  P  O  R  A  W
U  N  V  G  R  Q  A  P  N  X  B  H  S  U  F  V  E  Z  U  C  J  U  Y
J  G  X  D  J  I  T  S  Y  G  Q  W  U  O  I  K  B  T  W  A  I  S  P  N
F  Z  O  O  L  K  W  O  S  P  P  T  F  V  L  K  S  P  S  U  R  R  B  Q
A  Z  N  O  E  E  G  V  D  D  E  D  W  D  D  D  M  A  X  M  H  G  Y  T
K  J  R  A  B  P  Z  R  W  A  T  R  P  I  D  Y  I  Y  K  Z  Y  Z  L  B
Z  S  L  H  M  S  B  Q  Z  O  T  J  I  W  P  F  S  N  T  Y  L  U  O  B
Y  P  Y  V  M  I  N  K  R  E  P  E  Z  O  F  B  Q  F  G  A  D  U  A  P
Q  U  U  R  Z  N  O  Q  B  A  A  O  M  Y  D  U  R  R  J  M  C  V  U  A
O  D  H  N  C  Y  J  P  S  T  A  T  E  I  N  C  O  M  E  T  A  X  X  Y
U  R  M  H  N  T  U  F  F  W  M  C  C  M  K  J  N  D  N  N  G  L  S  S
I  F  R  P  D  E  D  U  C  T  I  O  N  S  Y  R  Y  N  K  Y  E  X  L  T
M  W  W  F  E  D  E  R  A  L  I  N  C  O  M  E  T  A  X  D  S  C  W  U
F  Q  J  C  O  O  U  R  A  D  S  B  O  L  U  E  S  X  T  V  T  J  R  B
L  Q  A  V  Q  E  F  T  Q  B  A  J  K  D  K  B  B  Y  N  F  G  C  E  B
N  U  U  V  J  I  B  T  L  U  I  T  E  P  U  G  W  T  H  K  H  E  D  M
E  H  P  M  U  G  A  Y  W  T  T  P  S  X  U  S  I  D  W  H  K  X  E  B
U  K  V  L  Z  Q  S  K  A  M  J  A  M  P  O  A  Z  B  X  E  P  P  Y  D
```

Pay Period	Year-to-Date	State Income Tax
Federal Income Tax	Net Pay	Gross Pay
Withholding	YTD	Pay Stub
Deductions	FICA	

Understanding Your Paycheck

Across

2. A tax levied by the federal government on your earnings, withheld from each paycheck, _____ Income Tax

6. Amounts subtracted from your gross pay, including taxes, insurance premiums, and retirement contributions.

8. The recurring schedule on which you receive your paycheck and for which your wages are calculated (e.g., weekly, bi-weekly, monthly), Pay _____

9. The cumulative total of your earnings and deductions from the beginning of the calendar year to the current pay period. (Abbrv.)

10. Stands for Federal Insurance Contributions Act, which funds Social Security and Medicare through payroll deductions. (Abbrv.)

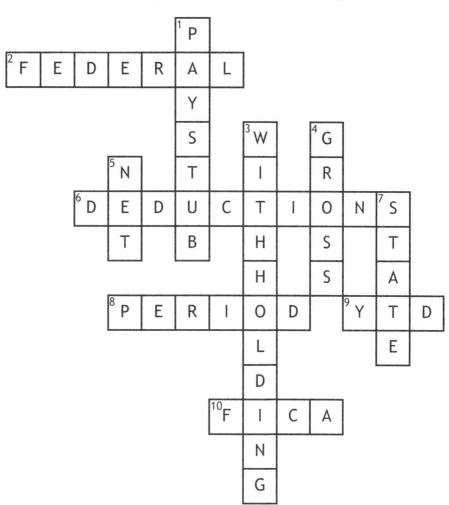

Down

1. A document that itemizes your pay, including gross wages, deductions, and net pay for a specific pay period. (2 words)

3. The amount of money taken out of your paycheck for taxes and other deductions before you receive it.

4. The total amount you've earned before any deductions are taken out, _____ Pay

5. Also known as "take-home pay," this is the amount you actually receive after all deductions have been subtracted from your gross pay, _____ Pay

7. A tax levied by most states on your earnings, also typically withheld from each paycheck, _____ Income Tax

I. Key Terms

1. Personal Income Tax: A form of direct taxation imposed by the government on an individual's earnings.

2. Taxable Income: The portion of your income subject to taxation, including wages, salaries, bonuses, and other forms of compensation.

3. Tax Bracket: Divisions of income that are taxed at different rates in a progressive tax system.

4. Deduction: A tool that can reduce your taxable income, potentially lowering the amount you owe.

II. Main Concept Overview

Personal income taxes are a form of direct taxation imposed by the government on an individual's earnings. They serve as a primary source of revenue for federal, state, and sometimes local governments.

III. Matching Section

B Withholding
C W-4 Form
A Taxable Income
D Tax Brackets
E Deductions

IV. Components of Personal Income Taxes

Component	Description
Taxable Income	The portion of your income subject to taxation, including wages, salaries, bonuses, and other forms of compensation.
Tax Brackets	The U.S. uses a progressive tax system, meaning tax rates increase as your income rises. Your income is divided into "brackets," each taxed at a different rate.
Deductions and Credits	Tools that can reduce your taxable income or tax liability, potentially lowering the amount you owe.
Withholding	The amount your employer deducts from each paycheck to cover your estimated tax liability.

V. True/False

T The U.S. uses a progressive tax system where tax rates increase as income rises.

T Filing your taxes correctly and on time helps you avoid costly fines and legal issues.

T Tax withholding serves as a pre-payment of your taxes.

T Understanding personal income taxes can help with financial planning.

F Personal income taxes only fund federal programs. (False: The article states they fund federal, state, and sometimes local governments.)

VI. Key Aspects of Personal Income Taxes

1. Financial Planning
2. Maximizing Your Money
3. Avoiding Penalties
4. Civic Responsibility

VII. Application Question

Sarah's annual income: $12 x 20 hours x 52 weeks = $12,480

Sarah might not owe federal income tax because:

1. Her income ($12,480) is less than the standard deduction ($12,550 for single filers in 2021).

2. The standard deduction reduces her taxable income to zero.

3. While she falls into the 10% federal tax bracket, the standard deduction eliminates her federal tax liability.

4. She would still see deductions for Social Security and Medicare taxes on her paycheck.

VIII. Reflection/Summary

(Answers will vary, but should include key points from the article such as the purpose of income taxes, how they work, and their importance. Students should relate this to future financial decisions like budgeting, financial planning, and understanding their paycheck deductions.)

Chapter 9: Lecture, Schedule, Discussion & Exploration

Part 1: Example Lecture

1. Introduction
   - Define personal income tax
   - Explain its importance in the U.S. financial system

2. Key Components of Personal Income Taxes
   - Taxable Income
     - Definition and examples
   - Tax Brackets
     - Explanation of progressive tax system
   - Deductions and Credits
     - Brief overview and distinction between the two
   - Withholding
     - Purpose and process

3. How Personal Income Taxes Work
   - W-4 form and its purpose
   - Process of filing a tax return
   - Paying taxes or receiving a refund

4. Real-World Application
   - Example of Sarah's part-time job
   - Calculation of taxable income and tax liability

5. Impact and Implications
   - Importance for financial planning
   - Role in funding public services

6. Conclusion
   - Recap key points
   - Emphasize the importance of understanding personal income taxes

Interesting Insights for Discussion

- The U.S. tax system is based on voluntary compliance, relying on citizens to report their income honestly.
- The modern income tax was first introduced in 1861 to help fund the Civil War.

Part 2: Class Schedule

1. Introduction to Personal Income Taxes
   - Brief lecture using the outline from Part 1

2. Article Reading
   - Students read the article on personal income taxes

3. Guided Notes Completion
   - Students fill out guided notes while discussing key points

4. Reflection Questions
   - Students answer reflection questions
   - Facilitate brief class discussion on responses

5. Hypothetical Scenarios
   - Present "what-if" scenarios
   - Group discussion on potential outcomes

6. Vocabulary Review
   - Quick review of key vocabulary terms

Part 3: Discussion Prompts and Further Exploration

1. Class Discussion Prompts:
   - How might understanding income taxes influence your future career choices?
   - Why is it important to keep track of your income and expenses?
   - How do income taxes contribute to our society?

2. Further Exploration:
   - Tax Deductions and Credits: Explore common deductions and credits that students might encounter in the future.
   - Historical Context: Investigate the history of income tax in the United States and how it has evolved.
   - Global Perspective: Compare the U.S. income tax system with those of other countries.

Additional Notes

- Encourage students to share personal experiences or knowledge about income taxes.
- Use visual aids such as charts or graphs to illustrate concepts like tax brackets and progressive taxation.
- Consider inviting a local tax professional as a guest speaker for real-world insights.
- Adapt the schedule as needed based on student engagement and understanding.
- Use the hypothetical scenarios as group work to promote peer learning and discussion.

Remember, the goal is to make personal income taxes relatable and understandable for high school students, preparing them for their future financial responsibilities.

Personal Income Taxes

```
P  K  F  G  4  C  T  T  A  X  A  B  L  E  I  N  C  O  M  E  P  P  W  M
M  R  O  R  U  Y  X  W  A  Y  F  S  F  W  R  L  W  W  4  L  K  W  O  A
X  W  O  F  T  P  E  R  S  O  N  A  L  I  N  C  O  M  E  T  A  X  I  I
U  R  R  G  C  A  T  A  X  B  R  A  C  K  E  T  I  C  E  G  S  D  W  M
I  H  E  S  R  O  X  G  G  X  P  E  B  H  F  U  D  L  M  4  A  X  4  C
O  H  V  X  M  E  P  R  A  G  B  T  H  G  A  F  G  H  E  H  O  A  V  W
X  K  S  A  H  G  S  D  E  K  D  P  V  M  T  U  L  A  M  N  N  C  M  C
F  4  V  G  M  L  B  S  T  T  R  U  T  P  4  W  M  F  I  H  R  C  K  G
W  P  M  H  C  D  S  X  I  I  U  D  E  W  I  T  H  H  O  L  D  I  N  G
V  U  I  C  U  R  D  U  M  V  K  R  I  T  T  S  D  A  X  P  F  O  M  B
M  Y  4  N  W  I  N  C  Y  T  E  C  N  G  W  M  R  C  D  S  I  Y  I  D
Y  H  L  K  L  G  W  E  C  L  T  T  B  4  D  E  S  U  V  P  L  A  M  U
V  A  X  B  N  P  D  B  L  Y  A  R  A  I  K  E  C  U  T  T  Y  W  G  K
M  R  W  U  V  S  D  L  M  H  X  K  F  X  A  R  D  S  V  L  G  X  X  K
H  S  R  H  4  G  4  A  A  P  C  X  I  U  S  X  C  U  I  S  M  4  A  V
T  E  F  R  I  4  G  T  B  G  R  A  B  H  G  Y  G  A  C  G  F  E  E  G
Y  H  K  H  W  C  A  O  W  G  E  U  W  K  U  A  S  M  K  T  G  I  G  I
B  K  C  B  F  U  N  I  N  D  D  C  S  4  Y  L  I  T  B  G  I  H  K  C
P  I  P  K  M  I  4  M  K  S  I  S  W  N  F  S  P  F  E  A  E  O  R  O
F  K  K  L  4  L  M  M  4  C  T  P  4  K  E  O  G  K  E  M  S  H  N  S
C  H  M  N  E  I  P  D  K  D  M  P  D  I  M  G  R  E  K  X  T  G  X  N
K  C  N  D  H  4  W  T  G  H  W  M  B  G  A  A  H  M  Y  A  4  X  F  U
V  N  F  S  T  A  N  D  A  R  D  D  E  D  U  C  T  I  O  N  S  A  K  E
A  A  Y  G  K  M  X  X  N  F  S  X  S  D  A  M  I  R  F  R  D  V  B  G
```

Deduction	Standard Deduction	Progressive Tax System
Tax Credit	Tax Return	Tax Bracket
Taxable Income	Personal Income Tax	W-4 Form
Withholding		

Personal Income Taxes

1 TAXABLE
2 DEDUCTION
3 W4FORM
4 BRACKET
5 RETURN
6 PROGRESSIVE
7 PERSONAL
8 CREDIT
9 DEDUCTION
10 WITHHOLDING

Across

7. A form of direct taxation imposed by the government on an individual's earnings, _____ Income Tax

8. A reduction in the amount of tax owed, differing from a deduction which reduces taxable income, Tax _____

9. A specific dollar amount that reduces your taxable income, an alternative to itemizing deductions, Standard _____

10. The amount your employer deducts from each paycheck to cover your estimated tax liability.

Down

1. The portion of your income subject to taxation, including wages, salaries, and bonuses, _____ Income

2. A reduction in taxable income, potentially lowering the amount of taxes owed.

3. A form filled out when starting a new job that helps your employer determine how much tax to withhold from your paycheck. (__-__ _____)

4. A range of incomes taxed at a specific rate in a progressive tax system, Tax _____

5. A form filed with the tax authority that reports income, expenses, and other relevant tax information, Tax _____

6. A system where tax rates increase as the taxable amount increases, _____ Tax System

I. Introduction

A. Employee benefits are forms of COMPENSATION provided in addition to regular salary or wages.

B. Benefits can significantly impact your overall FINANCIAL WELL-BEING and quality of life.

II. Understanding Employee Benefits

A. Employee benefits can be:
  1. MANDATORY: required by law
  2. VOLUNTARY: offered at employer's discretion

B. Benefits can account for up to 30% of an employee's total compensation package.

III. Types of Employee Benefits

A. HEALTH Insurance: Covers medical expenses, sometimes including dental and vision care.

B. RETIREMENT Plans: Help employees save for the future (e.g., 401(k)s, pension plans).

C. Paid Time Off (PTO): Includes VACATION DAYS, SICK LEAVE, and personal days.

D. Life and DISABILITY Insurance: Provides financial protection for employees and their families.

E. EDUCATIONAL Assistance: May include tuition reimbursement or professional development programs.

IV. The Hidden Value of Employee Benefits

A. TAX Advantages: Many benefits are tax-deductible or tax-deferred.

B. COST Savings: Employer-sponsored plans are often less expensive than individual plans.

C. Financial SECURITY: Benefits like retirement plans provide long-term security.

D. Work-Life BALANCE: Benefits like PTO can improve quality of life and job satisfaction.

V. Evaluating a Benefits Package

Steps to assess the value of employee benefits:

1. LIST ALL THE BENEFITS OFFERED BY THE EMPLOYER.
2. ESTIMATE THE MONETARY VALUE OF EACH BENEFIT.
3. ADD UP THE VALUES OF ALL BENEFITS.
4. ADD THIS TOTAL TO THE ANNUAL SALARY TO GET A MORE ACCURATE PICTURE OF TOTAL COMPENSATION.

VI. Emerging Trends in Employee Benefits

Match each trend with its description:

D Mental Health Support   A. Remote work options and flexible schedules
A Flexible Work Arrangements   B. Financial education and planning services
B Financial Wellness Programs C. Help with loan repayments
C Student Loan Assistance   D. Counseling services and mental health days
E Wellness Programs   E. Gym memberships, health screenings, or incentives for healthy behaviors

VII. True or False

T Employee benefits account for about 31% of the total compensation for civilian workers on average.

F All employee benefits are mandated by law.

T Some companies offer pet insurance as an employee benefit.

F The salary is always the most important factor when evaluating a job offer.

F Employer-sponsored health insurance is usually more expensive than individual plans.

VIII. Matching

Match each term with its correct description:

B Health Insurance   A. Helps employees save for future
A Retirement Plans   B. Covers medical expenses
D PTO   C. Protects against loss of income due to illness or injury

E Educational Assistance   D. Paid vacation, sick days, and personal time
C Disability Insurance   E. Supports continued learning and career growth

Example Lecture

1. Introduction
   - Define employee benefits: Additional compensation provided to employees beyond regular salary
   - Explain importance: Can significantly impact overall financial well-being and quality of life

2. Key Components of Employee Benefits
   - Health Insurance
     - Covers medical expenses, sometimes including dental and vision
     - Often less expensive than individual plans
   - Retirement Plans
     - Help employees save for the future (e.g., 401(k)s, pension plans)
     - May include employer contributions
   - Paid Time Off (PTO)
     - Includes vacation days, sick leave, and personal days
     - Promotes work-life balance
   - Life and Disability Insurance
     - Provides financial protection for employees and their families
   - Educational Assistance
     - May include tuition reimbursement or professional development programs

3. Value of Employee Benefits
   - Tax advantages
   - Cost savings
   - Long-term financial security
   - Improved work-life balance

4. Evaluating Benefits Packages
   - List all benefits offered
   - Estimate monetary value of each benefit
   - Add up values and compare to salary for total compensation

5. Emerging Trends in Employee Benefits
   - Mental health support
   - Flexible work arrangements
   - Financial wellness programs
   - Student loan assistance
   - Wellness programs

6. Conclusion
   - Emphasize importance of considering benefits when evaluating job offers
   - Encourage students to think about which benefits might be most valuable to them

Class Schedule

1. Introduction to Employee Benefits
   - Brief lecture using the outline above

2. Article Reading
   - Students read the article on Employee Benefits and Their Value

3. Guided Notes Completion
   - Students fill out guided notes while discussing key points
   - Facilitate brief discussions on each section

4. Reflection Questions
   - Students answer 2-3 reflection questions
   - Facilitate class discussion on responses

5. Hypothetical Scenarios
   - Present 1-2 "what-if" scenarios
   - Group discussion on potential outcomes

6. Vocabulary Review
   - Quick review of key terms
   - Can be done as a class or in small groups

Class Discussion Prompts

1. "How might the importance of different benefits change throughout your career?"
2. "What challenges might you face in comparing job offers with different benefits packages?"
3. "How do you think employee benefits reflect broader societal values or trends?"

Further Exploration

1. Historical changes in employee benefits: Explore how benefits have evolved over time and why.
2. International comparisons: Look at how employee benefits differ in other countries and why.
3. Gig economy and benefits: Discuss the challenges and opportunities for benefits in non-traditional employment structures.

Additional Notes

- Encourage students to share personal or family experiences with employee benefits when appropriate.
- Use the hypothetical scenarios to promote critical thinking and application of concepts.
- Consider inviting a human resources professional as a guest speaker to provide real-world insight.
- Remind students that benefits can significantly impact overall compensation and should be carefully considered in career decisions.

Employee Benefits and Their Value

```
O P Q G C P F C F Y P J Z R K E J D D A D C G Y
T L M V H T A M G X Q H A E A F Q D R X U G R Y
M M S N W C E I J C O M P E N S A T I O N U V F
Q D C U D C M V D I P Q X N F E J R X A Z S O F
S O G E H J B Z J T D K O Q C Q H N X G Y I L G
R I F H L H P C G J I R C L T K E F T H F H U M
N V V H R X C W X P Q M Y K A K A A O T T B N A
H F C V C I N V G V G C E Q F Z L U T W V B T R
W I I M X R O Z K E O Z P O Z Y T P A G B M A O
O B Z N J Y E C C J S L W N F H M L O O P R E
R Y R X A N N T B S W S U Q O F I A C J D E Y R
K Y Z G R N U A I W Z B J N S D N H O O Y M B O
L P V K C I C P F R W E Z C T P S Q M W T H E E
I J U M P D G I W I E X V B V A U E P C M A N O
F X U U X T P P A N N M D F S C R M E Q P Q E S
E T I Q C A O F G L J Q E L X A A Y N C G O F R
B K M Q X J N K T J S G Y N Y B N S S T M M I B
A A D Z P V M E K F B E S X T L C X A L N V T G
L B K V R A N Q M F K J C B S P E U T D F N S M
A Y I W Q D G Q X O X I G U B B L G I M K P F S
N M W V N H K X T N K Y C U R Y M A O Y T M F V
C M A N D A T O R Y B E N E F I T S N J A I R U
E Y I X P F L J R O U B S H P C T D I R N W Z O
F U V Q T P Z T G D X G Y H B X H Y A H Y Y H C
```

Compensation	Health Insurance	Retirement Plan
Paid Time Off	Financial Security	Work-Life Balance
Mandatory Benefits	Voluntary Benefits	Total Compensation
Voluntary	PTO	

Employee Benefits and Their Value

Across

7. An arrangement to provide people with income during retirement, _____ Plan

8. Additional benefits offered at the employer's discretion, _____ Benefits

9. Payment or reward for services or employment.

10. Employee benefits required by law, _____ Benefits

Down

1. The equilibrium between one's job and personal life, _____-_____ Balance

2. The state of having stable income or resources to support one's standard of living, Financial _____

3. The complete pay package, including all benefits and salary, Total _____

4. Additional compensation provided to employees beyond regular salary.

5. Coverage that pays for medical and surgical expenses, _____ Insurance

6. Compensated leave from work for vacation, illness, or personal reasons. (Abbrv.)

I. Key Terms

1. Emergency Fund: A dedicated savings account set aside specifically for unexpected expenses or financial emergencies.
2. Liquidity: Easy accessibility of funds, typically in a savings account.
3. Financial Security: Safety net provided during unexpected situations.

II. Main Concept Overview

An emergency fund is a dedicated savings account set aside specifically for unexpected expenses or financial emergencies. It serves as a financial buffer, protecting you from life's unpredictable events.

III. Matching Section

1. C
2. A
3. B
4. D
5. E

IV. True/False Questions

1. True
2. True
3. False
4. False
5. True

V. Application Question

Sarah's emergency fund helps her replace her crashed laptop without derailing her budget or resorting to high-interest credit card debt. This demonstrates how an emergency fund can turn a potential crisis into a manageable situation.

VI. Reflection/Summary

Three real-world situations where an emergency fund could be useful:
1. Job loss
2. Medical emergencies
3. Home repairs
(Other acceptable answers: car troubles, family emergencies)

Starting an emergency fund as a high school student can benefit you in the future by:
- Developing the habit of saving early
- Providing financial stability and peace of mind
- Setting you up for a lifetime of financial wellness
- Allowing you to face life's challenges with confidence
- Positioning you to tackle other financial goals in the future

(Note: Exact wording may vary, but answers should reflect these key points from the article.)

Part 1: Example Lecture

Introduction
- Define emergency fund: A dedicated savings account for unexpected expenses or financial emergencies
- Explain importance: Provides financial security and reduces stress during unexpected situations

Key Components of Emergency Funds
1. Liquidity
   - Easily accessible, typically in a savings account
   - Allows quick access during emergencies

2. Adequacy
   - Typically 3-6 months of living expenses
   - Amount may vary based on individual circumstances

3. Separation
   - Keep distinct from regular savings
   - Helps avoid temptation to use for non-emergencies

Real-World Applications
- Car repairs
- Medical emergencies
- Job loss
- Unexpected travel for family emergencies

Impact and Implications
- Reduces financial stress
- Helps avoid high-interest debt
- Provides flexibility in decision-making during crises

Conclusion
- Emergency funds are crucial for financial stability
- Starting early, even with small amounts, can make a significant difference

Interesting Insights

1. Only 39% of Americans could cover a $1,000 emergency expense from savings (2021 Bankrate survey)
2. The concept of emergency funds gained popularity during the Great Depression

Part 2: Class Schedule

1. Introduction to Emergency Funds
   - Brief lecture using the outline from Part 1
2. Article Reading
   - Students read the article on Emergency Funds
3. Guided Notes Completion
   - Students fill out guided notes while discussing key points
   - Facilitate class discussion on main concepts
4. Reflection Questions
   - Students answer 2-3 reflection questions
   - Lead class discussion on student responses
5. Hypothetical Scenarios
   - Present 1-2 "what-if" scenarios
   - Group discussion on potential outcomes and decision-making
6. Vocabulary Reinforcement
   - Review key vocabulary words as a class
   - Students create their own examples using the terms

Part 3: Discussion Prompts and Further Exploration

Class Discussion Prompts:
1. Why do you think many people struggle to maintain an emergency fund?
2. How might cultural or family attitudes towards money influence one's approach to emergency funds?
3. In what ways could technology make it easier or harder to maintain an emergency fund?

Further Exploration:
1. Budgeting Techniques: Explore various budgeting methods that can help allocate money for emergency funds.
2. Psychology of Saving: Investigate the psychological factors that influence saving behavior and how to overcome barriers.
3. Financial Products: Research different types of savings accounts or other financial products suitable for emergency funds.

Additional Notes

- Encourage students to share personal experiences or observations related to financial emergencies
- Use the hypothetical scenarios as opportunities for role-playing or problem-solving exercises
- Consider inviting a local financial professional as a guest speaker to provide real-world insights
- Adapt the schedule as needed, potentially extending the lesson over multiple class periods for more in-depth exploration

Emergency Funds

```
L H P O J M R I Y P R T F O J N W O K N X M D G
D I B F F I N A N C I A L S E C U R I T Y G X R
U V N U R R E H N I L G L L Y Y Y W D J Z E G F
M L G H D X F I N A N C I A L S T A B I L I T Y
K L W R Z G A P E E G A X D Z M B C V M I X V H
Y I K Z X Q E O Z I Z Z G A W D M V S J Z T T E
Z K E T A W H T Y R E O C N L M Z E P B J A H X
V Q M D B A W Z O D I L R V K E Y I I G A I U P
R Y E A J N U D D M V S S S L O K O G H A E P E
U N R Z Z E Z T Y Q M V K P U L T G O I I D V N
L X G Y W Q B M O W J A N M K S U B F H A D B S
Q U N E S O D U X V M T D D P A L N S C Y R H J E
I V Y J D Z S V H A D N I O B H L G L S M T H K
D U F C O W B X K T V Y C C C L H I E Q U A Q Z
I V U M Q B K F P R Q T I G T K C Z M M E W N
T P N L U A D A M D F S H G Q R Y M I N E P D A
Y T D A H Q B T I F F D N J V T A B L V C N Y O
O L K M J K I J A K H D T X R Q W N W P J M T D
K P H X F I N A N C I A L G O A L F S E C B A F
S C I C A L F D R E B H B I I Y Z V R F N Q U Q
N K I X O L F S A V I N G S A S E Q W E E A A I
R L N Q K O X Q M O H S D K C Z N J Q V Z R P N
```

Risk Management

Financial Stability

Expenses

Liquidity

Financial Goal

Financial Security

Savings

Automatic Transfer

Emergency Fund

Budget

Emergency Funds

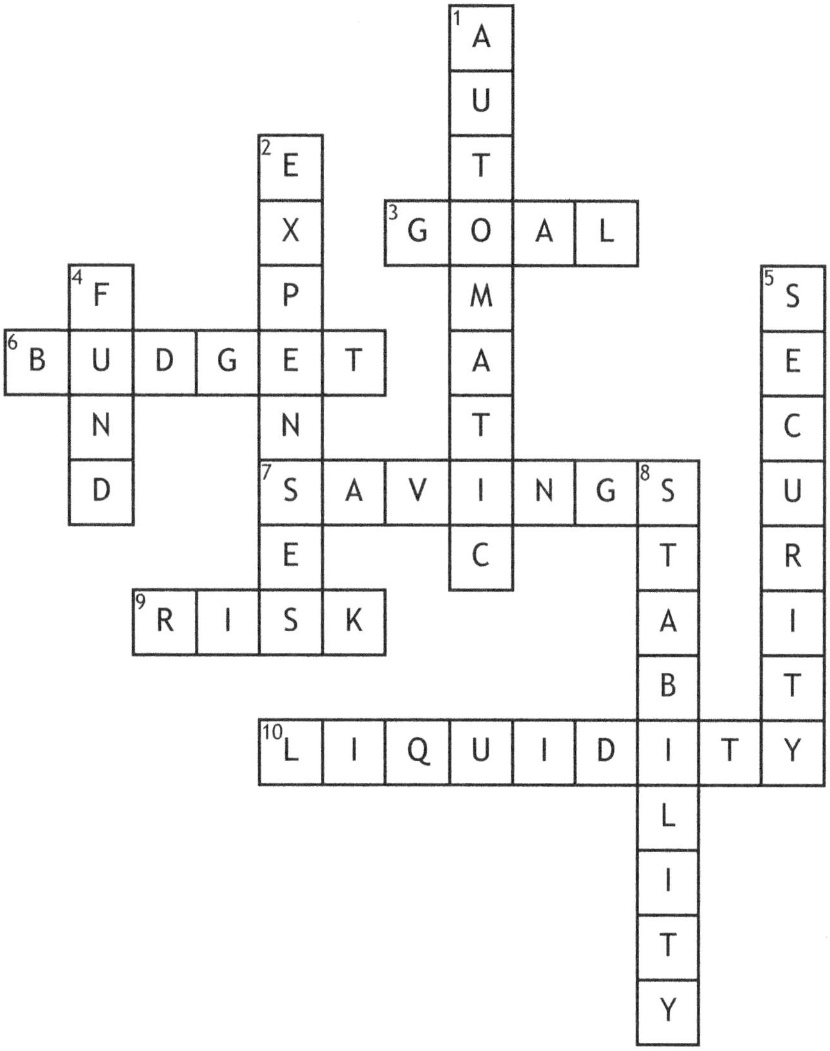

Across

3. A specific, measurable objective related to money management, such as building an emergency fund, Financial _____

6. A financial plan that allocates income towards expenses, savings, and debt repayment.

7. Money set aside for future use, typically in a bank account or other low-risk, accessible location.

9. The practice of identifying, assessing, and controlling threats to one's financial well-being, _____ Management

10. The ease with which an asset can be converted into cash without significant loss in value.

Down

1. A pre-arranged movement of funds from one account to another, often used for regular savings contributions, _____ Transfer

2. The costs incurred for goods or services in daily living or to run a business.

4. A dedicated savings account set aside specifically for unexpected expenses or financial emergencies, Emergency _____

5. The state of having stability in one's financial situation, often achieved through proper planning and risk management, Financial _____

8. The ability to consistently meet financial obligations and weather unexpected financial challenges, Financial _____

Puzzle grid answers:

- 1 Down: AUTOMATIC
- 2 Down: EXPENSE
- 3 Across: GOAL
- 4 Down: FUND
- 5 Down: SECURITY
- 6 Across: BUDGET
- 7 Across: SAVINGS
- 8 Down: STABILITY
- 9 Across: RISK
- 10 Across: LIQUIDITY

I. Key Terms

1. Saving: Setting aside a portion of your income for future use
2. Investing: Putting your money into assets that have the potential to grow in value over time
3. Compound Interest: Interest earned not just on your initial investment, but also on the accumulated interest over time

II. Main Concept Overview

Saving and investing are two fundamental pillars of personal finance that can significantly impact your financial well-being. While saving is crucial for emergency funds and short-term goals, investing helps in growing your wealth over time.

III. Matching Section

B Emergency Fund   A. Ownership shares in companies
A Stocks   B. Financial safety net for unexpected expenses
D Bonds   C. Professionally managed collections of stocks, bonds, or other assets
C Mutual Funds   D. Loans to governments or corporations
E Real Estate   E. Property investments, including physical real estate or REITs

IV. Saving

A. Importance of Saving:
1. Emergency Fund
2. Short-term Goals
3. Peace of Mind

B. Strategies for Effective Saving:
1. Set Clear Goals
2. Pay Yourself First
3. Automate Your Savings

V. Investing

A. Importance of Investing:
1. Wealth Building
2. Beating Inflation
3. Achieving Long-term Goals

B. Common Types of Investments:
1. Stocks
2. Bonds
3. Mutual Funds
4. Real Estate

VI. True or False

T Compound interest is essentially "interest on interest".
T Investments with higher potential returns usually carry higher risks.
T Diversifying your investments helps spread out risk.
F Saving is only important for long-term financial goals.
F It's recommended to start investing with large amounts of money.

VII. Fill in the Table

Aspect	Saving	Investing
Primary Purpose	Set aside money for future use	Grow wealth over time
Time Frame	Short-term goals	Long-term financial objectives
Examples	Emergency fund, buying a new smartphone	Stocks, bonds, mutual funds, real estate

VIII. Application Question

Explain the concept of compound interest using the example provided in the article. How does this demonstrate the power of investing over time?

Answer: The article provides an example where you invest $1,000 at an annual return of 7%. After one year, you'd have $1,070. In the second year, you'd earn interest on $1,070, not just your original $1,000. This demonstrates the power of investing over time because the compounding effect can lead to significant growth over long periods. Your money earns returns not just on your initial investment, but also on the accumulated interest, accelerating wealth growth.

Part 1: Example Lecture

Introduction to Saving and Investing

1. Introduction
   - Define saving and investing
   - Explain their importance in personal finance
   - Highlight the impact on short-term and long-term financial well-being

2. Key Components of Saving
   - Emergency fund
   - Short-term goals
   - Strategies for effective saving

3. Key Components of Investing
   - Types of investments (stocks, bonds, mutual funds, real estate)
   - Risk and reward balance
   - Long-term wealth building

4. The Power of Compound Interest
   - Definition and explanation
   - Example: $1,000 investment at 7% annual return

5. Getting Started with Saving and Investing
   - Assess your financial situation
   - Start small and be consistent
   - Importance of education and professional advice

Interesting Insights

- Compound interest is often called the "eighth wonder of the world"
- The earlier you start investing, the more time your money has to grow

Part 2: Class Schedule

1. Introduction to Saving and Investing
   - Brief lecture using the outline from Part 1
2. Article Reading
   - Students read the article on "Unlocking Your Financial Future: The Power of Saving and Investing"
3. Guided Notes Completion
   - Students fill out guided notes while discussing key points
   - Facilitate class discussion on responses
4. Reflection Questions
   - Students answer reflection questions
   - Facilitate brief class discussion on responses
5. Hypothetical Scenarios
   - Present "what-if" scenarios
   - Group discussion on potential outcomes
6. Vocabulary Review
   - Quick review of key terms
   - Suggest assigning crossword puzzle as homework

Part 3: Discussion Prompts and Further Exploration

1. Class Discussion Prompts:
   - How might understanding saving and investing change your current financial habits?
   - What are some challenges young people face when trying to save or invest?
   - How can technology help or hinder our saving and investing efforts?

2. Further Exploration:
   - Different types of investment accounts (e.g., 401(k), IRA)
     - Connect to long-term investing and retirement planning
   - The role of financial institutions in saving and investing
     - Explore how banks, credit unions, and investment firms facilitate saving and investing

Additional Notes

- Encourage students to share personal experiences or observations related to saving and investing
- Use the hypothetical scenarios as group activities to promote collaborative problem-solving
- Consider inviting a local financial advisor as a guest speaker for a future class
- Suggest students use online savings calculators to visualize compound interest growth
- Adapt the schedule as needed, potentially extending to a two-day lesson for deeper exploration

Remember, the goal is to make saving and investing relatable and interesting to high school students. Emphasize real-world applications and encourage critical thinking about personal finance decisions.

Saving and Investing

```
V Z C U C L C S U R I C H P Z T V N U M X R E K
J H J R A S X R O R S U R Z J S R T Y H S I F Q
F T B P Y W H B Y H G O B H Z R U P K E U I L V
S F O U Y Y J J O L M U T U A L F U N D S B L H
B I N V E S T I N G J K F U E M T K R R J T B R
D P D Z Q P F Z M S S M G G V A L X C I Q Y F Z
G X S G J P C E V D O O H T T U H R Z S V D D N
Y M X O I I H H G T B R L Z P B D O R K E P Q T
L I N H W J Q M P P Q L H Z R B X R D T Z J C X
D I C O M P O U N D I N T E R E S T Z O F Y L A
Z I Q C M J P T A B G M E Y X A O A F L Z H S D
E G V U L G X I X S Y W B S H G E V I E V R O B
M D P E I Z R Q E A V P S V B E G W R R Y H E Y
E M L W R D Z L B V L F V I T V X G H A V P Z A
R M E X Y S I I T I W N T H T D X A W N Z T D D
G W R X B H I T K N O V I S C R Q M S C R S J C
E X B N I I C F Y G Z H V E E Y J H T E T I F G
N Q O G E G B D I W Y I T U V I O K O P A R T F
C R K I X Y G W H C E Y B G S D C Y C S O Q T Z
Y R B U G I Z E N X A H B F C Y H V K S M A D H
F E N Z V D P E C U D T G U M A E W S M N V Q D
U O R W Y M C C R Y I I I A Y V H I V W V Y P T
N K X K Z Y S U S Q R V B O Z S J K M E G A M I
D A K O M Q I Y J D K W T F N D A R X X C K F E
```

Compound Interest

Liquidity

Stocks

Saving

Risk Tolerance

Mutual Funds

Diversification

Emergency Fund

Bonds

Investing

Saving and Investing

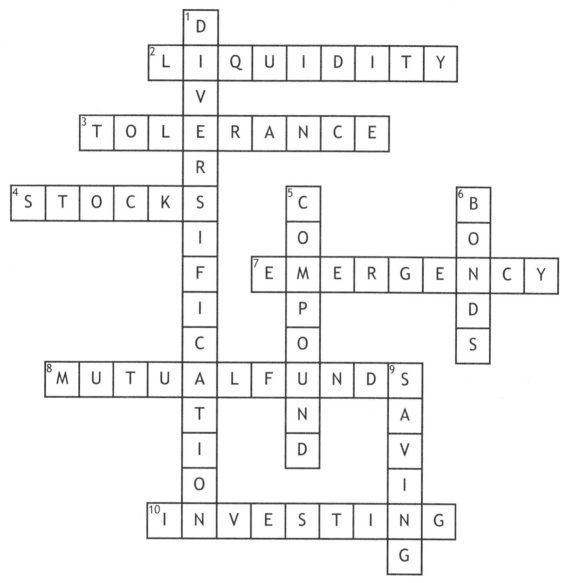

Across

2. The ease with which an asset can be converted into cash without significant loss in value.

3. The degree of variability in investment returns that an investor is willing to withstand, Risk _____

4. Ownership shares in a company.

7. Money set aside for unexpected expenses or financial emergencies, _____ Fund

8. Professionally managed collections of stocks, bonds, or other assets. (2 words)

10. Putting money into assets with the potential to grow in value over time.

Down

1. Spreading investments across various assets to manage risk.

5. Interest earned not just on the initial investment, but also on accumulated interest over time, _____ Interest

6. Loans made to governments or corporations.

9. The practice of setting aside a portion of income for future use.

I. Key Terms

1. Risk: The chance that an investment's actual return will be different from what you expected.
2. Return: The gain or loss on an investment over a specific period, usually expressed as a percentage of the amount invested.
3. Diversification: Spreading investments across different types of assets to reduce the impact of poor performance in any single investment.
4. Asset Allocation: Dividing investments among different asset categories based on goals, risk tolerance, and investment timeline.
5. Time Horizon: The length of time you plan to keep your money invested.

II. Main Concept Overview

The relationship between risk and return in investments is that higher risk generally leads to higher potential return. This means that investments with higher potential returns usually come with greater risk of loss.

III. Matching Section

C. Market Risk: Risk that the entire market will decline
E. Interest Rate Risk: Risk related to changes in interest rates
B. Inflation Risk: Risk that returns won't keep up with inflation
A. Liquidity Risk: Risk of not being able to sell quickly without loss
D. Company Risk: Risk specific to a particular company's performance

IV. Fill in the Table

Aspect	Low-Risk Investments	High-Risk Investments
Example	Savings accounts, bonds	Stocks, cryptocurrency
Potential Return	Low	High
Safety of Capital	High	Low
Best for	Short-term goals	Long-term goals

V. True/False

False - Diversification means investing all your money in one promising company.

True - The longer your investment time horizon, the more risk you can generally afford to take.

False - Low-risk investments always provide better returns than high-risk investments.

True - Asset allocation involves dividing investments among different asset categories.

True - The stock market has historically provided an average annual return of about 10% over the long term.

VI. Application Question

Suggested answer: For a short-term goal like buying a laptop in 6 months, a low-risk investment would be most appropriate. This could be a savings account or a short-term certificate of deposit. While the return might be low, the principal would be safe and available when needed. High-risk investments like stocks are not suitable for short-term goals due to market volatility and the risk of losing money in the short term.

VII. Reflection/Summary

Key points to include:
- Risk and return are generally positively correlated in investments.
- Higher risk investments offer potential for higher returns but also greater potential for losses.
- Low-risk investments offer more stability but typically lower returns.
- Diversification and asset allocation are strategies to manage investment risk.
- The appropriate level of risk depends on individual factors like investment goals and time horizon.

Understanding these concepts can help in making more informed investment decisions, balancing risk and potential return based on personal financial goals and circumstances.

Example Lecture Outline

1. Introduction
   - Define risk and return in investments
   - Explain the importance of understanding these concepts for personal finance

2. Key Components of Risk and Return
   - The Risk-Return Relationship
     - Higher risk generally leads to higher potential return
     - Lower risk usually means lower potential return
   - Types of Investment Risks
     - Market risk
     - Interest rate risk
     - Inflation risk
     - Liquidity risk
     - Company risk
   - Strategies for Managing Risk
     - Diversification
     - Asset allocation
     - Time horizon considerations

3. Real-World Applications
   - Discuss the tech stock example from the article
   - Relate to students' potential investment decisions (e.g., saving for college vs. long-term retirement planning)

4. Impact and Implications
   - Discuss how understanding risk and return affects financial decision-making
   - Emphasize the importance of aligning investments with personal goals and risk tolerance

5. Conclusion
   - Recap key points about risk and return
   - Encourage students to apply these concepts in their future financial planning

Interesting Insights

- The stock market has historically provided an average annual return of about 10% over the long term, but with significant short-term ups and downs.
- Warren Buffett, one of the world's most successful investors, follows a strategy of investing in companies he understands, demonstrating that knowledge can help manage risk.

Class Schedule

1. Introduction to Risk and Return
   - Brief lecture using the outline above

2. Article Reading
   - Students read the article on Understanding Risk and Return in Investments

3. Guided Notes Completion
   - Students fill out guided notes while discussing key points

4. Reflection Questions
   - Students answer 2-3 reflection questions
   - Facilitate brief class discussion on responses

5. Hypothetical Scenarios
   - Present 1-2 "what-if" scenarios
   - Group discussion on potential outcomes

6. Vocabulary Reinforcement
   - Quick review of key vocabulary terms

Discussion Prompts

1. How might your personal goals affect the level of risk you're willing to take in investments?
2. Why is diversification important in investing?
3. How could understanding risk and return help you make better financial decisions in the future?

Further Exploration

1. Different types of investments (stocks, bonds, mutual funds, etc.) and their risk-return profiles
2. Historical performance of various asset classes and what it teaches us about risk and return
3. The role of financial advisors in helping individuals manage investment risk

Additional Notes

- Encourage students to share their thoughts and experiences throughout the lesson
- Use the hypothetical scenarios to stimulate discussion and critical thinking
- Consider adapting the schedule for different class lengths by adjusting activity durations
- Assess student understanding through their participation in discussions and completion of guided notes

Remember, the goal is to help students grasp the fundamental relationship between risk and return in investments and how this knowledge can inform their future financial decisions.

Understanding Risk and Return in Investments

```
Y D N S U E D U W D I V E R S I F I C A T I O N
W E H X O L B Y A T K F E Z U Q G L F A J I O J
U S U H C N B B O F W B V Y Q S R J J B M L Q S
M V O L A T I L I T Y Y P K C V T Y N M X H H K
D D P O R T F O L I O N S I P Z Z F I E G Y A G
I W T B M U M Z T Z A W F T J H T V A C H J A W
N G O D R A A G D V R J I H Z O C Z G J N U A R
F Q Y I K A R B V R Y X V B O O O D O Q I J L
L C F U U N N K N H O D A H W J H X V J C K D I
A Y O J H I T E E O F H N V W A D S S E H B Q Q
T K G A H T Y E T T Q A Y Y N S Y F W L R U U U
I Y J M X Z V T Y V R Q H Z J S K X Q U I P E I
O T E P Z A J W W R V I A V N E C C S N Z I X D
N Y W N I V Q S M U E J S Y M T C J H R M E M I
Y I N F L A T I O N R I S K P A X J H X U B G T
O T H K K U B Y G I Y A F D D L R L R Z D F E Y
Y B Z H X Q C X O G G L A I O L E A O S S U K K
H B U V V R P H Q O X C C K L O T D B M I U Y H
Y E Q K Y Z G B F N S W J V J C U K T O Z H U P
F P P L R Q C V X C P I T G E A R T R R J H I F
E Z T I M E H O R I Z O N H S T N C Q N T O A U
R H Z H Q J W V F N O E N V Z I R Y P V H X M B
R R C D W G H F K Y J A F C I O Q H P U R M H S
T Q L P A O D N U T K N D I P N G S A O P L J H
```

Asset Allocation

Time Horizon

Market Risk

Inflation Risk

Portfolio

Inflation

Volatility

Liquidity

Diversification

Return

Understanding Risk and Return in Investments

Across

6. The gain or loss on an investment over a specific period, usually expressed as a percentage.

7. The risk that the entire market will decline, affecting most stocks and investments, _____ Risk

8. The length of time you plan to keep your money invested, Time _____

9. How quickly and easily an investment can be sold or converted to cash.

10. The risk that your investment returns won't keep pace with inflation, _____ Risk

Down

1. Spreading investments across different types of assets to reduce risk.

2. A collection of investments owned by an individual or organization.

3. Dividing investments among different asset categories based on goals and risk tolerance, _____ Allocation

4. The degree of variation in the price of an investment over time.

5. The chance that an investment's actual return will be different from what you expected.

I. Key Terms

1. Stocks: Ownership shares in a company
2. Bonds: Debt instruments issued by corporations, governments, or other entities
3. Mutual Funds: Pooled investments that invest in a diversified portfolio of stocks, bonds, or other securities

II. Main Concept Overview

Investing plays a crucial role in building wealth and achieving financial goals. The three primary investment vehicles discussed are stocks, bonds, and mutual funds.

III. Stocks

A. Definition: Stocks represent ownership shares in a company.
B. When you purchase a stock, you become a partial owner of that business.
C. Two primary ways to make money from stocks:
    1. Capital appreciation
    2. Dividends
D. Factors affecting stock value (list four):
    1. Company performance
    2. Economic conditions
    3. Industry trends
    4. Investor sentiment

IV. Bonds

A. Definition: Bonds are debt instruments issued by corporations, governments, or other entities to raise funds.
B. Key components of bonds:
    1. Face value: The amount the bond is worth at maturity
    2. Coupon rate: The interest rate paid by the bond
    3. Maturity date: When the bond's principal is to be repaid
C. Risks associated with bonds (list three):
    1. Interest rate risk
    2. Credit risk
    3. Inflation risk

V. Mutual Funds

A. Definition: Mutual funds pool money from many investors to invest in a diversified portfolio of stocks, bonds, or other securities.
B. Types of mutual funds (list four):
    1. Stock funds

2. Bond funds
3. Balanced funds
4. Index funds
C. Advantages of mutual funds (list three):
  1. Diversification
  2. Professional management
  3. Accessibility
D. Potential drawbacks of mutual funds (list three):
  1. Fees
  2. Lack of control
  3. Potential tax inefficiency

VI. Matching

Match each term with its correct description:

B Stocks   A. Lending money to organizations
A Bonds   B. Ownership shares in a company
C Mutual Funds   C. Pooled investments in various securities

VII. True or False

T Stocks have historically provided higher returns compared to other investment vehicles.
T Bonds are generally considered less risky than stocks.
T Mutual funds allow investors to benefit from professional management.
T Index funds aim to track the performance of a specific market index.
F Diversification is one of the disadvantages of mutual funds.

VIII. Reflection/Summary

List four reasons why understanding stocks, bonds, and mutual funds is crucial for personal finance:

1. Informed decision-making
2. Risk management
3. Goal achievement
4. Financial literacy

Part 1: Example Lecture Outline

1. Introduction
   - Define investing: Using money to buy assets with the expectation of generating income or profit
   - Explain importance: Building wealth and achieving financial goals

2. Key Investment Vehicles
   a. Stocks
      - Definition: Ownership shares in a company
      - Ways to make money: Capital appreciation and dividends
      - Risk level: Higher risk, potential for higher returns
   b. Bonds
      - Definition: Debt instruments issued by organizations
      - Key components: Face value, coupon rate, maturity date
      - Risk level: Generally lower risk, steady income
   c. Mutual Funds
      - Definition: Pooled investments managed professionally
      - Types: Stock funds, bond funds, balanced funds, index funds
      - Benefits: Diversification, professional management, accessibility

3. Real-World Applications
   - Building a diversified portfolio
   - Example: Sarah's investment strategy (50% stocks, 30% bonds, 20% mutual funds)

4. Impact and Implications
   - Risk management through diversification
   - Aligning investments with financial goals and risk tolerance

5. Conclusion
   - Recap key points about stocks, bonds, and mutual funds
   - Encourage further exploration of investment options

Interesting Insights

   - Historically, stocks have outperformed other asset classes over long periods
   - Mutual funds allow small investors to access professionally managed, diversified portfolios

Part 2: Class Schedule

1. Introduction to Investment Vehicles
   - Brief lecture using the outline from Part 1
2. Article Reading
   - Students read the article on stocks, bonds, and mutual funds
3. Guided Notes Completion
   - Students fill out guided notes while discussing key points
   - Facilitate class discussion on responses
4. Reflection Questions
   - Students answer reflection questions
   - Facilitate class discussion on responses
5. Hypothetical Scenarios
   - Present "what-if" scenarios
   - Group discussion on potential outcomes
6. Vocabulary Reinforcement
   - Students complete crossword puzzle
   - Review answers as a class

Part 3: Discussion Prompts and Further Exploration

1. Class Discussion Prompts:
   - How might your age affect your investment choices?
   - What are some potential advantages and disadvantages of investing in individual stocks versus mutual funds?
   - How could economic events, like changes in interest rates, affect different types of investments?
   - Why is it important to consider both risk and potential return when making investment decisions?

2. Further Exploration:
   - The role of financial advisors in investment planning
     - Connection: Discuss how professional advice relates to the management of mutual funds
   - Impact of global events on investment markets
     - Connection: Explore how events can affect stock prices and bond yields
   - Ethical investing and socially responsible funds
     - Connection: Relate to the discussion of different types of mutual funds

Additional Notes

- Encourage students to share personal experiences or knowledge about investing
- Use real-world examples from current news to illustrate investment concepts
- Consider inviting a guest speaker (e.g., local financial advisor) for a future class
- Remind students that investment knowledge is crucial for long-term financial planning

Navigating the Investment Highway

```
U I O F Q Q F I R D H B E L J T K K L J J Y J Y
Q N W Z S F P H K N R B H Q Z P W I U P W W Z O
V E W K Y T D O A D K B S G B L G H R Q D D D Q T
D U E M D I O Y M D I M M L Z K C E P B U U P Z
G X D Z B U D C B J Z V J O F K Z G M S N I D T
R L K B F Z R C K O B X E Q R A T Z U U Y O G S
O V G O D F T J K W N Z S R I N M B O M O X P R
L M D I V I D E N D U D N S S N E B I D D Q P X
Y L Y M K O W U B U R E Z B K I R I S B E W O D
A M F P E C E I W U X R W N T C F F P G S I R F
D Z U F S P O P Z B Q X W L O L L I R U R E T D
V U C T C L S A F P D E B B L I I U C Q Q N F H
N D U A U M R G P P P S S V E M Y Q I A S G O S
O F T X U A N N U M N I B E R D H T U E T Q L E
U E T W M O L B D F P N C E A O A U A I I I M
V A F U N K B F M O R Y O F N Y M I L G D M O L
R H G E T S U X U N Y K F B C R W D L R Y I I N
S Q W P C W C X W N O N T Z E J Q M P J J A T U
Q H C O S S M F Z H D U E B Z B A X O V W O J Y
Q E M Q P J M U V R E J Q V V T K Y F A O I C X
L A J O C E C V A M A G H R I Y G V D H U C Y N
F W C V M V O A S S E T A L L O C A T I O N U B
D K R S Q C A P I T A L A P P R E C I A T I O N
O Q B O Z I O E P Z P S U N Q L B V I L J B R A
```

Capital Appreciation

Risk Tolerance

Asset Allocation

Liquidity

Dividend

Portfolio

Diversification

Mutual Fund

Bond

Stock

Navigating the Investment Highway

Across

6. The increase in the price or value of assets, Capital _____

8. The degree of variability in investment returns that an investor is willing to withstand, Risk _____

9. Ownership shares in a company.

10. A distribution of a portion of a company's earnings to shareholders.

Down

1. The practice of spreading investments among various financial instruments to reduce risk.

2. The ease with which an asset can be converted into cash without affecting its market price.

3. The process of dividing investments among different asset categories such as stocks, bonds, and cash, _____ Allocation

4. An investment vehicle that pools money from many investors to invest in a diversified portfolio of stocks, bonds, or other securities. (2 words)

5. A debt instrument issued by corporations, governments, or other entities to raise funds.

7. A collection of financial investments like stocks, bonds, commodities, cash, and cash equivalents.

I. Key Terms

1. Insurance: A contract between you and an insurance company to cover specific financial losses
2. Premium: Regular payments you make to maintain your insurance coverage
3. Deductible: The amount you must pay out-of-pocket for covered services before your insurance starts to pay
4. Copayment: Fixed amounts you pay for specific services
5. Coinsurance: A percentage of the cost that you're responsible for after meeting your deductible

II. Main Concept Overview

Insurance is a contract between you and an insurance company. You pay regular premiums, and in return, the insurer agrees to cover specific financial losses you might face.

III. Types of Insurance

A. Auto Insurance
1. Liability Coverage: Covers damages you cause to others in an accident, including both property damage and bodily injury
2. Collision Coverage: Pays for damage to your own vehicle in the event of a collision with another vehicle or object
3. Comprehensive Coverage: Protects your car from non-collision related incidents such as theft, vandalism, natural disasters, or damage from falling objects

B. Health Insurance
1. Premiums: The regular payments you make to maintain your insurance coverage
2. Deductibles: The amount you must pay out-of-pocket for covered services before your insurance starts to pay
3. Copayments: Fixed amounts you pay for specific services
4. Network: A group of healthcare providers who have agreed to provide services at negotiated rates

C. Life Insurance
1. Term Life Insurance: Provides coverage for a specific period, typically 10, 20, or 30 years
2. Whole Life Insurance: Covers you for your entire life and includes an investment component known as cash value

IV. Matching Section

B Liability Coverage
A Collision Coverage
C Comprehensive Coverage
D Term Life Insurance
E Whole Life Insurance

V. True/False

T Auto insurance is mandatory for drivers in most states.
T Young adults can stay on their parents' health insurance until age 26.
T Term life insurance provides coverage for a specific period.
T Premiums are the regular payments you make to maintain your insurance
    coverage.
T It's important to review and update your insurance coverage regularly.

VII. Application Question

(Possible answers, student responses may vary)
1. Premiums: Important because they determine the ongoing cost of maintaining coverage.
2. Deductibles: Important because they affect out-of-pocket costs before insurance kicks in.
3. Network: Important because using in-network providers typically results in lower out-of-pocket costs.

VIII. Reflection/Summary

(Possible answer, student responses may vary)
Understanding insurance is crucial for financial health because it helps manage risk and provides protection against unexpected financial losses. Insurance offers both financial security by covering potentially large expenses (like car accidents, medical bills, or providing for dependents after death) and peace of mind by reducing worry about these potential financial burdens. As the article concludes, having the right insurance allows you to navigate life's uncertainties with greater confidence.

Part 1: Example Lecture

Introduction
- Define insurance as a contract between an individual and an insurance company
- Explain its importance in managing financial risks

Key Components of Insurance
1. Auto Insurance
   - Liability coverage
   - Collision coverage
   - Comprehensive coverage

2. Health Insurance
   - Premiums
   - Deductibles
   - Copayments and coinsurance
   - Provider networks

3. Life Insurance
   - Term life insurance
   - Whole life insurance

Real-World Applications
- Discuss how auto insurance protects in case of accidents
- Explain how health insurance makes medical care more affordable
- Describe how life insurance provides for dependents

Impact and Implications
- Discuss how insurance affects personal financial planning
- Explain the consequences of being underinsured or uninsured

Conclusion
- Summarize the importance of understanding different types of insurance
- Encourage students to consider their current and future insurance needs

Interesting Insights

1. The concept of insurance dates back to ancient times, with early forms of marine insurance in Babylonia around 2000 BC.
2. The average American family pays more than $19,000 per year in insurance premiums, highlighting the significant role insurance plays in personal finance.

Part 2: Class Schedule

1. Introduction to Insurance
   - Brief lecture using the outline from Part 1
2. Article Reading
   - Students read the article on insurance basics
3. Guided Notes Completion
   - Students fill out guided notes while discussing key points
   - Facilitate class discussion on main concepts
4. Reflection Questions
   - Students answer reflection questions
   - Lead class discussion on responses, encouraging personal connections
5. Hypothetical Scenarios
   - Present "what-if" scenarios
   - Group discussion on potential outcomes and decision-making
6. Vocabulary Review
   - Review key terms using the vocabulary list
   - Consider using a quick matching game or flashcard activity

Part 3: Discussion Prompts and Further Exploration

Class Discussion Prompts:
1. How might your insurance needs change as you become more independent?
2. What factors should you consider when choosing between different insurance plans?
3. How can insurance contribute to your overall financial well-being?

Further Exploration:
1. The role of government in insurance (e.g., National Flood Insurance Program, Social Security)
   - Connects to the concept of shared risk and mandatory insurance programs
2. Emerging trends in insurance (e.g., usage-based auto insurance, telemedicine in health insurance)
   - Shows how technology is changing the insurance landscape
3. Insurance fraud and its impact on premiums
   - Highlights the ethical aspects of insurance and why premiums might increase

Additional Notes
- Encourage students to share personal experiences or knowledge about insurance
- Use real-world examples and current events to make the topic more relatable
- Consider inviting a local insurance agent as a guest speaker for a future class
- Assess understanding through class participation, guided notes completion, and responses to reflection questions
- Adapt the schedule as needed, potentially extending the lesson over two class periods for more in-depth discussion

Remember, the goal is to help students understand the basics of insurance and its importance in their financial lives. Encourage critical thinking about how insurance relates to their current and future financial decisions.

The Basics of Insurance

```
A L S G M J T A U H X U J Q D S V Q T U W A T Q
C Q J O B N F G D I G V Z F E P F S A D M K J U
X C S C W H O L E L I F E I N S U R A N C E L K
T Y O X G Q O Y D P K P V L E W O C W E S U T P
P J Y M C E F I I P B D E D U C T I B L E T W X
C L J I P J L P D I N S U R A N C E O U T T C E
E B Z M I R V L Q L A O H Y D O V L G R E E G Z
M Z Y I F Q E F V P E V R G V I L I U N X R D I
N S X O X F C H H U E W D Z M Y Y A S V V M K N
Q X G W K R W O E Z K P D S U Y V B T T U L L P
T Y I C L M I A P N N K F Y C Y C I V K Y I D T
R K P K J E L J W A S C Z O G Z L L D H S F M P
F G S T B Y I J R L Y I M E J D C I L R M E B H
Y B X Q D D N N F C O M V U F R V T V G Z I R P
F F U C X X J K S Z U V E E E Z Y Y P O E N B B
S P B Z N K M F O M C V Z N C G S C X B C S X B
G W R W Y T D T P M C I N W T O J O G A Q U J N
T F W E H X T J Q L U P R Y O I V P W H R D S
P D P H M N H C Q N Q X Y K I R B E T X K A S U
R E I X Z I H T X T O C F D O C O R R Y E N X O
J U L R O V U S B Q E T F T M E X A B A X C H X
C O J R Q A P M Q U N E T W O R K G G V G E K W
X W V V Z H R Y A V Z W I K Z N N E K L H E T B
R I S K M A N A G E M E N T V Q P R T B P D H A
```

Liability Coverage	Comprehensive Coverage	Term Life Insurance
Whole Life Insurance	Risk Management	Network
Copayment	Deductible	Premium
Insurance		

The Basics of Insurance

Across

2. The regular payments you make to maintain your insurance coverage.

4. Insurance that covers you for your entire life and includes an investment component, _____ _____ Insurance

8. Insurance that protects against theft, vandalism, and other non-collision incidents, _____ Coverage

9. Insurance that pays for damage you cause to others in an accident, _____ Coverage

10. The practice of identifying potential financial losses and taking action to reduce them, _____ Management

Down

1. The amount you must pay out-of-pocket for covered services before your insurance starts to pay.

3. Fixed amounts you pay for specific services in health insurance.

5. This financial product helps manage risk and provide peace of mind.

6. A group of healthcare providers who have agreed to provide services at negotiated rates.

7. Insurance that provides coverage for a specific period, _____ _____ Insurance

I. Key Terms

1. Credit Score: A three-digit number that represents your creditworthiness
2. Credit Report: A detailed record of your credit history

II. Main Concept Overview

A credit score is a THREE-digit number, typically ranging from 300 to 850, that represents your CREDITWORTHINESS.

It acts as a financial TRUST indicator – the HIGHER the number, the more TRUSTWORTHY you appear to potential lenders.

III. Credit Score Factors

Fill in the percentage that each factor contributes to your credit score:

1. Payment history: 35%
2. Credit utilization: 30%
3. Length of credit history: 15%
4. Types of credit accounts: 10%
5. Recent credit inquiries: 10%

IV. Credit Report Contents

List five components included in a credit report:

1. Open and closed credit accounts
2. Payment history on each account
3. Credit limits and balances
4. Personal information like addresses and employment history
5. Public records such as bankruptcies or tax liens

V. Matching

Match each term with its correct description:

B Equifax	A. Detailed record of your credit history
C Credit Score	B. One of the three major credit bureaus
A Credit Report	C. Three-digit number representing creditworthiness
D TransUnion	D. Another major credit bureau

VI. True/False

FALSE Credit scores only affect loan approvals and interest rates.

TRUE Checking your own credit report is considered a "soft inquiry" and doesn't affect your score.

TRUE It's a good idea to keep old credit accounts open even if you're not using them regularly.

TRUE Your payment history has the most significant impact on your credit score.

TRUE Credit reports are compiled by three major credit bureaus.

VII. Application Question

Describe three specific actions you can take to improve or maintain a good credit score:

1. Pay bills on time, every time
2. Keep credit card balances low
3. Don't close old credit accounts

(Also acceptable: Limit new credit applications, Regularly check your credit report for errors)

VII. Reflection/Summary

In your own words, explain why understanding credit scores and reports is important for your financial future:

Answers will vary, but should mention how credit scores affect financial opportunities and decision-making.

How might your credit score affect your life in the next 5-10 years? List two potential impacts:

Answers may include:

1. Ability to get approved for loans (e.g., mortgage, car loan) and the interest rates offered
2. Renting an apartment
3. Employment opportunities, especially for financial positions
4. Insurance premiums in some states
5. Avoiding deposits on utilities when moving to a new place

Example Lecture Outline

1. Introduction
   - Define credit scores and credit reports
   - Explain their importance in personal finance

2. Key Components of Credit Scores
   - Payment history (35%)
   - Credit utilization (30%)
   - Length of credit history (15%)
   - Types of credit accounts (10%)
   - Recent credit inquiries (10%)

3. Understanding Credit Reports
   - Contents of a credit report
   - The three major credit bureaus
   - How to obtain a free credit report

4. Real-World Applications
   - Impact on loan approvals and interest rates
   - Influence on renting, employment, and insurance

5. Building and Maintaining Good Credit
   - Paying bills on time
   - Keeping credit card balances low
   - Managing credit applications

6. Conclusion
   - Recap key points
   - Emphasize the long-term impact of credit management

Interesting Insights to Share

1. The concept of credit scoring was introduced by the Fair Isaac Corporation (FICO) in 1989, revolutionizing the lending industry.

2. While credit scores typically range from 300 to 850, a perfect 850 score is extremely rare, achieved by less than 1.5% of consumers.

Class Schedule

1. Introduction to Credit Scores and Reports
   - Brief lecture using the outline from Part 1
2. Article Reading
   - Students read the article on credit scores and reports
3. Guided Notes Completion
   - Students fill out guided notes while discussing key points
   - Facilitate class discussion on responses
4. Vocabulary Review
   - Review key vocabulary terms using the provided list
   - Consider using a quick matching game or flashcards
5. Hypothetical Scenarios Discussion
   - Present "what-if" scenarios
   - Facilitate small group discussions on potential outcomes
   - Share group insights with the class
6. Reflection Questions
   - Students answer reflection questions individually
   - Discuss selected responses as a class

Discussion Prompts

1. How might understanding credit scores change your financial decisions now and in the future?
2. What challenges might you face in building a good credit score as a young adult?
3. How could improving financial literacy about credit benefit society as a whole?

Further Exploration

1. The history and evolution of credit scoring systems
   - This topic can provide context for how credit scoring has changed over time and its growing importance in the financial world.
2. The debate around the use of credit scores in non-financial decisions (e.g., employment)
   - This exploration can help students understand the broader implications of credit scores and the ethical considerations surrounding their use.
3. International credit scoring systems and their differences from the U.S. system
   - This can broaden students' understanding of credit and how it's managed globally, especially relevant in our interconnected world.

Additional Notes

- Encourage students to share personal experiences or observations related to credit, keeping discussions respectful and privacy-conscious.
- Consider inviting a local financial advisor or bank representative as a guest speaker for real-world insights.
- Remind students that while building credit is important, it's equally crucial to use credit responsibly and avoid unnecessary debt.
- Adapt the schedule as needed for different class lengths, potentially extending the hypothetical scenarios or reflection questions sections for longer classes.

Credit Scores and Reports

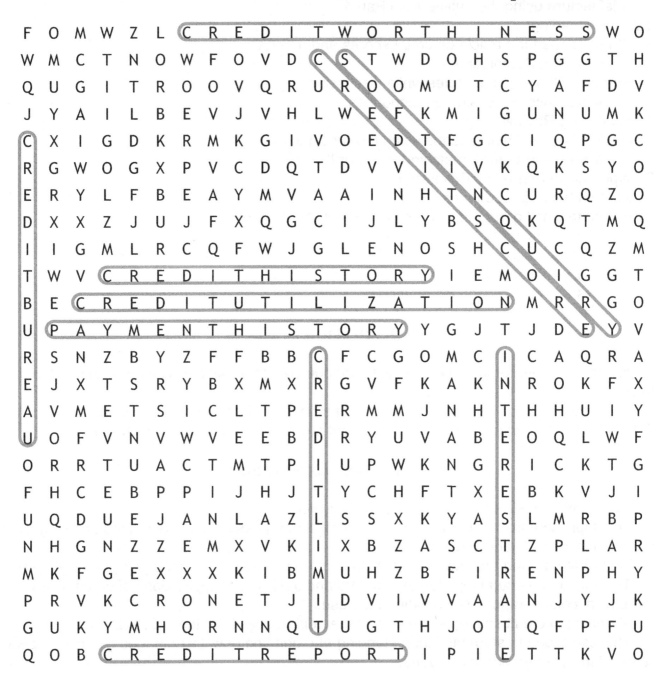

Credit Score

Credit Report

Credit Bureau

Credit Utilization

Payment History

Credit Limit

Interest Rate

Soft Inquiry

Credit History

Creditworthiness

Credit Scores and Reports

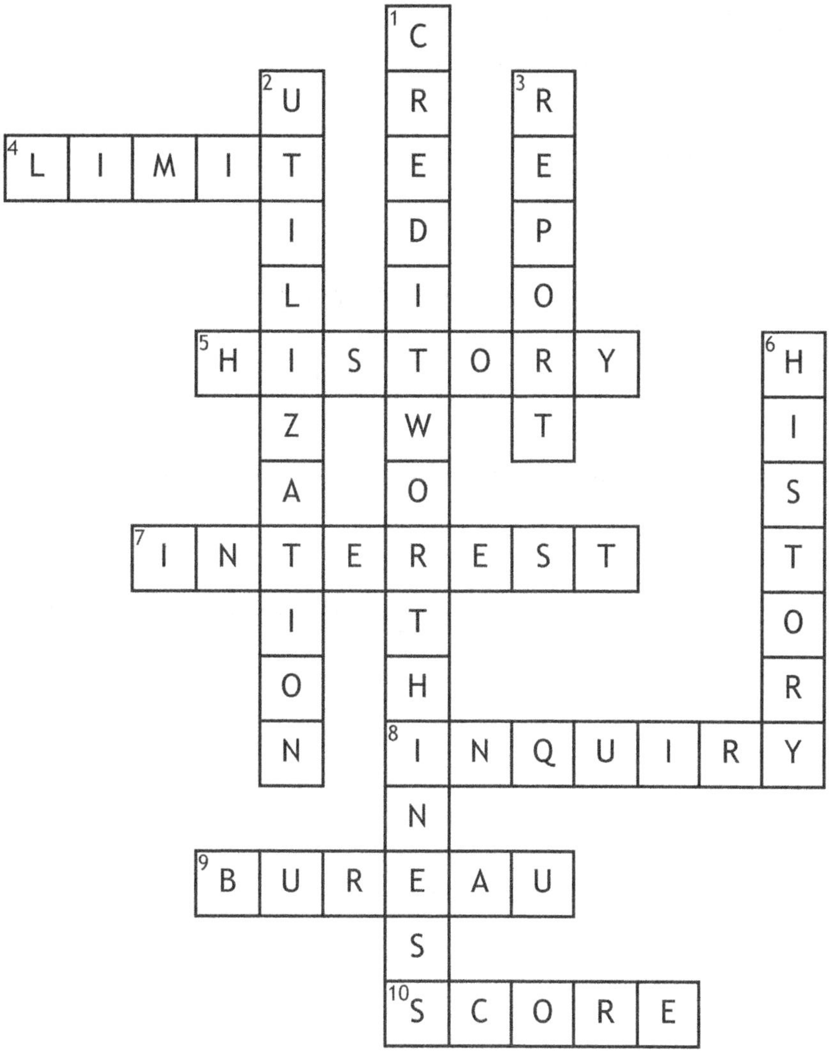

Across

4. The maximum amount you can borrow on a credit card or line of credit, Credit _____

5. The length of time you've been using credit, Credit _____

7. The percentage of a loan charged as interest to the borrower, _____ Rate

8. A credit check that doesn't affect your credit score, Soft _____

9. An agency that collects and maintains consumer credit information, Credit _____

10. A three-digit number representing an individual's creditworthiness, Credit _____

Down

1. A measure of how suitable an individual is to receive financial credit.

2. The amount of credit you're using compared to your credit limits, Credit _____

3. A detailed record of an individual's credit history, Credit _____

6. A record of whether you've paid your bills on time, Payment _____

Crossword grid answers:
- 4 Across: LIMIT
- 5 Across: HISTORY
- 7 Across: INTEREST
- 8 Across: INQUIRY
- 9 Across: BUREAU
- 10 Across: SCORE
- 1 Down: CREDITWORTHY
- 2 Down: UTILIZATION
- 3 Down: REPORT
- 6 Down: HISTORY

I. Key Terms

1. Credit Card: A financial tool that allows you to borrow money from a financial institution to make purchases.
2. Interest: The charge applied to the remaining balance if you don't pay the full amount.
3. Credit Score: A measure of creditworthiness that can be positively or negatively impacted by credit card use.

II. Main Concept Overview

Credit cards allow you to borrow money from a financial institution to make purchases. You're expected to pay back this amount, typically on a monthly basis.

If you don't pay the full amount, you'll be charged interest on the remaining balance.

III. Benefits and Risks of Credit Cards

A. Benefits:
1. Building credit
2. Convenience
3. Rewards
4. Emergency Fund (or financial safety net)

B. Risks:
B Debt Accumulation
C Credit Score Damage
A Overspending

IV. Tips for Responsible Credit Card Use (True/False)

F 1. It's okay to only make minimum payments each month.
T 2. You should aim to use less than 30% of your credit limit.
T 3. Regularly checking your transactions is important.
F 4. Understanding your card's terms and conditions isn't necessary.
F 5. Cash advances are a good way to use your credit card.

V. Application Question

Answers will vary. Look for responses that demonstrate understanding of responsible credit card use (paying full balance, staying within budget) and potential consequences of irresponsible use (debt accumulation, damaged credit score).

VI. Reflection/Summary

Answers will vary. Look for summaries that touch on key points such as:
- Paying the full balance each month
- Keeping utilization below 30%
- Understanding terms and conditions
- Avoiding cash advances
- Budgeting before using the card
- The long-term impact on credit scores and financial opportunities

Students should relate these concepts to future financial decisions such as getting loans, renting apartments, or even job applications.

Part 1: Example Lecture

Introduction
- Define credit cards: Financial tools that allow borrowing money for purchases
- Explain importance: Building credit history, financial flexibility, potential rewards

Key Components of Responsible Credit Card Use
1. Understanding Credit Cards
   - How they work: Borrowing and repayment
   - Interest charges on unpaid balances

2. Benefits and Risks
   - Benefits: Building credit, convenience, rewards, emergency fund
   - Risks: Debt accumulation, credit score damage, overspending

3. Best Practices
   - Pay in full and on time
   - Stay below 30% credit utilization
   - Monitor statements regularly
   - Understand terms and conditions

4. Building a Positive Credit History
   - Importance of credit scores
   - Long-term impact on financial opportunities

Real-World Applications
- Alex and Jordan example: Contrast responsible and irresponsible use
- Discuss potential scenarios students might encounter (first job, college expenses)

Impact and Implications
- How credit card use affects future financial opportunities
- Importance of establishing good habits early

Conclusion
- Recap key points of responsible credit card use
- Emphasize long-term benefits of wise credit management

Interesting Insights

1. The average credit card debt for Americans is over $6,000. Responsible use from the start can help avoid this common pitfall.
2. Some employers check credit reports in hiring processes. Good credit habits can potentially impact job opportunities.

Part 2: Class Schedule

1. Introduction to Credit Cards
   - Brief lecture using the outline from Part 1
2. Article Reading
   - Students read the article on responsible credit card use
3. Guided Notes Completion
   - Students fill out guided notes while discussing key points
   - Facilitate class discussion on responses
4. Reflection Questions
   - Students answer 2-3 reflection questions
   - Lead brief class discussion on responses
5. Hypothetical Scenarios
   - Present 1-2 "what-if" scenarios
   - Group discussion on potential outcomes and solutions
6. Vocabulary Reinforcement
   - Quick review of key vocabulary terms
   - Consider using a matching game or flashcards for engagement

Part 3: Discussion Prompts and Further Exploration

Class Discussion Prompts:
1. Why do you think it's important to learn about credit cards now, even if you don't have one yet?
2. What are some situations where using a credit card might be better than using cash or a debit card?
3. How could credit card use impact your goals after high school (e.g., college, travel, first apartment)?

Further Exploration

1. Credit Reports: Explore how credit reports work and what information they contain. This connects to the concept of credit scores discussed in the article.
2. Types of Credit Cards: Investigate different types of credit cards (secured, student, rewards) and their pros and cons. This expands on the basic credit card concept introduced in the article.

Additional Notes

- Encourage open discussion throughout the lesson, using personal experiences or observations to make the content relatable.
- Adapt the schedule as needed. For longer classes, consider adding a group activity where students create their own "responsible credit use" guidelines.
- Use real credit card statements (with personal information removed) to make concepts more tangible.
- Consider inviting a guest speaker from a local bank or credit union to provide real-world insights.

Remember, the goal is to create an engaging, informative lesson that prepares students for responsible financial management in their future.

Responsible Credit Card Use

```
J  C  C  A  I  W  Q  E  I  T  L  K  W  C  W  U  E  S  B  M  X  D  Z  P
J  W  R  Z  A  R  D  X  E  A  P  Y  H  A  R  O  B  T  F  P  H  L  J  Z
F  T  K  Z  M  N  P  F  B  F  A  V  O  R  D  E  X  I  Y  A  K  K  D  J
Q  Q  M  S  J  S  N  B  E  O  F  N  C  F  P  P  D  W  A  Q  T  Z  N  K
W  X  C  K  K  J  R  U  I  N  T  E  R  E  S  T  N  I  G  Z  A  C  B  T
X  O  C  C  R  Q  G  U  A  O  O  M  R  S  L  K  Y  G  T  P  M  H  P  B
R  E  R  H  R  S  D  K  Q  L  Q  T  P  R  Y  J  F  M  Q  L  J  D  E  H
O  S  E  R  F  E  S  V  I  S  P  V  T  R  R  R  S  M  K  Q  I  G  R  D
P  L  D  D  T  V  D  C  V  C  R  E  D  I  T  C  A  R  D  M  Z  M  P  V
N  R  I  C  R  E  D  I  T  S  C  O  R  E  X  P  L  H  Z  U  Y  R  I  M
M  G  T  Y  P  U  I  J  T  Q  Y  J  U  C  O  H  D  K  N  D  X  U  A  T
L  G  U  J  Z  X  C  O  K  H  L  C  C  R  E  J  M  S  P  K  O  V  K  Q  F
S  G  T  Y  V  S  E  C  I  V  I  A  G  M  J  N  V  J  P  V  V  P  E  P
C  T  I  V  R  V  I  M  D  W  D  S  M  S  P  Q  T  Q  W  X  I  N  S  M
A  O  L  C  E  X  Q  A  W  I  K  S  T  S  S  U  C  A  L  A  Y  C  W  C
S  J  I  L  W  O  A  P  R  S  M  X  N  O  W  S  G  Z  G  F  G  Z  Z  A
H  P  Z  E  A  C  P  R  W  A  A  Q  N  F  R  A  B  J  Z  E  O  C  U  U
A  M  A  R  R  B  N  K  S  Z  Q  X  I  F  S  Y  N  U  L  B  R  L  H  J
D  N  T  S  D  H  M  K  Z  Q  I  X  E  L  Q  U  P  T  B  C  G  A  G  A
V  Q  I  Z  S  D  F  T  S  N  T  X  X  D  L  Y  A  J  T  F  Y  F  T  B
A  G  O  R  S  R  M  I  N  I  M  U  M  P  A  Y  M  E  N  T  G  Z  X  E
N  I  N  S  J  I  I  Q  Z  M  K  F  W  J  S  J  V  N  L  Y  K  R  Q  T
C  S  H  J  Q  D  T  S  F  K  V  R  T  X  V  U  I  K  N  K  N  X  J
E  M  B  D  M  U  V  P  C  G  C  O  J  I  K  F  I  E  K  I  R  Z  N  S
```

Credit Score	Credit Limit	Minimum Payment
Credit Utilization	Annual Percentage Rate	Cash Advance
Credit History	Rewards	APR
Interest	Credit Card	

Responsible Credit Card Use

Across

5. The cost of borrowing money, typically expressed as a percentage of the amount borrowed.

8. A record of a person's ability to repay debts and demonstrated responsibility in repaying them, Credit _____

9. The yearly interest rate charged on outstanding credit card balances. (Abbrv.)

10. When you use your credit card to withdraw cash or transfer money to your checking account, Cash _____

Down

1. The maximum amount a financial institution will allow you to borrow on a credit card, Credit _____

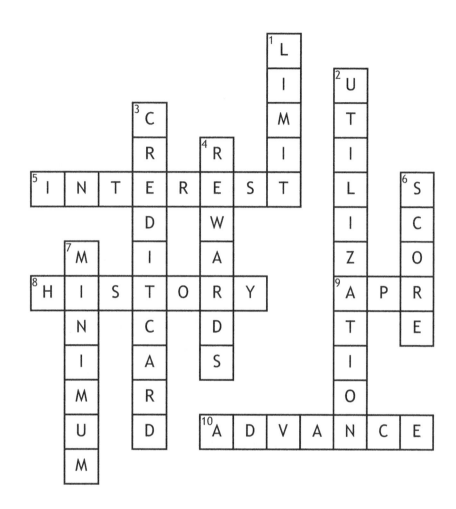

2. The ratio of your credit card balance to your credit limit, expressed as a percentage, Credit _____

3. A financial tool that allows you to borrow money from a financial institution to make purchases. (2 words)

4. Incentives offered by credit card companies, such as cash back or travel miles, for using their card.

6. A numerical representation of a person's creditworthiness, based on their credit history, Credit _____

7. The smallest amount of money that you are required to pay on your credit card bill each month, _____ Payment

I. Key Terms

1. Loan: A sum of money borrowed from a lender that the borrower agrees to repay over time, typically with interest.
2. Principal: The original amount borrowed.
3. Interest Rate: The percentage charged on the borrowed amount.
4. Term: The length of time for loan repayment.
5. Monthly Payment: The amount paid each month, including both principal and interest.

II. Main Concept Overview

A loan is a sum of money borrowed from a lender that the borrower agrees to repay over time, typically with interest.

Loans enable significant purchases or investments while spreading the cost over time.

III. Matching Section

C Student Loans   A. Vehicle serves as collateral
A Auto Loans   B. Often the largest loan in a person's lifetime
B Mortgage Loans   C. Come in federal and private types
E Federal Loans   D. Usually have terms of 3-6 years
D Private Loans   E. May offer forgiveness programs for certain professions

IV. Fill in the Table

Complete the table with information about different loan types:

Loan Type	Typical Term	Interest Rates	Collateral
Student	10-25 years	Lower (federal), Higher (private)	None
Auto	3-6 years	Moderate	The vehicle
Mortgage	15-30 years	Varies	The property

V. True/False

T Federal student loans generally have lower interest rates than private student loans.

F Auto loans typically have longer terms than mortgage loans.

T The interest rate on a fixed-rate mortgage remains the same for the entire loan term.

T FHA loans are government-backed loans with more lenient requirements.

T A larger down payment on an auto loan can potentially secure a better interest rate.

VI. Application Question

Before taking out any loan, the article mentions four important steps to consider. List three of these steps and explain why each is important.

Possible answers (any three of the following):

Step 1: Assess the financial situation and determine affordable borrowing amounts
Importance: This helps ensure that you don't borrow more than you can afford to repay, reducing the risk of financial stress.
Step 2: Shop around and compare offers from multiple lenders
Importance: This allows you to find the best terms and interest rates, potentially saving money over the life of the loan.
Step 3: Understand all terms and conditions, including fees and penalties
Importance: This helps avoid surprises and ensures you know exactly what you're agreeing to when taking out the loan.
Step 4: Consider the long-term impact on financial health
Importance: This helps you understand how the loan will affect your overall financial situation, including future goals and opportunities.

VII. Reflection/Summary

Based on the information in the article, summarize how student loans, auto loans, and mortgage loans can impact a person's financial health. Consider both positive and negative effects mentioned in the article.

Key points to include:
- Positive impacts: building credit history, enabling important life goals
- Negative impacts: potential financial stress, limiting future opportunities if borrowing is excessive
- Student loans: can provide access to education and increase earning potential, but high debt levels can delay other financial milestones
- Auto loans: allow for reliable transportation, potentially improving job prospects and quality of life
- Mortgages: offer a path to homeownership and building equity, but represent a long-term financial obligation
- All loans affect debt-to-income ratios and require budgeting for monthly payments
- Importance of considering how loan payments fit into overall financial plans

Part 1: Example Lecture Outline

1. Introduction
   - Define loans and their role in personal finance
   - Explain the importance of understanding different loan types

2. Key Components of Loans
   - Principal: The original borrowed amount
   - Interest Rate: The cost of borrowing, expressed as a percentage
   - Term: Length of time for repayment
   - Monthly Payment: Amount paid each month (principal + interest)

3. Student Loans
   - Federal Student Loans
     - Lower, fixed interest rates
     - More flexible repayment options
     - Potential loan forgiveness programs
   - Private Student Loans
     - Offered by banks, credit unions, and online lenders
     - Generally higher interest rates
     - May require a co-signer

4. Auto Loans
   - Typically secured loans (vehicle as collateral)
   - Terms usually range from 3-6 years
   - New vs. used car loan considerations

5. Mortgage Loans
   - Used to purchase real estate, typically a home
   - Long-term loans (usually 15-30 years)
   - Types: Fixed-rate, Adjustable-rate, FHA, VA

6. Impact and Implications of Loans
   - Building credit history
   - Enabling major life goals (education, transportation, homeownership)
   - Long-term financial commitments and responsibilities

7. Conclusion
   - Recap key differences between loan types
   - Emphasize importance of informed borrowing decisions

Interesting Insights

- The average student loan debt in the U.S. is around $30,000 per borrower.
- Mortgage loans are often the largest loans most people will take in their lifetime.

Part 2: Class Schedule

1. Introduction to Loans
   - Brief lecture using the outline from Part 1
2. Article Reading
   - Students read the article on Types of Loans
3. Guided Notes Completion
   - Students fill out guided notes while discussing key points
   - Facilitate brief discussions on each loan type
4. Reflection Questions
   - Students answer two reflection questions
   - Facilitate class discussion on responses
5. Hypothetical Scenarios
   - Present two "what-if" scenarios
   - Group discussion on potential outcomes
6. Vocabulary Review
   - Quick review of key vocabulary terms
   - Students create their own examples using the terms

Part 3: Discussion Prompts and Further Exploration

1. Class Discussion Prompts:
   - How might your choice of career affect your approach to student loans?
   - What factors would you consider when deciding between a new or used car loan?
   - How does the concept of building home equity through a mortgage differ from renting?

2. Further Exploration:
   - Credit Scores: Explore how credit scores affect loan terms and approval
   - Loan Repayment Strategies: Discuss various methods for efficient loan repayment
   - Financial Technology: Examine how online lending platforms are changing the loan landscape

Additional Notes

- Encourage students to share personal or family experiences with loans to make the content more relatable
- Use the hypothetical scenarios as group activities to promote collaborative problem-solving
- Consider inviting a guest speaker (e.g., local bank representative) to provide real-world insights
- Adapt the schedule as needed, potentially extending discussions on topics that resonate most with your students

Remember, the goal is to create an engaging, interactive lesson that helps students understand the practical implications of different loan types in their lives.

Financing Your Future - Student, Auto, and Mortgage Loans

```
G J R M B F S C O K I G W I Z O R J B W S Z X J
S V H X I C P I F J V I H M F X L W Q U F F X V
F E D E R A L S T U D E N T L O A N E L O V M I
M C W P R W G V X V R Y I C X Z K J O I J P A C
K V P P K H C Z L F K J D I V D M L Y Q C W Y J
D J R H M K E G J E A R K U O V S N G F O V I B
Z S I F N U D V A U I M J E M M E R P C L Z D F
A Q V L R D O U W O X T I P V C I D O N L B M A
T I A X J H J N J O N M M O R T G A G E A Q T W
I R T R L L I F E H F D U Q V I X S F Z T T R I
Q K E F W O T O W B V E G B U X N G T M E Z S J
Q P S A I I B L V K I Q Y C I Y P C Z L R X E K
W E T L M X N I X H N A S W J Z H T I N A N D C
W W U C Y Q E T Y A R F L L L S E L E P L H Z Q
L R D D Y W R D E X X H O L U L Z O H R A N K L
L K E J M F G Z R R H S X M T M L A Y M L Z D
I M N P S B B A Z A E V U K W M R L V G E Y V N
B D T A N G G A Q Q T S H T S Q U V O G K I Z P
G M L A U O L I P M G E T B R S K D K A S D Y Q
X L O L U X X F G L O Y L R Z H D S I P N S I N
Z Z A Y B S Q L B Q D G K O A N F P F Q P K L Q
I M N J P C O H A Y D G R C A T G F H V V R U B
V X E Z K L W D B H S B C Q I N E G S O U A Z X
V W E Y D Y V R R Q H M E U K Q T T S D L H C
```

Interest Rate

Federal Student Loan

Private Student Loan

Fixed-Rate Loan

Mortgage

Collateral

Term

Principal

Loan

Financing Your Future - Student, Auto, and Mortgage Loans

Across

4. The original amount borrowed in a loan.

5. An asset that a borrower offers as security for a loan, which can be seized by the lender if the borrower fails to repay the loan.

8. A loan used to purchase real estate, typically a home, where the property serves as collateral.

9. A loan for education expenses offered by banks, credit unions, and online lenders, often with higher interest rates than federal loans, _____ Student Loan

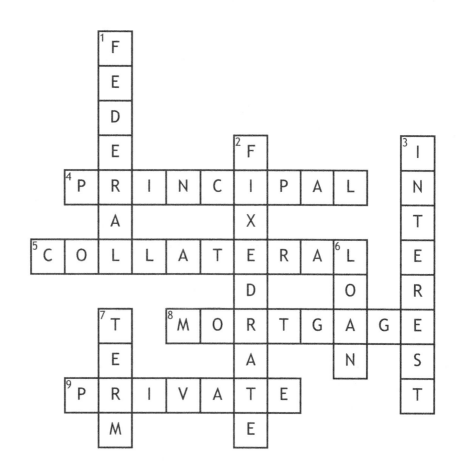

Down

1. A loan for education expenses provided by the government, generally with lower interest rates and more flexible repayment options, _____ Student Loan

2. A loan where the interest rate remains the same for the entire loan term, _____-_____ Loan

3. The percentage charged on the borrowed amount of a loan, _____ Rate

6. A sum of money borrowed from a lender that the borrower agrees to repay over time, typically with interest.

7. The length of time for loan repayment.

I. Key Terms

1. Debt: Money owed to another person or institution
2. Budget: A financial roadmap that helps you understand your income and expenses
3. Debt Snowball: Pay off the smallest debt first while making minimum payments on others
4. Debt Avalanche: Focus on the debt with the highest interest rate first
5. Creditor: The person or institution to whom money is owed

II. Main Concept Overview

Debt management is crucial because high levels of debt can limit your ability to save for important goals, negatively impact your credit score, cause stress and affect your mental health, and restrict your career and lifestyle choices.

III. Matching Section

A. Know What You Owe
B. Create a Budget
C. Debt Snowball
D. Debt Avalanche
E. Negotiate with Creditors

IV. True/False

T Paying only the minimum on your debts can keep you in debt for years.
F Creditors are never willing to work with you on your debt.
T Increasing your income can accelerate your debt repayment.
T It's crucial to avoid accumulating new debt while paying off existing debt.
T A budget helps you understand your income and expenses.

V. Fill in the Table

Managing Debt	Reducing Debt
Know What You Owe	Negotiate with Creditors
Create a Budget	Consider Debt Consolidation
Pay More Than the Minimum	Increase Your Income
Use the Debt Snowball or Avalanche Method	Avoid Taking on New Debt

VI. Application Question

The debt snowball method involves paying off the smallest debt first while making minimum payments on others. This method provides quick wins and motivation. For example, if someone has three debts - $500 on a store card, $2000 on a credit card, and $10,000 in student loans - they would focus on paying off the $500 store card first. Once that's paid off, they would move on to the $2000 credit card, and finally the student loans. This method can be motivating because the person sees progress quickly by completely eliminating smaller debts, which can provide encouragement to continue tackling larger debts.

VII. Reflection/Summary

The six steps for creating your own debt management plan, as outlined in the article, are:
1. List all your debts
2. Create a budget
3. Choose a debt repayment strategy (snowball or avalanche)
4. Look for ways to reduce interest rates or consolidate debt
5. Find opportunities to increase income
6. Track your progress and celebrate milestones

These steps are relevant now and in the future because they provide a structured approach to managing finances and dealing with debt. Even if a student doesn't have debt now, understanding these principles can help them make informed decisions about taking on and managing debt in the future, such as with student loans or credit cards. It also introduces important financial literacy concepts like budgeting and income management that are valuable throughout life.

Part 1: Example Lecture

1. Introduction
   - Define debt as money owed to another person or institution
   - Explain the importance of debt management in personal finance

2. Key Components of Debt Management
   - Understanding Your Debt
     - Know what you owe (creditors, amounts, interest rates)
     - Recognize the impact of debt on financial health
   - Creating a Budget
     - Track income and expenses
     - Allocate funds for debt repayment
   - Debt Repayment Strategies
     - Debt Snowball: Pay smallest debt first
     - Debt Avalanche: Focus on highest interest rate
   - Increasing Income and Reducing Expenses
     - Find ways to earn extra money
     - Cut unnecessary expenses

3. Strategies for Reducing Debt
   - Negotiate with creditors
   - Consider debt consolidation
   - Avoid taking on new debt

4. Impact and Implications
   - Effect on credit score
   - Influence on future financial opportunities

5. Conclusion
   - Recap key strategies for managing and reducing debt
   - Emphasize the importance of proactive debt management

Interesting Insights

- The psychological boost of the debt snowball method can lead to long-term success in debt repayment
- Effective debt management skills learned in youth can lead to lifelong financial stability

Part 2: Class Schedule

1. Introduction to Debt Management
   - Brief lecture using the outline from Part 1

2. Article Reading
   - Students read the article on Strategies for Managing and Reducing Debt

3. Guided Notes Completion
   - Students fill out guided notes while discussing key points
   - Facilitate class discussion on main concepts

4. Reflection Questions
   - Students answer 2-3 reflection questions
   - Lead class discussion on student responses

5. Hypothetical Scenarios
   - Present 1-2 "what-if" scenarios
   - Group discussion on potential solutions and outcomes

6. Vocabulary Reinforcement
   - Review key vocabulary terms as a class
   - Students create their own examples using the terms

Part 3: Discussion Prompts and Further Exploration

1. Class Discussion Prompts:
   - How might your approach to spending change if you had debt to repay?
   - Why is it important to understand debt management before taking on student loans?
   - How could the skills learned in debt management apply to other areas of life?

2. Further Exploration:
   - Credit Scores: Explore how debt management affects credit scores and why they're important
   - Student Loans: Discuss different types of student loans and repayment options
   - Financial Technology: Investigate how apps and online tools can assist in debt management

Additional Notes

- Encourage students to share personal experiences or observations about debt management
- Use the hypothetical scenarios to stimulate problem-solving discussions
- Emphasize the long-term benefits of good debt management skills
- Consider inviting a financial professional as a guest speaker for real-world insights

Strategies for Managing and Reducing Debt

```
S N I H N S D B B L T W W V N R N O M T M G F T
F R G F Y A X C D V V N I H D G F Q R J H W T J
K Z K O Z Z R H W F H T L W G Y J B I J C F X F
W Y I E Q X T M L X R F T Z W Y K M W C R W W I
M P X I O E C D I B E M G J Z A S T D O E M G N
W R F F Y W R L J N H B V N E P U R W N D Q D A
P C V W O I E D C O I D K O J V V W H S I X S N
R U V L Y N D R F E W M A N Y H L Z D O T X U C
E J I L Y T I Y P R V N U Q Y G L Q G L S D D I
M R P N H E T Y E A E E T M C J U Z C I C G Q A
S V V X K R O K G P H L X F P B X O P D O G O L
W M Z Y N E R D W M R S K K C A O G H A R J W F
Z Z B A E S A Y N X P P P W K H Y Y G T E M I R
S Y H N J T D K A I X U B Q Q L P M Q I J I S E
F F O S X T R S A D O U J W A Z N S O E O N I X E
Q U T G I A N L I U K O F D N G I G T N B O H D
N A A B X T D E B T A V A L A N C H E P T V Y O
Q O Y F O E X X F H L Z N B T O A J Z C B L V M
D E B T C O N S O L I D A T I O N K Z K Y A E I
M I F Y D U C A V G O W S D G Q U J O C I M R T
L M Q Z I Q Z W W I E D E B T S N O W B A L L M
M T P Y I B N W V R D P O V Q K M F K P W H O N
T W B E E U U L G E B U D G E T N A Y H Q B E F
L G X S L V A T I W S G Q C U E Q C Q I A V L L
```

Debt Snowball

Debt Avalanche

Debt Consolidation

Minimum Payment

Financial Freedom

Interest Rate

Consolidation

Creditor

Credit Score

Budget

Strategies for Managing and Reducing Debt

Across

2. The person or institution to whom money is owed.

7. A numerical representation of a person's creditworthiness, affected by their debt management practices. (2 words)

9. The percentage of a loan that a lender charges as interest to the borrower. (2 words)

10. The smallest amount of money that must be paid on a debt each month to keep the account in good standing, _____ Payment

Down

1. The process of combining multiple debts into a single loan, often with a lower interest rate, Debt _____

3. A debt repayment strategy where you focus on paying off the debt with the highest interest rate first, Debt _____

4. A financial plan that helps you understand and manage your income and expenses.

5. Money owed to another person or institution.

6. The state of having sufficient personal wealth to live without having to work actively for basic necessities, Financial _____

8. A debt repayment strategy where you pay off the smallest debt first while making minimum payments on others, Debt _____

I. Key Terms

1. Predatory Lending: Unfair, deceptive, or fraudulent practices of some lenders during the loan origination process.
2. Balloon Payments: Loans with low initial payments that suddenly skyrocket.
3. Phishing: Fake emails or websites posing as legitimate institutions to steal your data.
4. Ponzi Scheme: Investment frauds promising high returns, paid using money from new investors.
5. Identity Theft: Criminals use your personal information to open accounts or make purchases in your name.

II. Main Concept Overview

Predatory lending and financial scams are significant threats to financial well-being. They operate by tricking you into parting with your money or personal information and often target financially vulnerable individuals, specific communities, the elderly, or those with limited financial literacy.

The two main categories discussed in the article are:
1. Predatory Lending
2. Financial Scams

III. Predatory Lending

Fill in the table with the red flags of predatory lending:

Red Flag	Description
Excessive Interest Rates	Rates above 36% for personal loans can be predatory
Pressure Tactics	Lender rushes you to sign without fully understanding terms
Balloon Payments	Loans with low initial payments that suddenly skyrocket
Prepayment Penalties	Hefty fees for paying off your loan early
No Credit Check	Often masks sky-high interest rates

IV. Financial Scams

Match each type of financial scam with its description:

C Phishing   A. Investment frauds promising high returns

A Ponzi Scheme   B. Criminals use your information to open accounts or make purchases

B Identity Theft   C. Fake emails or websites posing as legitimate institutions

D Advance Fee Fraud   D. Scammers ask for upfront payments for prizes or services that never materialize

V. True or False

T Legitimate financial institutions will always give you time to make informed decisions.

F If an offer sounds too good to be true, it's still worth considering.

F Sharing personal or financial details is safe as long as you're dealing with a bank.

T Creating a "Financial Red Flags" list can help protect you from scams.

T Predatory lending operates in a legal gray area.

VI. Protecting Yourself

List four ways to protect yourself from predatory lending and financial scams:

1. Be Skeptical
2. Guard Your Information
3. Research
4. Take Your Time

(Note: The article provides these four specific ways to protect yourself)

VII. Reflection

(Answers will vary. Look for responses that demonstrate understanding of the impact of predatory lending and financial scams on personal finance decisions.)

Remember, your financial journey is a marathon. Take it one step at a time, and don't hesitate to seek advice from trusted sources when in doubt.

Part 1: Example Lecture

Introduction
- Define predatory lending and financial scams
- Explain their importance in personal finance education

Key Components of Predatory Lending and Financial Scams
1. Predatory Lending Tactics
    - Excessive interest rates
    - Pressure tactics
    - Hidden fees and charges
2. Common Financial Scams
    - Phishing
    - Identity theft
    - Ponzi schemes
3. Red Flags to Watch For
    - Too good to be true offers
    - Pressure to act immediately
    - Requests for personal information

Real-World Applications
- Example of Sarah's payday loan experience
- Recent news stories about financial scams

Impact and Implications
- Personal financial consequences
- Broader economic impact on communities

Conclusion
- Importance of financial literacy in protection
- Empowering students to make informed decisions

Interesting Insights

1. Predatory lending often targets specific communities, perpetuating cycles of poverty.
2. The rise of cryptocurrency has led to new forms of financial scams, highlighting the need for continuous education in this field.

Part 2: Class Schedule

1. Introduction to Predatory Lending and Financial Scams
   - Brief lecture using the outline from Part 1
2. Article Reading
   - Students read the article on predatory lending and financial scams
3. Guided Notes Completion
   - Students fill out guided notes while discussing key points
4. Hypothetical Scenarios Discussion
   - Present "what-if" scenarios
   - Facilitate class discussion on potential response
5. Reflection Questions
   - Students answer selected reflection questions
   - Brief sharing of responses
6. Vocabulary Review
   - Quick review of key terms

Part 3: Discussion Prompts and Further Exploration

1. Class Discussion Prompts:
   - How might predatory lending affect different communities differently?
   - What role does technology play in both facilitating and preventing financial scams?
   - How can we balance the need for accessible credit with protection against predatory practices?

2. Further Exploration:
   - Consumer protection laws and regulations: Explore how legislation aims to prevent predatory lending and financial scams.
   - Financial technology (FinTech) and fraud: Investigate how new financial technologies are changing the landscape of personal finance and creating new challenges in fraud prevention.
   - Psychology of scams: Delve into the psychological tactics scammers use to manipulate their targets.

Additional Notes

- Encourage students to share relevant personal experiences or stories they've heard, fostering a collaborative learning environment.
- Use the hypothetical scenarios as opportunities for role-playing exercises, allowing students to practice responding to potential scams.
- Consider inviting a guest speaker from a local bank or consumer protection agency to provide real-world insights.
- Emphasize the ongoing nature of financial education, encouraging students to stay informed about new types of scams and predatory practices.
- Adapt the lesson timing as needed, potentially extending the hypothetical scenarios or reflection questions sections if students are particularly engaged.

Remember, the goal is to equip students with practical knowledge and critical thinking skills to protect themselves in real-world financial situations. Encourage questions and foster an open discussion throughout the lesson.

Safeguarding Your Financial Future

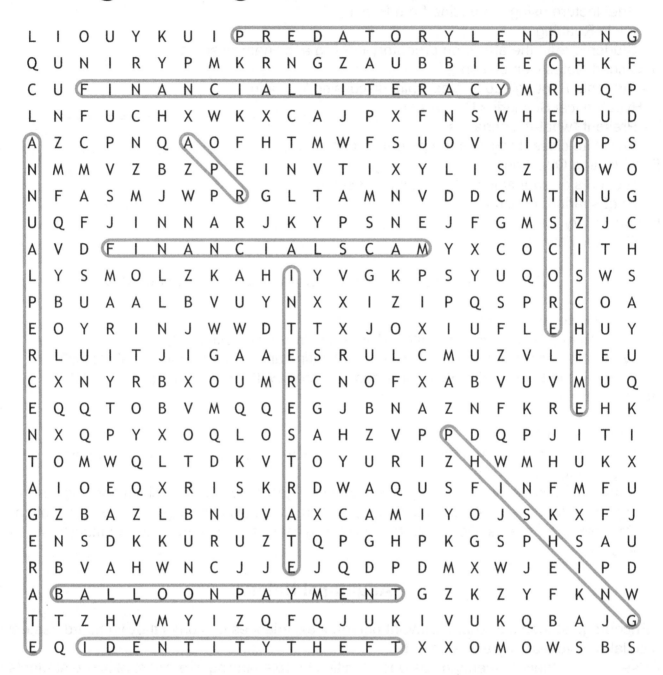

Predatory Lending

Identity Theft

Ponzi Scheme

Phishing

Financial Scam

Balloon Payment

Financial Literacy

Credit Score

Interest Rate

Annual Percentage Rate

APR

Safeguarding Your Financial Future

Across

4. The fraudulent acquisition and use of a person's private identifying information, usually for financial gain, _____ Theft

6. The yearly cost of a loan, including interest and fees, expressed as a percentage. (Abbrv.)

7. A fraudulent investing scam promising high rates of return with little risk to investors, _____ Scheme

8. The fraudulent practice of sending emails or messages purporting to be from reputable companies to induce individuals to reveal personal information.

9. Fraudulent schemes designed to trick people into parting with their money or personal information, Financial _____

10. Unfair, deceptive, or fraudulent practices of some lenders during the loan origination process, _____ Lending

Down

1. A numerical expression based on a statistical analysis of a person's credit files, representing their creditworthiness. (2 words)

2. The percentage of a loan amount that a lender charges for borrowing money, _____ Rate

3. A large payment due at the end of a loan term, much larger than the regular payments, _____ Payment

5. The possession of skills and knowledge that allows an individual to make informed and effective decisions with their financial resources, Financial _____

Crossword Grid

- 1 Down: CREDITSCORE
- 2 Down: INTEREST
- 3 Down: BALLOON
- 4 Across: IDENTITY
- 5 Down: LITERACY
- 6 Across: APR
- 7 Across: PONZI
- 8 Across: PHISHING
- 9 Across: SCAM
- 10 Across: PREDATORY

I. Key Terms

1. Retirement Planning: The process of determining retirement income goals and the actions and decisions necessary to achieve those goals.

2. Compound Interest: A financial principle that allows your money to grow exponentially over time.

3. 401(k): Employer-sponsored retirement account that allows you to contribute pre-tax dollars from your paycheck.

4. Individual Retirement Account (IRA): Personal retirement savings account that comes in two main types: Traditional and Roth.

5. Social Security: A government program that provides a basic level of income in retirement, based on your work history and the amount you've paid into the system over your career.

II. Main Concept Overview

Retirement planning is the process of determining retirement income goals and the actions and decisions necessary to achieve those goals. It involves making strategic financial decisions today that will impact your quality of life in the future.

III. Matching Section

D Traditional IRA
A Roth IRA
B 401(k)
C Social Security
E Compound Interest

IV. Fill in the Table

Step	Description
1	Assess current financial situation
2	Set retirement goals
3	Calculate retirement needs
4	Choose appropriate investments
5	Make regular contributions
6	Review and adjust plan

V. True/False

False Retirement planning is only necessary for people nearing retirement age.

True The power of compound interest means that starting to save early can result in significantly more savings.

False 401(k) plans are personal retirement accounts that are not connected to your employer.

True Inflation can erode the purchasing power of your retirement savings over time.

False Once you create a retirement plan, you don't need to review or adjust it.

VI. Reflection/Summary

Student answers will vary but should touch on key points such as:
- The importance of starting retirement planning early
- Understanding different retirement savings vehicles (401(k), IRAs, Social Security)
- The power of compound interest
- The need to set goals, make regular contributions, and adjust the plan over time
- Consideration of challenges like inflation and healthcare costs

Students might relate this to other financial concepts like budgeting, saving, or investing, and discuss how retirement planning fits into their overall financial goals.

Part 1: Example Lecture

Introduction
- Define retirement planning: The process of determining retirement income goals and the actions necessary to achieve them
- Explain its importance: Ensures financial security and desired lifestyle in later years

Key Components of Retirement Planning
1. Setting Retirement Goals
   - Consider desired lifestyle, travel plans, hobbies
   - Estimate future expenses

2. Saving and Investing
   - Importance of starting early
   - Power of compound interest
   - Different investment vehicles (401(k), IRA, etc.)

3. Understanding Retirement Accounts
   - 401(k) plans: Employer-sponsored, potential matching
   - Individual Retirement Accounts (IRAs): Traditional vs. Roth
   - Social Security: Basic government-provided retirement income

4. Managing Risks
   - Diversification of investments
   - Adjusting risk tolerance over time
   - Planning for inflation and healthcare costs

Real-World Applications
- Discuss how early planning affects long-term financial security
- Provide examples of how small, consistent savings can grow over time

Impact and Implications
- Emphasize how retirement planning affects quality of life in later years
- Discuss the potential consequences of inadequate planning

Conclusion
- Recap key points of retirement planning
- Encourage students to start thinking about their long-term financial future

Interesting Insights

1. The concept of retirement is relatively new, becoming widespread in the U.S. only after the introduction of Social Security in 1935.
2. Due to increasing life expectancies, many people may spend a third of their lives in retirement, highlighting the importance of proper planning.

Part 2: Class Schedule

1. Introduction to Retirement Planning
   - Brief lecture using the outline from Part 1
2. Article Reading
   - Students read the article on Basics of Retirement Planning
3. Guided Notes Completion
   - Students fill out guided notes while discussing key points
   - Facilitate class discussion on responses
4. Reflection Questions
   - Students answer reflection questions
   - Facilitate class discussion on responses
5. Hypothetical Scenarios
   - Present "what-if" scenarios
   - Group discussion on potential outcomes
6. Vocabulary Reinforcement
   - Students complete crossword puzzle
   - Review answers as a class

Part 3: Discussion Prompts and Further Exploration

Class Discussion Prompts:
1. How might retirement look different for your generation compared to your parents' or grandparents'?
2. What are some potential challenges to saving for retirement that are unique to your generation?
3. How can understanding compound interest change the way you think about saving and investing?

Further Exploration

1. Investment strategies for retirement: Explore different asset allocation models and how they change as a person nears retirement.
2. Impact of healthcare costs on retirement planning: Investigate how rising healthcare costs affect retirement savings needs.
3. International retirement systems: Compare the U.S. retirement system with those of other countries to gain a global perspective.

Additional Notes

- Encourage students to share personal observations or family experiences related to retirement planning
- Use the hypothetical scenarios as opportunities for role-playing or small group discussions
- Consider inviting a financial planner as a guest speaker for a future class to provide real-world insights
- Adapt the schedule as needed for different class lengths, potentially spreading the material over two sessions for shorter class periods

Remember, the goal is to make retirement planning relatable and relevant to high school students, emphasizing the long-term benefits of early planning and consistent saving.

Basics of Retirement Planning

```
S  O  H  E  U  R  I  Y  V  R  I  S  K  T  O  L  E  R  A  N  C  E  G  E
M  C  R  Y  D  E  0  Y  C  C  K  K  4  A  E  H  T  I  L  U  F  M  K  I
H  K  L  P  C  T  1  O  C  A  U  G  T  S  1  4  N  1  S  E  U  D  U  D
I  O  R  R  D  I  V  E  R  S  I  F  I  C  A  T  I  O  N  F  F  E  G  G
1  1  0  0  C  R  0  M  L  1  4  G  A  E  D  V  L  H  C  C  T  H  R  G
C  D  T  P  1  E  C  P  Y  D  M  M  E  F  H  O  T  O  A  L  R  R  N  C
4  T  Y  U  M  O  1  L  P  K  S  C  T  N  I  L  R  E  E  Y  F  N  M
L  Y  K  A  U  E  M  K  M  P  D  L  M  V  4  Y  N  P  H  O  K  O  D  G
H  R  D  U  G  N  P  M  L  4  P  L  C  4  G  F  Y  A  M  C  1  4  V  R
M  G  F  S  G  T  O  E  K  O  U  1  S  O  O  U  A  H  4  I  R  R  G  4
L  R  Y  O  D  P  U  P  M  Y  N  M  0  C  V  G  D  G  A  E  4  I  1  C
F  Y  Y  C  V  L  N  N  C  C  E  G  R  F  U  S  4  G  F  0  0  T  D  C
4  H  E  I  D  A  D  K  V  G  M  K  E  C  M  I  I  N  L  D  1  E  0  D
4  N  O  A  E  N  I  K  E  P  P  D  R  V  L  4  0  P  0  C  K  0  M  M
C  M  U  L  D  N  N  T  I  E  L  H  Y  O  I  4  K  4  0  A  P  M  1  N
D  I  S  S  U  I  T  S  4  V  O  V  O  R  K  T  N  M  E  G  L  T  V  L
A  N  P  E  L  N  E  Y  I  0  Y  U  R  S  C  R  Y  S  C  Y  A  I  G  I
O  F  4  C  P  G  R  O  S  1  E  E  Y  P  E  4  0  R  C  O  N  M  G  R
E  L  S  U  H  C  E  G  Y  S  R  F  F  T  M  0  H  0  I  0  K  U  S  A
M  A  0  R  A  1  S  E  U  E  M  L  C  H  L  N  O  A  C  S  E  M  T  P
T  T  D  I  U  O  T  C  C  L  A  M  D  P  F  Y  O  U  L  0  K  H  4  Y
P  I  4  T  A  S  D  V  Y  1  T  D  C  R  M  I  C  A  T  C  O  N  K  O
F  O  Y  Y  F  P  Y  D  F  N  C  4  4  C  M  H  O  4  D  G  O  P  E  4
M  N  1  V  R  L  C  E  0  K  H  C  C  4  M  H  Y  L  V  1  M  H  1  T
```

Retirement Planning	Compound Interest	401(k) Plan
Risk Tolerance	Employer Match	Longevity Risk
Diversification	Inflation	Social Security
IRA		

Basics of Retirement Planning

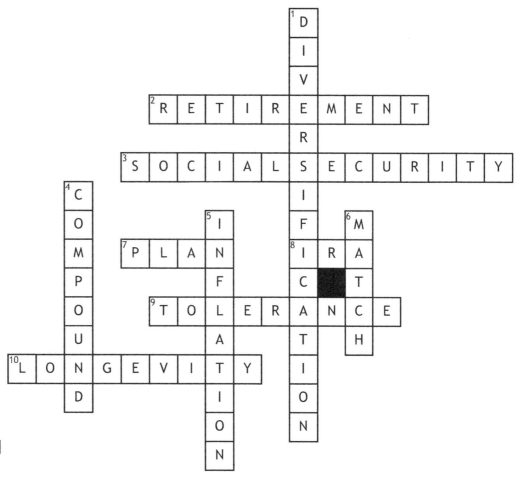

Across

2. The process of determining retirement income goals and the actions and decisions necessary to achieve those goals, _____ Planning

3. A government program that provides a basic level of income in retirement, based on your work history and the amount you've paid into the system over your career. (2 words)

7. An employer-sponsored retirement account that allows you to contribute pre-tax dollars from your paycheck, 401(k) _____

8. A personal retirement savings account that comes in two main types: Traditional and Roth, (Abbrv.)

9. The degree of variability in investment returns that an investor is willing to withstand, Risk _____

10. The risk of outliving one's savings in retirement due to increased life expectancy, _____ Risk

Down

1. The practice of spreading your investments across various financial instruments to minimize risk.

4. A financial principle that allows your money to grow exponentially over time, _____ Interest

5. The rising cost of goods and services over time, which can erode the purchasing power of your savings.

6. A contribution made by an employer to an employee's retirement account, typically a percentage of the employee's contribution, Employer _____

I. Key Terms

1. Banking Services: Financial products and tools offered by banks and credit unions to help individuals and businesses manage their money.

2. Checking Account: An account that allows you to deposit money, write checks, and use debit cards for everyday transactions and bill payments.

3. Savings Account: An account that helps you set aside money and earn interest, ideal for emergency funds and short-term savings goals.

4. Online and Mobile Banking: Services that allow you to manage your accounts, pay bills, and transfer money from your device, offering convenience and 24/7 access to your finances.

5. Credit Card: A financial tool that allows you to make purchases on credit and can help build credit history when used responsibly.

II. Main Concept Overview

Banking services are financial products and tools offered by banks and credit unions to help individuals and businesses manage their money. These services go beyond just storing cash; they include options to help you save, spend, borrow, and grow your money efficiently.

III. Importance of Banking Services

1. Financial Independence: Learning to manage your own money is a key step towards adulthood.

2. Building Credit: Starting with a checking account can lead to responsible credit card use, helping you build a good credit score for the future.

3. Saving for Goals: Banking services can help you save and track your progress towards financial goals.

4. Security: Banks offer protection for your money that you can't get by keeping cash under your mattress.

IV. True or False

F 1. Banking services only include storing your cash.

T 2. A checking account serves as your financial command center.

F 3. Credit cards always help build a good credit history, regardless of how they're used.

T 4. Online banking allows you to manage your accounts 24/7.

F 5. When comparing banking services, you should only consider the minimum balance requirements.

V. Comparing Banking Services

When comparing banking services, it's important to consider:

1. Minimum balance requirements
2. Fees (including hidden ones)
3. Interest rates
4. Online and mobile banking features
5. ATM access

VI. Application Question

If you're starting with a small amount of money and value no fees, Bank A might be better for you. This is because Bank A offers no minimum balance requirement and waives the monthly fee for students. This makes it more accessible and affordable for someone just starting out with banking who may not have a large initial deposit or consistent income to maintain a minimum balance.

VII. Reflection/Summary

Two ways understanding banking services can benefit high school students:

1. It helps in building good financial habits early, setting a foundation for future financial success.

2. It enables students to start saving for goals (like college or a car) more effectively by choosing the right accounts and services.

Comparing banking services helps make informed financial decisions by allowing you to choose services that best fit your specific needs and financial situation. It ensures you're aware of all costs and benefits associated with different accounts, helping you avoid unnecessary fees and maximize the benefits of your banking relationship.

Part 1: Example Lecture

Introduction
- Define banking services as financial products and tools offered by banks and credit unions
- Explain their importance in personal finance management

Key Components of Banking Services
1. Checking Accounts
   - Everyday transactions and bill payments
   - Features: debit cards, check writing, online/mobile access
2. Savings Accounts
   - Setting aside money and earning interest
   - Emergency funds and short-term goals
3. Online and Mobile Banking
   - 24/7 account access and management
   - Features: bill pay, transfers, mobile check deposit
4. Credit Cards and Personal Loans
   - Borrowing options for various needs
   - Importance of responsible use for credit building

Real-World Applications
- Managing part-time job earnings
- Saving for college or a car
- Building credit history for future financial opportunities

Impact and Implications
- Financial independence and decision-making skills
- Long-term financial health and stability
- Protection and security of funds

Conclusion
- Recap the importance of understanding banking services
- Encourage students to start exploring banking options

Interesting Insights

1. Did you know? The first ATM was installed in 1967, revolutionizing access to banking services.
2. Fun fact: Some banks now offer special teen accounts with parental monitoring features, combining financial independence with guidance.

Part 2: Class Schedule

1. Introduction to Banking Services
   - Brief lecture using the outline from Part 1
2. Article Reading
   - Students read the article on Understanding and Comparing Banking Services
   - Encourage highlighting or noting unfamiliar terms
3. Guided Notes Completion
   - Students fill out guided notes while discussing key points
   - Facilitate brief class discussion on main concepts
4. Reflection Questions
   - Students answer 2-3 reflection questions
   - Share responses in small groups or with a partner
5. Hypothetical Scenarios
   - Present 1-2 "what-if" scenarios
   - Group discussion on potential outcomes and decisions
6. Vocabulary Review
   - Quick review of key terms
   - Could use a rapid-fire Q&A format or matching game

Part 3: Discussion Prompts and Further Exploration

Class Discussion Prompts:
1. How might your banking needs change as you transition from high school to college or work?
2. What are the pros and cons of online-only banks versus traditional brick-and-mortar banks?
3. How can responsible use of banking services contribute to your overall financial well-being?

Further Exploration

1. Cryptocurrency and Digital Banking: Explore how new technologies are changing the banking landscape.
2. Consumer Protection in Banking: Investigate laws and regulations that protect consumers in their banking activities.
3. Global Banking Systems: Compare banking services and practices in different countries to understand cultural and economic influences on banking.

Additional Notes

- Encourage students to share personal experiences or questions about banking throughout the lesson.
- Consider inviting a local bank representative as a guest speaker for a future class.
- Adapt the schedule for longer classes by expanding discussion time or including a hands-on activity, such as comparing real bank account options online.
- For shorter classes, focus on the article, guided notes, and one hypothetical scenario, assigning reflection questions as homework.
- Assess understanding through class participation, completion of guided notes, and quality of responses to reflection questions and scenarios.

Understanding and Comparing Banking Service

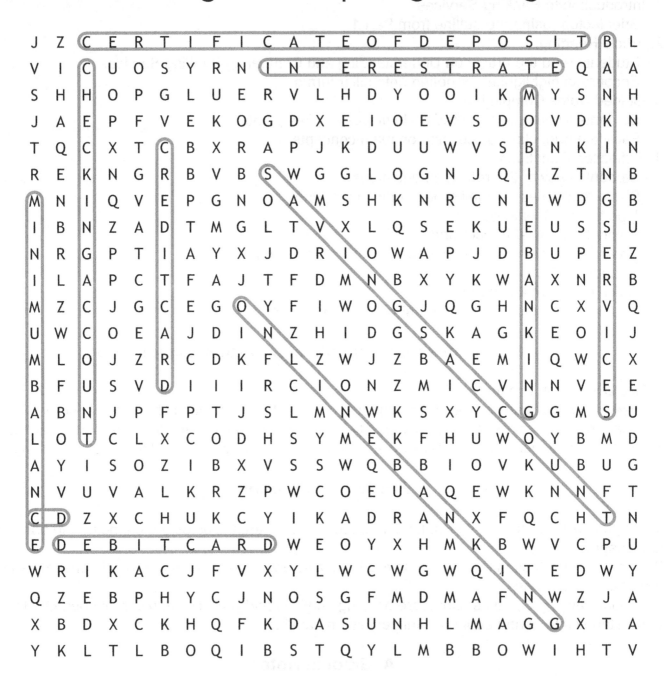

Banking Services

Checking Account

Savings Account

Online Banking

Mobile Banking

Minimum Balance

Debit Card

Credit Card

Certificate of Deposit

CD

Interest Rate

Understanding and Comparing Banking Service

Across

2. An account that allows you to deposit money, write checks, and use debit cards for everyday transactions and bill payments, _____ Account

6. A service that allows you to manage your accounts, pay bills, and transfer money through the internet, _____ Banking

7. A payment card that allows the cardholder to borrow funds to pay for goods and services, _____ Card

9. An account that helps you set aside money and earn interest, ideal for emergency funds and short-term savings goals, _____ Account

10. A service that enables you to perform banking activities through a smartphone or tablet app, _____ Banking

Down

1. The percentage of an amount of money that is paid for its use, typically expressed as an annual percentage of the principal amount. (2 words)

3. A savings account that holds a fixed amount of money for a fixed period of time, typically offering higher interest rates than regular savings accounts. (Abbrv.)

4. Financial products and tools offered by banks and credit unions to help individuals and businesses manage their money, _____ Services

5. A payment card that deducts money directly from a checking account to pay for purchases, _____ Card

8. The lowest amount of money required to keep an account open or avoid fees, as specified by a financial institution, _____ Balance

Crossword grid solution:

- 2 Across: CHECKING
- 6 Across: ONLINE
- 7 Across: CREDIT
- 9 Across: SAVINGS
- 10 Across: MOBILE
- 1 Down: INTEREST RATE
- 3 Down: CD
- 4 Down: BANKING
- 5 Down: DEBIT
- 8 Down: MINIMUM

I. Key Terms

1. Consumer Rights: Legal protections designed to ensure fair and ethical treatment of customers in the marketplace.
2. Consumer Responsibilities: Actions consumers should take to maintain a fair and efficient marketplace.
3. Consumer Bill of Rights: Introduced by President John F. Kennedy in 1962, the basis for consumer rights in the United States.

II. Main Concept Overview

Consumer rights and responsibilities are crucial for empowering smart shoppers in the marketplace. They help ensure fair and ethical treatment of customers and promote informed financial decisions.

III. Matching Section

B Right to safety   A. Freedom to select from various options
C Right to be informed   B. Products should not pose unnecessary risks
A Right to choose   C. Access to accurate information about products
D Right to be heard   D. Ability to voice complaints and seek resolution
E Informed consumer   E. Researching before making purchases

IV. Four Fundamental Consumer Rights

1. The right to safety
2. The right to be informed
3. The right to choose
4. The right to be heard

V. True or False

T Consumer responsibilities include using products as intended.
T The right to safety means products should not pose unnecessary risks to health or well-being.
T Consumers have a responsibility to report fraudulent or deceptive practices.
T Understanding contracts is a consumer responsibility.
T Consumer rights apply to various types of purchases, including buying a smartphone.

VI. Fill in the Table

Complete the table with examples of how consumer rights and responsibilities apply when purchasing a smartphone:

Consumer Right/ Responsibility	Example for Smartphone Purchase
Right to safety	Expect that the phone won't overheat or explode during normal use
Right to be informed	The store must provide accurate information about the phone's features, warranty, and return policy
Consumer responsibility	Research different phone models and read reviews before making a decision
Right to be heard	If the phone is defective, you have the right to complain and seek a resolution

VII. Application Question

Based on the article, list three steps you can take to become a more empowered consumer. How might these steps help you make better financial decisions?

Possible answers include:
1. Stay informed about consumer protection laws and rights in different industries.
2. Read the fine print and review contracts carefully before signing.
3. Ask questions to seek clarification on products, services, or policies.
4. Document everything, keeping records of purchases, warranties, and communication with businesses.
5. Know where to turn by familiarizing yourself with consumer protection agencies and resources.

These steps can help make better financial decisions by:
- Increasing awareness of rights and protections
- Avoiding hidden fees or unfavorable terms
- Ensuring understanding of what is being purchased
- Providing evidence in case of disputes
- Knowing how to seek help if issues arise

VIII. Reflection/Summary

Student summaries should touch on key points such as:
- Consumer rights protect customers in the marketplace
- Consumer responsibilities ensure consumers play their part in maintaining a fair market
- Understanding both rights and responsibilities leads to better financial decisions
- Exercising consumer rights and fulfilling responsibilities contributes to a fair and ethical marketplace for everyone
- Being an informed and responsible consumer helps improve product quality and prevent fraud

Students should also reflect on how these concepts apply to their own experiences as young consumers.

Part 1: Example Lecture

Introduction
- Define consumer rights and responsibilities
- Explain their importance in personal finance and the marketplace

Key Components of Consumer Rights and Responsibilities
1. Four Fundamental Consumer Rights
   - Right to safety
   - Right to be informed
   - Right to choose
   - Right to be heard

2. Consumer Responsibilities
   - Being an informed consumer
   - Reading and understanding contracts
   - Using products and services as intended
   - Reporting fraudulent or deceptive practices

3. Real-World Applications
   - Smartphone purchase example
   - Online shopping scenarios

4. Impact and Implications
   - Better financial decisions
   - Increased consumer confidence
   - Improved product quality
   - Fraud prevention

Conclusion
- Summarize the importance of understanding consumer rights and responsibilities
- Encourage students to apply these concepts in their daily lives

Interesting Insights

1. The Better Business Bureau receives over 1 million consumer complaints annually, highlighting the importance of consumer awareness.
2. Many countries have adapted the original Consumer Bill of Rights to address modern challenges like e-commerce and data privacy.

Part 2: Class Schedule

1. Introduction to Consumer Rights and Responsibilities
   - Brief lecture using the outline from Part 1
2. Article Reading
   - Students read the article on Consumer Rights and Responsibilities
3. Guided Notes Completion
   - Students fill out guided notes while discussing key points
   - Facilitate class discussion on responses
4. Reflection Questions
   - Students answer reflection questions
   - Facilitate class discussion on responses
5. Hypothetical Scenarios
   - Present "what-if" scenarios
   - Group discussion on potential outcomes
6. Vocabulary Reinforcement
   - Students complete crossword puzzle
   - Review answers as a class

Part 3: Discussion Prompts and Further Exploration

Class Discussion Prompts:
1. How might understanding consumer rights change your approach to making purchases?
2. What challenges do you think consumers face in the digital age?
3. How can fulfilling consumer responsibilities contribute to a fairer marketplace?

Further Exploration

1. Consumer Protection Laws: Explore specific laws that protect consumers in your state or country.
2. Digital Consumer Rights: Investigate how consumer rights apply to digital products and services.
3. Consumer Advocacy Groups: Research organizations that work to protect consumer rights and their impact on policy-making.

Additional Notes

- Encourage students to share personal experiences related to consumer rights throughout the lesson.
- Adapt the schedule as needed, potentially extending the hypothetical scenarios section if students are particularly engaged.
- Consider inviting a guest speaker from a local consumer protection agency for a future class.

Remember to use all activities as opportunities for class discussion and to assess student understanding throughout the lesson. Emphasize the real-world applications of these concepts to make the material more relevant and engaging for students.

Consumer Rights and Responsibilities

```
C O N S U M E R P R O T E C T I O N A G E N C Y
O I F S A E L B O Q L J J X K P D S L Q O Q Q D
N Z U H K O W Z L M W R Y J M Y N B X M N T C G
S R I G H T T O B E H E A R D L E Y K I T T S M
U L Q N X P H B I N R C K C S L E K Y Z A V I A
M E E O F O M P Z K Y I W Z L X W A P H Y N D R
E N B A O N D A I C R G I O D B V R S P S L K E
R Q H E L X R T R L R O L H Y X G V V Z O C D T
R G Z T I S I M I P J K N D T G J Z F Z Z V I P
E W Y R Y L D J E Y C Q Q S M T Q N B T S Y G L
S Z C C B V O B C D V X N R U K O A I Q J L J A
P G E F Q Q K Z M O C M E W E M A S J X T H X C
O P N L N Y F G F D Q O Y V M Q E A A E X S E E
N P N R P G B H M H V X N I P L B R Q F M Q J E
S B K H W V L R O D K N C S W P O F R D E F J Z
I I D S P I R H O K O U P A U X B M E I L T J O
B V N L C O G X G C V C G S N M V Y B J G U Y C
I U S H V V R N W J S A U J C W E V I W Z H T A
L M T M Z I O F B G X A B D O B P R H D E Z T A
I H O C O N S U M E R B I L L O F R I G H T S S
T R I G H T T O B E I N F O R M E D X L P L J Z
I U I G O J F C D J J Z Q B P M I G D K X A A R
E J S F D A O K R I G H T T O C H O O S E F D S
S Q S C L T J D N V P Y J Y P X A Q A N B I M V
```

Consumer Rights	Consumer Responsibilities	Consumer Bill of Rights
Right to Safety	Right to Be Informed	Right to Choose
Right to Be Heard	Informed Consumer	Consumer Protection Agency
Marketplace		

Consumer Rights and Responsibilities

Across

3. Legal protections designed to ensure fair and ethical treatment of customers in the marketplace, Consumer _____

5. The consumer protection ensuring freedom to select from a variety of options in the marketplace without undue pressure or manipulation, Right to _____

8. The arena, physical or digital, where goods and services are bought and sold.

10. Actions and obligations of consumers to maintain a fair and efficient marketplace, Consumer _____

Down

1. A set of principles introduced by President John F. Kennedy in 1962, forming the basis for consumer protections in the United States, Consumer _____ __ _____

2. Government organizations responsible for protecting consumer interests and enforcing consumer rights, Consumer _____ Agency

4. The consumer protection ensuring that products and services do not pose unnecessary risks to health or well-being, Right to _____

6. The consumer protection providing the ability to voice complaints and seek resolution for legitimate grievances, Right to Be _____

7. A shopper who researches products and services before making purchases, _____ Consumer

9. The consumer protection guaranteeing access to accurate information about products and services, including prices, terms, and conditions, Right to Be _____

Crossword solution grid:

- 1 Down: BILL
- 2 Down: PROTECTION
- 3 Across: RIGHTS
- 4 Down: SAFETY
- 5 Across: CHOOSE
- 6 Down: HEARD
- 7 Down: INFORMED
- 8 Across: MARKETPLACE
- 9 Down: INFORMED
- 10 Across: RESPONSIBILITIES

I. Key Terms
1. Financial Advisor: A professional who provides financial advice and guidance.
2. Credentials: Recognized certifications or qualifications in financial matters.
3. Conflict of Interest: A situation where an advisor's personal interest might interfere with providing unbiased advice.
4. Fee-only Advisor: An advisor who charges a flat rate or percentage of assets managed.
5. Red Flags: Warning signs to watch out for when evaluating financial advice.

II. Main Concept Overview
Evaluating financial information and advice is crucial because it can save you from costly mistakes and help you make informed decisions about your money.

The goal of evaluating financial advice is not to find perfect advice, but to gather enough reliable information to make confident choices about your financial future.

III. Matching Section
C. Certified Financial Planner (CFP)
B. Chartered Financial Analyst (CFA)
A. Credentials
D. Transparency
E. Compensation

IV. True or False
F Professional financial advisors are the only reliable source of financial information.
T It's important to approach all financial advice with a critical eye and healthy skepticism.
F Doing your own research is unnecessary if you have a certified financial advisor.
T Even good financial advice may not be right for everyone's specific situation.
T Promises of guaranteed high returns with little or no risk are a common red flag.

V. Fill in the Table: Key Factors in Evaluating Financial Information

Factor	Example from the article
Credentials and Qualifications	Look for advisors with recognized financial certifications such as CFP or CFA
Experience and Track Record	Consider how long they've been providing financial advice and their past performance
Potential Conflicts of Interest	Be aware of how financial advisors are compensated (e.g., commissions vs. fee-only)
Transparency and Communication	Ability to explain complex concepts in understandable terms and be open about fees and strategies

VI. Application Question

(Answers will vary, but should include points such as:)
- Recognize the promise of "guaranteed" high returns with no risk as a red flag
- Be skeptical of advice from social media influencers who may not have proper credentials
- Research the investment opportunity independently using reputable sources
- Consider seeking a second opinion from a certified financial advisor
- Avoid making quick decisions without thorough research

VII. Reflection/Summary

(Answers will vary, but may include points such as:)
1. It's important to consider the credentials and qualifications of financial advisors.
2. Be aware of potential conflicts of interest in financial advice.
3. Always do your own research and consider multiple sources of information.

How these skills might impact future financial decision-making:
These skills can help in making more informed and confident financial decisions, avoiding potential scams or unsuitable advice, and developing a more critical approach to evaluating financial information from various sources.

Part 1: Example Lecture

Introduction
- Define financial information and advice
- Explain the importance of evaluating financial advice in personal financial management

Key Components of Evaluating Financial Advice
1. Sources of Financial Advice
   - Professional advisors
   - Online resources
   - Personal networks
2. Credentials and Qualifications
   - Importance of recognized certifications
   - Experience and track record
3. Identifying Conflicts of Interest
   - Different compensation models
   - Potential biases in advice
4. Recognizing Red Flags
   - Unrealistic promises
   - Pressure tactics
   - Lack of transparency

Real-World Applications
- Evaluating investment opportunities
- Choosing financial advisors
- Making informed financial decisions

Impact and Implications
- Long-term financial health
- Protection against fraud and poor advice
- Improved financial literacy and confidence

Conclusion
- Recap the importance of critical evaluation
- Encourage ongoing learning about personal finance

Interesting Insights

1. The financial advice industry is rapidly changing with the rise of robo-advisors and AI-powered financial planning tools.
2. Studies show that individuals who regularly seek and evaluate financial advice tend to have better long-term financial outcomes.

Part 2: Class Schedule

1. Introduction to Evaluating Financial Advice
   - Brief lecture using the outline from Part 1
2. Article Reading
   - Students read the article on evaluating financial information and advice
3. Guided Notes Completion
   - Students fill out guided notes while discussing key points
   - Facilitate class discussion on responses
4. Reflection Questions
   - Students answer 2-3 reflection questions
   - Share responses in small groups or as a class
5. Hypothetical Scenarios
   - Present 1-2 "what-if" scenarios
   - Group discussion on potential outcomes and decision-making processes
6. Vocabulary Review
   - Quick review of key vocabulary terms
   - Could use a rapid-fire Q&A format or a quick matching game

Part 3: Discussion Prompts and Further Exploration

Class Discussion Prompts:
1. Why do you think it's important to evaluate financial advice, even if it comes from a trusted source?
2. How might social media influence the way people receive and perceive financial advice?
3. What skills do you think are most important when evaluating financial information?

Further Exploration

1. The psychology of financial decision-making: Explore how emotions and cognitive biases can affect our financial choices.
2. The evolution of financial advice: Investigate how technology is changing the landscape of financial advising, including the rise of robo-advisors.
3. Regulation in the financial advice industry: Research the laws and regulations that govern financial advisors and how they protect consumers.

Additional Notes

- Encourage students to share personal experiences or observations related to financial advice, creating a more engaging and relatable discussion.
- Consider inviting a guest speaker (e.g., a local financial advisor or banker) to provide real-world insights.
- Use current events or recent financial news stories to illustrate the importance of evaluating financial information.
- Adapt the schedule as needed for different class lengths. For shorter classes, focus on the article, guided notes, and one or two key activities.
- Assess student understanding through their participation in discussions, completion of guided notes, and responses to reflection questions and hypothetical scenarios.
- Emphasize that evaluating financial advice is an ongoing skill that students will use throughout their lives, not just for major financial decisions.

Evaluating Financial Information and Advice

```
Z Y A Y S Y Q V O X Y D V T L G Z C N R X F D T
N I X Q O C L J N A G Q L Z J P E K W I V A M R
Q W T M M S T B J Q U L Z C K K E V E S I D S A
C F M W I A B J T Z W U N C E A C Q W K U I B N
E O V O W O H U X J W C J I P S N D F T K Y C S
Y X N D T Y C P L F P D W P L V T O E O N Y M P
F Z F F U B Q R V V Q V D P O R K P E L C U F A
I X I I L W R H E V J J R P O X K T O E Z O R R
N S N B J I A K V D E B D A Q B A X N R N M L E
A R A M E C Y D P E Z E H V D F H L A D O R N N
N O N S H G C T K B H N N H H R M Y N M Z O C C
C J C R N M F J O B Q V T I V O L L A C R C Z Y
I P I E E Z P Q J F H S U I F M A C D E U O I A
A M A D V D Q F R H I E P H A V O C V H B W O G
L F L D Z B F L S Q T N Z O I L D Q I H H H U R
A M L A V R M L O C R I T G L L S I S E U P O E
D I I S N N G Y A K M U W E A M Y G O X R Q K T
V Z T P Y R H D H G C J N Z R D I T R Q F X L T
I W E X O I N L X Y S C R J Q E B S I I T R V J
S S R S X J E Y Z W Z H L N B H S E N Z L Q F U
O B A C W K O L S M V D G A J I C T U M N P I L
R R C A E U X S Q D L V T P M O D U K H Q P E O
X B Y X D I V E R S I F I C A T I O N P J H E K
H A X K J U T C O E W T F Y S Q K X M N G X T V
```

Financial Literacy

Financial Advisor

Conflict of Interest

Fee-only Advisor

Risk Tolerance

Red Flags

Diversification

Transparency

CFP

Credentials

Evaluating Financial Information and Advice

Across

3. A financial advisor who is compensated solely by fees paid by clients, rather than commissions on financial products sold, ___-_____

4. The quality of being open, clear, and honest in communication and business practices.

6. A situation where a person's personal interest might interfere with their professional responsibilities, _____ of Interest

7. Warning signs or indicators of potential problems or issues, particularly in financial advice or investments. (2 words)

9. The degree of variability in investment returns that an individual is willing to withstand, _____ Tolerance

10. The practice of spreading investments among different financial instruments to reduce risk.

Down

1. The ability to understand and effectively use various financial skills, including personal financial management and investing, Financial _____

2. Professional qualifications or achievements that demonstrate a person's expertise in a particular field.

5. A professional certification for financial advisors who have met specific education and experience requirements. (Abbrv.)

8. A professional who provides guidance and advice on managing finances and investments, Financial _____

Crossword grid solution

1 Down: LITERACY
2 Down: CREDENTIALS
3 Across: FEE ONLY
4 Across: TRANSPARENCY
5 Down: CFP
6 Across: CONFLICT
7 Across: RED FLAGS
8 Down: ADVISOR
9 Across: RISK
10 Across: DIVERSIFICATION

I. Key Terms

1. Comprehensive Financial Plan: A detailed strategy that outlines your current financial situation, defines your financial goals, and charts a course to achieve those goals.
2. Net Worth: A snapshot of your current financial position, listing all your assets (what you own) and liabilities (what you owe).
3. Budget: A detailed plan of your income and expenses, helping you understand and control your cash flow.
4. Financial Goals: The destinations on your financial journey. They can be short-term, medium-term, or long-term.

II. Main Concept Overview

A comprehensive financial plan is a detailed strategy that outlines your current financial situation, defines your financial goals, and charts a course to achieve those goals.

III. Matching Section

C Financial Goals
D Net Worth Statement
A Budget
B Savings and Investment Strategy
E Retirement Planning

A. A detailed plan of income and expenses
B. Strategy to grow wealth over time
C. Destinations on your financial journey
D. Snapshot of current financial position
E. Ensuring funds for life after work

IV. True or False

False A comprehensive financial plan is a one-time document that never needs to be updated.
True The net worth statement lists all your assets and liabilities.
False Budgeting is not an important part of a comprehensive financial plan.
True Risk management includes insurance policies to protect you and your assets.
True A good financial plan often leads to increased savings.

V. Application Question

Sarah, a 28-year-old marketing professional, created a comprehensive financial plan. How did this plan help her achieve her financial goals? Provide at least two specific examples from the article.

Sample Answer: Sarah's comprehensive financial plan helped her achieve her financial goals in two main ways:
1. It helped her realize she was spending too much on discretionary items and not saving enough for her goal of buying a house. By adjusting her budget and setting up automatic savings, she was able to save $20,000 for a down payment in just two years.
2. The plan also helped her start contributing to her retirement account early, putting her on track for a comfortable retirement.

VI. Reflection/Summary

Summarize the main benefits of having a comprehensive financial plan in your own words. How might creating such a plan impact your own financial decisions?

Sample Answer: The main benefits of having a comprehensive financial plan include:
1. Clarity and direction in your financial life
2. Improved decision making aligned with long-term goals
3. Reduced financial stress
4. Increased savings
5. Better preparedness for expected and unexpected life events

Creating such a plan might impact my own financial decisions by helping me prioritize my financial goals, make more informed choices about spending and saving, and feel more confident about my financial future. It could also motivate me to start saving for important long-term goals like retirement earlier than I might have otherwise.

Example Lecture Outline

1. Introduction
   - Define comprehensive financial plan
   - Explain its importance in personal finance
   - Highlight its role in achieving financial goals

2. Key Components of a Comprehensive Financial Plan
   - Financial Goals
     - Short-term, medium-term, long-term
   - Net Worth Statement
     - Assets and liabilities
   - Budget
     - Income and expenses
   - Savings and Investment Strategy
     - Risk tolerance and time horizons

3. The Process of Creating a Financial Plan
   - Assess current financial situation
   - Define financial goals
   - Develop strategies
   - Implement the plan
   - Monitor and adjust

4. Benefits of a Comprehensive Financial Plan
   - Clarity and direction
   - Improved decision making
   - Reduced financial stress
   - Increased savings
   - Better preparedness for life events

5. Real-World Application
   - Sarah's example: saving for a house and retirement

6. Conclusion
   - Emphasize the ongoing nature of financial planning
   - Encourage students to start their own financial plans

Interesting Insights

1. A comprehensive financial plan can serve as a powerful tool for achieving both short-term desires and long-term dreams, much like a roadmap for a lifelong journey.
2. Financial planning isn't just for adults with full-time jobs; students can benefit greatly from starting early, even with small amounts of money.

Class Schedule

1. Introduction to Comprehensive Financial Planning
   - Brief lecture using the outline
2. Article Reading
   - Students read the article on Creating a Comprehensive Financial Plan
3. Guided Notes Completion
   - Students fill out guided notes while discussing key points
4. Reflection Questions
   - Students answer reflection questions
   - Facilitate brief class discussion on responses
5. Hypothetical Scenarios
   - Present "what-if" scenarios
   - Group discussion on potential outcomes
6. Vocabulary Review
   - Review key terms as a class

Class Discussion Prompts

1. Why do you think it's important to start financial planning at a young age?
2. How might creating a financial plan change the way you think about money?
3. What challenges do you think people face when trying to stick to a financial plan?

Further Exploration

1. Budgeting Tools: Introduce students to various budgeting apps or spreadsheets they can use to start their own budgets.
   - Connection: This practical tool directly relates to the budgeting component of a comprehensive financial plan.

2. Career Planning: Discuss how career choices can impact long-term financial plans.
   - Connection: Career decisions significantly affect income potential, which is a crucial factor in financial planning.

Additional Notes

- Encourage students to think about their own financial goals during the lesson.
- Consider inviting a local financial planner as a guest speaker for a future class.
- Adapt the schedule as needed. For longer classes, expand the discussion sections or add a hands-on budgeting activity.
- Use the hypothetical scenarios to promote group problem-solving and discussion.
- Emphasize that financial planning is an ongoing process and that plans should be regularly reviewed and adjusted.

Remember, the goal is to make financial planning relevant and accessible to high school students, setting them up for future financial success.

Creating a Comprehensive Financial Plan

```
L C B R J N T I O G H X X K B J O H Z R A I F S
R O V U O X N Q L I A B I L I T Y S M C K N D R
R I O X D C X I A O A C K Y J K D H X W B D Y K
B E S B G G S D U L B O F H N G A C G P F B P S
W K J K Z Z E I E C O C A N V A A X R Z F R Z J
F A E K M G D T B Q Q X D R V P A D L Y X E O C
V F C C O A I Y Y L K Z S R X F T N X S D T Z X
D W Z Y Y X N F I N A N C I A L P L A N E I N H
Q Q S U M T V A N I J V T E S E F Q U Q Z R R C
B Z N F W P E A G D T K Z W W S I D E G B E J W
R X H X K B S X X E B Z S W B J N P S M F M J X
W Y G Z L E T S L T M X C N Z S A J T O Q E Y Y
M U Y U U O M E L Y R E U L Y B N B A N Y N I M
T A W A D S E T O V K J N K M C C Q T X M T K R
A V K F A V N Y X R L F H T M M I D E R L P N M
X I T K Z R T N S X M N U I C Y A G P L I L A N
H H T K O J S G I U N V Z U U S L X L Q B A Y E
H G C W P F T M D K Y E F U L C G S A M O N O T
K P N I M Q R C C E P F Q O K D O M N D L N C W
G L D H O T A Q I N V R Z R I S A C N Y B I G O
L K X Z R G T N E P S F I M C J L W I O K N C R
I Y G K J T E W X S Y T A G B Y S H N D T G V T
N E H R O J G L P B W R H E O V H S G T G O O H
V Y L Q X F Y S Z A H S P O N K K K J L K Y A Y
```

Financial Plan	Financial Goals	Risk Management
Retirement Planning	Estate Planning	Investment Strategy
Liability	Asset	Net Worth
Budget		

Creating a Comprehensive Financial Plan

Across

2. Any debt or financial obligation you owe to others.

6. The destinations on your financial journey, which can be short-term, medium-term, or long-term, Financial _____

7. The process of planning for the transfer of your assets after your death, including wills and trusts, _____ Planning

8. A plan for growing your wealth over time, considering factors like risk tolerance and time horizons, _____ Strategy

9. A detailed plan of your income and expenses, helping you understand and control your cash flow.

10. A snapshot of your current financial position, listing all your assets (what you own) and liabilities (what you owe). (2 words)

Down

1. A strategy to ensure you have enough funds to maintain your desired lifestyle after you stop working, _____ Planning

3. The process of identifying potential financial risks and taking steps to minimize their impact, often through insurance, Risk _____

4. Anything of value that you own, such as cash, investments, or property.

5. A detailed strategy that outlines your current financial situation, defines your financial goals, and charts a course to achieve those goals, Financial _____

INTRODUCE | REINFORCE | HOMEWORK | REMEDIATION | HOME | SPED
Introducing The 25x Series Of Workbooks For Middle & High School

Current Titles Available & Launching Now on Amazon & TPT:

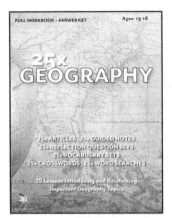

25x: Geography

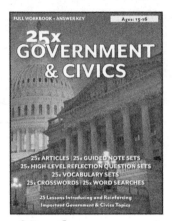

25x: Government & Civics

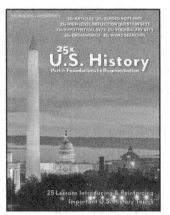

25x: U.S. History Part 1

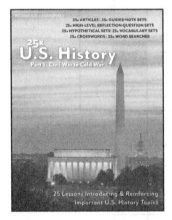

25x: U.S. History Part 2

25x: Economics (HS)

25x: Life Skills (HS)

Current Titles In Production For Fall 2025

25x: Chemistry (HS)

25x: World History

25x: Soft Skills (MS & HS)

25x: Consumer Science (HS)

25x: Money Skills (MS & HS)

25x: Career & Technical Education

25x: Physics

Current Titles In Production For Summer 2025

High School

25x: Astronomy

25x: Law

25x: Entrepreneurship

25x: Graphic Design

25x: Programming

25x: Web & Internet

25x: Electronics

25x: Network Security

Middle School

25x: ELA-Literature

25x: Decision Making

25x: Money Matters

25x: Online Life

*Mathematics Titles
In Development*

Written & Produced By Award-Winning & Recognized Teachers With 20+ Years Of Classroom Experience

Inspired Educators Reflection Journal, Now Available On Amazon

Introducing - Inspired Educators K-12 Professional Development (PD Credit Available)

Empower teachers with the resources to nurture resilience and longevity.

Introducing the *Inspired Educators K-12 Professional Development Series!* Designed for educators, this unique program offers five 60-90 minute sessions that focus on nurturing teacher mental and emotional well-being.

Join us for engaging sessions delivered through Zoom, in-person, or via our convenient online course system. By completing the optional reflection journal, educators can earn one professional development credit.

The Five Sessions Are: 1. The Importance of Self-Care, 2. The Importance of Letting Go, 3. Raising Self-Awareness as an Educator, 4. Maintaining a Positive Mindset, and 5. Maintaining a Growth Mindset

Introducing - Let It Go: 7-Steps to Keeping Your Cool for High School Stu dents!

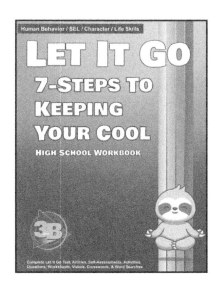

Let It Go: 7-Steps To Keeping Your Cool Workbook for High School Students. TPT & Amazon

This comprehensive workbook is written specifically for grades 9-12 and contains 10 complete lessons for students looking to improve their social emotional learning.

Let It Go teaches students to take back control from their Defense Cascade (fight-flight-freeze response) and remain calm, cool, and collected when facing any situation. The program is designed with real solutions that teach students how to regulate their emotions, build self-awareness, and maintain a positive mindset. Not only does this program give students the skills they need to manage difficult situations in life but also gives them practical solutions to help them live their very best lives.

Our Lessons On:
TeachersPayTeachers (TPT)
https://www.teacherspayteachers.com/store/3andb

Our Workbooks On:
Amazon
https://amzn.to/3ygpsvk

To learn more about our resources visit our website: 3andB.com

Made in the USA
Monee, IL
19 November 2024